Philip Kerr & Ceri Jones

Straightforward

Intermediate Student's Book

MACMILLAN

Contents

		Reading & Listening	Speaking	Writing (in the Workbook)
1A	R	*Liars!*	Discussing what people are most likely to lie about	A description of a best friend
	L	Radio review of TV programme: *How Michael Portillo became a single mum*	Talking about yourself **Did you know?** British political parties	
1B	R	*Are you British enough?*	Discussing answers to a British culture quiz Devising a quiz about culture in your country	
1C	L	Three conversations in an office	Talking about first impressions	
2A	R	*Lawyer gives up job to cycle around South America*	Discussing travelling	A description of a town or city
	L/R	Three unusual journeys	Talking about a film or book of a long journey	
2B	R	An excerpt from a web diary about a trip round Australia	Talking about Australia Planning a journey across your country	
2C	L	Three conversations about trying to get somewhere	Talking about daily transport **Did you know?** New York & London taxis	
3A	R	*Paradise Ridge*	Discussing where you live	Advantages and disadvantages
	L	Interviews with residents talking about disadvantages of living in Paradise Ridge	Designing a luxury holiday home	
	L	Interviews with people who live in unusual homes		
3B	R	*6 things you probably didn't know about beds and bedrooms*	Talking about sleeping & dreaming	
3C	L	Three conversations at a dinner party	Describing a recent dinner party **Did you know?** Food in Britain	
4A	R	*Lottery winners and losers*	Inventing a story about a lottery winner	A narrative: Lottery winner
4B	L	Conversation: discussing things in common	Identifying & discussing coincidences	
4C	R	*The world's luckiest man*	Inventing a bad luck story	
	L	Three bad luck stories	**Did you know?** Superstitions in Britain	
5A	R	*Catch them young*	Planning & presenting an advertisement for a mineral water	An advertisement
	L	A phone call: credit card telesales	Carrying out a market research survey	
5B	R	*Office stereotypes*	Planning an office party	
5C	L	Ordering office supplies over the phone	Roleplay: phone conversation ordering office supplies **Did you know?** London's Mayfair district	
6A	R	Questionnaire: *What kind of holiday person are you?*	Roleplay: making plans with other holiday makers	An extract from a holiday brochure
	L	Six short interviews at the airport	Planning a holiday for a family group	
6B	R	*Emerald Tours*	Discussing the perfect day out **Did you know?** Cork – European capital of culture	
6C	L	Enquiring about flights over the phone	Discussing the different ways men & women think	

Lesson	Grammar	Vocabulary	Functional language	Pronunciation
7A Life changes p66	Present perfect continuous 1	Phrasal verbs with *live* Metaphor		
7B Happy birthday p70	Present perfect continuous 2	Life stages		
7C Dilemmas p72		Exclamations with *what*	Giving advice	Intonation (feelings)
7 Language reference p74				
8A Breaking news p76	*Would* Unreal conditions 1	Newspapers		/ʊ/ & /uː/
8B Speeding p80		Compound nouns (driving)	Offers	
8C Bank robbers p82	Unreal conditions 2	Law & order		
8 Language reference p84				
9A Shops & shoppers p86	Articles & determiners Quantifiers 1	Containers Shopping		*of*
9B E-shopping p90	Quantifiers 2	Collocations with *take*		
9C Telephone bills p92		Prepositional phrases	Complaints	
9 Language reference p94				
10A Secrets p96	Modals of speculation 1 (present time) Modals of speculation 2 (present time)	Illusions Word families		Sentence stress
10B Mysteries p100	Modals of speculation (past time)	Verbs followed by infinitive		
10C Strictly confidential p102		Idioms	Advantages & disadvantages	
10 Language reference p104				
11A Olympic dreams p106	Passive Verbs with two objects	Sport Nouns & adjectives (describing people)		
11B The sporting year p110	Causative	Services		/ɪə/ & /eə/
11C Sport relief p112		*Make & do*	Question tags (checking)	
11 Language reference p114				
12A Money matters p116	Reported speech & thought Reported questions	Verb collocations (money)		
12B Sue! p120	*Tell* & *ask* with infinitive	Reporting verbs		
12C Gifts of gold p122			Social expressions	Intonation (social expressions)
12 Language reference p124				

Communication activities p126   Tapescripts p135   Irregular verb list p155   Unit reviews p156

4

		Reading & Listening	Speaking	Writing (in the Workbook)
7A	R	*Redundancy was the best thing that ever happened to me*	Discussing important life events	A letter of advice
	L	Interview with a househusband	*Did you know?* Legal ages in England & Wales	
7B	R	*Maria prepares to celebrate her 110th birthday*	Discussing different stages of life	
			Talking about changes in students' lifetimes	
7C	L	Conversation about a dilemma at work	Discussing personal dilemmas	
			Roleplay: giving advice about a problem	
8A	L	Interview with an investigative journalist	Planning the front page for a newspaper	A funny crime story
	R	Newspaper reports	Discussing three related newspaper articles	
			Did you know? Rupert Murdoch	
8B	L	Two conversations involving driving offences	Discussing the seriousness of driving offences	
			Discussing the advantages & disadvantages of a life without cars	
8C	R	Newspaper article about idiot robbers	Talking about films with robberies	
			Continuing a dialogue from a film	
9A	R	*Checking out the check out*	Planning a shopping centre	A letter of complaint
	L	Interview with a shopaholic		
9B	R	*Eezeemall.com*	Devising a quiz to test whether classmates are technophobes or cybernauts	
9C	L	Three conversations about problems with phones & phone bills	Choosing a ring tone, fascia & logo for classmates' mobile phones	
			Roleplay: making a complaint	
			Did you know? Red phone boxes	
10A	R	*The tricks of the trade*	Performing a magic trick	A narrative
	L	Radio phone-in: *The Da Vinci Code*	Discussing conspiracy theories	
			Did you know? Glastonbury	
10B	R	*The Return of Martin Guerre*	Solving a mystery	
10C	L	Conversation about the installation of spy software at work	Discussing confidential information	
			Roleplay: debate about installing CCTV cameras in secondary schools	
11A	R	*Louise's Olympic dream*	Talking about sports & how to play them	A description of a sporting event
	R	*Olympic gymnast calls for a divorce*	Planning & presenting an Olympic bid	
	L	Interview with a psychologist about child sports stars		
11B	R	Extracts from a guide book about sporting events	Interviewing each other about services	
11C	L	Conversations about a sponsored bike ride	Discussing ways to raise money for charity	
			Did you know? The British royal family & charity	
12A	R	*I never thought it would happen to me*	Ordering important things in life	Writing a report
	R	*The money survey*	Discussing answers to a survey about money	
	L	A conversation about the results of the money survey	Asking & answering questions about money	
12B	R	Five crazy litigation stories	Deciding how much money to award in a litigation case	
12C	L	Three conversations in an office	Choosing presents for special occasions	
			Did you know? US Congressional gold medal	

1A | Double lives

SPEAKING

1 Work in small groups. Look at the list and decide which things are the most important when you are describing who you are.

- name
- age
- job
- nationality
- marital status
- qualifications
- friends
- salary

2 Discuss these questions.

- Which information in exercise 1 are you most interested in when you meet someone for the first time?
- Which of these things do you think people are most likely to lie about?
- Talk about the most honest person you know.

3 Put the following in order of seriousness (1 = most serious ➜ 6 = least serious).

☐ lying about why you are late for work/school
☐ lying about your age to get into a nightclub
☐ lying about your qualifications to get a job
☐ lying to your partner about another person
☐ lying to a friend about their new hairstyle
☐ lying to a member of your family about a present that you didn't like

READING

1 Look at the photo and answer the questions.

- Who do you think the man is speaking to?
- Is he speaking honestly?

2 Read the texts and say if the sentences are true (T) or false (F).

1 It is possible to spot a liar because of his body language.
2 Liars sometimes speak less quickly.
3 Will has a two-year-old son.
4 Will does not have a job.
5 A young boy discovers the truth about Will.
6 Most of the world's top ten lies are about money.

● Four-page special!

Liars!
How to spot them

He thinks he's getting away with it, but his body and his voice are giving him away. He's stumbling over his words. He's fidgeting and nervous. His hands won't stay still and his palms are probably sweaty as well. He seems to be smiling, but there's a little bit of tension around his lips and his nose. Although the bottom half of his face is forming a smile, it hasn't reached his eyes. He's looking at you straight in the eyes and he appears to be 100% sincere, but the tone of his voice has dropped and the rhythm of his speech has slowed down. There's no doubt about it: he's lying.

Learn to spot the telltale signs – read more on page 2

Screen liars

'She's erm ... delightful.'

'I love kids,' says Will (played by Hugh Grant in the hit film *About A Boy*). 'Yeah, I like messing around with them, you know. I have a two-year-old, Ned. He's got blue eyes.' Will is looking for a girlfriend, but all the women he knows at the moment are either married or divorced, and they all have children. Will is 38, he has no family and no job, and he specializes in doing nothing. He lives off the royalties of a hit song that his father wrote years and years ago. So Will invents an imaginary son and goes to single-parent meetings. He is soon dating a lot of pretty young single mums. But things get complicated one day, when a young boy arrives at Will's home and says, 'You don't have a kid. You've been lying to me, my mum and my mum's friend.'

Read about more screen liars on page 3

※ The world's top ten lies ※

1 I love you.
2 You look great.
3 I'll call you tomorrow.
4 We never got the letter.
5 I'm not feeling very well.
6 I had no choice.
7 We had a lovely time.
8 I missed you.
9 It wasn't me.
10 I won't be long.

Read the top 100 on page 4

3 Find words in the texts that match the definitions 1–5.

1 moving your body nervously
f _ _ _ _ _ _ _ _
2 wet because you are hot
s _ _ _ _ _
3 honest
s _ _ _ _ _ _
4 wasting time/playing
m _ _ _ _ _ _ a _ _ _ _ _
5 depends on something for money
l _ _ _ _ o _ _

4 Work in pairs. Discuss these questions.

● What other sentences would you expect to see in the top 100 lies?
● Do you know any other films where a liar is the central character? Tell your partner.

GRAMMAR: stative & dynamic verbs

1 Look at the verbs in italics. Circle the stative verbs and underline the dynamic verbs.

1 Every morning Gerald *puts on* a suit and tie, *kisses* his wife goodbye and *goes* to work.
2 Or, at least, that's what his wife *thinks*, and that's what Gerald *wants* his wife to believe.
3 In fact, Gerald *feeds* pigeons in the park or *does* crosswords in the local library.
4 His wife *goes* shopping every Saturday and *buys* new furniture for the house with her credit card.
5 She *doesn't know* that they *don't have* any more money.

Use dynamic verbs

● in either the simple or the continuous form.
● to describe an action.
   *Will **is looking for** a girlfriend.*

Use stative verbs

● in the simple form, not usually in the continuous form.
● to describe emotions, opinions, the senses, and states that do not change.
   *I **love** kids.* Not *I am loving kids.*
   *He **appears to be** 100% sincere.* Not *He is appearing to be 100% sincere.*

Common stative verbs:

agree   appear   be   believe   belong   cost   dislike
forget   hate   have   know   like   love   matter
mean   need   own   prefer   realize   remember
seem   think   understand   want   spend

> **SEE LANGUAGE REFERENCE PAGE 14**

2 Walter Mitty is the hero of a short story by James Thurber. His life is sad and ordinary, but most of the time he lives in a dream world, as the heroic Captain Mitty. Correct three mistakes with stative or dynamic verbs in the two paragraphs from the story.

1 The weather is getting worse and the plane is not having enough fuel to return to base. But, Captain Mitty, who is sitting at the controls, is not knowing the meaning of the word *fear*. He is understanding that there is only one way to save everyone's life. 'We're going through,' he announces.

2 'I am being accurate at 100 metres. I never miss.' Mitty is holding a heavy automatic and the crowd believe him. The courtroom is in chaos. Mitty is needing to find a way out, but he is not wanting to use the gun.

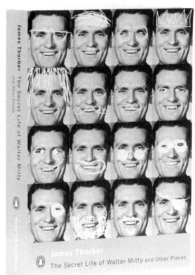

3 Work in pairs, A and B. You are going to describe a moment of Mitty's real and imaginary life using both dynamic and stative verbs.

A: Turn to page 126 and describe what is happening.
B: Turn to page 134 and describe what is happening in Mitty's imagination.

SPEAKING

1 Turn to page 126. Choose one sentence and complete it so that it is true for you. Complete the other sentences so that they are not true for you!

2 Works in pairs. Tell your partner your sentences from exercise 1. Can he/she guess which sentence is true?

LISTENING & SPEAKING

1 Work in pairs. Discuss these questions.

- What do you think the following people do on a typical working day?
  a) a mother of four small children
  b) a member of parliament
- Whose lifestyle is more similar to yours? In what ways?

2 Work in pairs. Read the TV review. What do you think the main differences between Michael Portillo and Jenny Miner's lifestyles will be?

Tonight • BBC2 9pm

In tonight's **How Michael Portillo Became a Single Mum**, politician Michael Portillo adds new skills to his CV. The son of a Spanish political refugee, Michael Portillo has had a long career in politics. In the 1990s, he became Secretary of State for Defence. In 2001, he tried to become leader of the Tory party. Tonight, he makes his first appearance in the wonderful world of reality TV when he volunteers to look after Jenny Miner's four children for a week. It's a rare chance to see a politician at work in the real world.

3 🔘 1.1 Listen to the first part of a review of the TV programme. Check the answers you gave in exercise 2.

4 🔘 1.2 Listen to the second part of the review and answer the questions.

1 Did the reviewer like Michael Portillo before the programme?
2 Did the reviewer like him after the programme?
3 Did Michael Portillo admit that he had problems?
4 Did Tasha and her friends like him?
5 Did he enjoy working at the supermarket?
6 What did Portillo try to persuade the youngest child to do?
7 Did Portillo find it easy to look after Ellie?
8 Who was the reviewer's favourite character in the programme?

5 🔘 1.1–1.2 Listen again and complete the sentences.

1 Michael Portillo volunteered **to step into single mum Jenny Miner's** _____ for a week.
2 Life as a single mum is going to be **a real** _____-opener.
3 It is one of **the high** _____ of his week.
4 It looks as if **he's bitten off more than he can** _____.
5 All his people skills and lessons in political diplomacy **will get him** _____.

6 Work in pairs. Explain the meaning of the phrases in bold in exercise 5.

7 Which politician in your country would you like to see in a similar TV programme? Why?

GRAMMAR: present simple & present continuous

1 Choose the correct phrases to complete the rules below. Then choose examples from the sentences highlighted in tapescripts 1.1–1.2 on page 135.

Use the *present simple / present continuous*
- to talk about facts (things that are always true) and permanent situations.
  Example _____
- to talk about habits and actions that happen regularly.
  Example _____

Use the *present simple / present continuous*
- to talk about actions that are happening at the moment of speaking.
  Example _____
- to talk about temporary situations and activities.
  Example _____

Usually use stative verbs in the *present simple / present continuous*.
  Example _____ Not *is wanting to*

⊙ FOR THE PRESENT SIMPLE AND THE PRESENT CONTINUOUS WITH FUTURE MEANINGS, SEE PAGE 64

⊙ SEE LANGUAGE REFERENCE PAGE 14

2 Choose the correct verb forms to complete the article.

> **Faking it** is the hit TV series where people learn a new job in just a few weeks and then try to persuade experts that it's their real job! In this week's episode, a volunteer (1) *has / is having* four weeks to learn a new skill. This week's volunteer, Tim Hutch, usually (2) *works / is working* as a music teacher in a secondary school. In *Faking it*, he becomes a rock star. When you see him in the programme, he (3) *plays / is playing* live on stage in a rock band! In his real job as a music teacher, he (4) *teaches / is teaching* kids to play classical guitar. That's the only instrument he can play. But in *Faking it* he (5) *learns / is learning* to play the bass guitar. Tim Hutch has many challenges to face, but the thing he most (6) *wants / is wanting* to learn is how to dance in time. Don't miss it!

3 Write six sentences about yourself using these time expressions.

> now   usually   once a week
> this week   never   at the moment

Vocabulary: verbs with two meanings

> Some verbs can be both stative and dynamic, but the meaning changes. You can use the verbs *think*, *see* and *have* in the simple and continuous forms, but with different meanings.
>
> I **see** *what the problem is now.*
> (= I understand what the problem is now.)
> I'**m seeing** *a TV reviewer at ten tomorrow.*
> (= I have arranged to meet her.)

> ❯ See Language Reference page 14

1 Choose the correct verb to complete the sentences.

1 I *think / am thinking* this is probably the best programme I've seen all year.
2 I don't know if Portillo *thinks / is thinking* about starting a new career.
3 I *see / am seeing* what you mean.
4 I *am seeing / see* two politicians for a meeting tomorrow.
5 Jenny Miner *has / is having* four children.
6 Look at Portillo. He *has / is having* a really good time at the party.

2 Work in pairs. Explain the meaning of each use of the verbs in exercise 1.

3 Complete the sentences with *see*, *have* or *think* in the present simple or present continuous.

see
1 He _____ his doctor next week.
2 She _____ why he lied to her but she isn't going to forgive him.

have
1 He _____ £5 in his pocket.
2 She _____ a party at her flat on Saturday.

think
1 He _____ about getting his hair cut this weekend.
2 She _____ reality TV shows should be banned.

4 Work in pairs. Use the three verbs from exercise 3 to make sentences that are true for you. Then tell your partner about yourself.

> *I think a lot of programmes on TV are very funny.*
> *I'm thinking of going on holiday to Greece next year.*

Did you know?

1 Work in pairs. Read the information and discuss these questions.

For nearly one hundred years, only two British political parties have governed Britain. The Labour Party is a socialist party and its leaders have included Tony Blair and Harold Wilson. The Conservatives (also known as Tories) are traditionally more right-wing. Winston Churchill and Margaret Thatcher are perhaps the most famous leaders of the Tory Party so far. The Liberal Democrats are the third biggest political party in Britain. Their leaders have included David Steele and Charles Kennedy.

● What are the main political parties in your country?
● What are the differences between them?
● What other political parties are there?
● Who are the most famous members of these political parties?

1B | Britishness

SPEAKING & VOCABULARY: self-image

1 Complete the sentences in column A with a phrase from column B.

A	B
1 I think of myself as *a Scot,*	a *an old-age pensioner – I'm too busy for that.*
2 I would describe myself	b as *quite fit for my age.*
3 I don't see myself as	c but *I've lived in England for 25 years.*
4 I'm proud to be the	d *grandmother of two very clever girls.*
5 *My family* is the most	e important thing to me.
6 My neighbours probably see	f *live in such a nice house.*
7 I consider myself lucky to	g me *as a very friendly person.*

2 Change the words in italics in exercise 1 to make sentences that are true for you. Compare your sentences with a partner.

I think of myself as a European, but I've lived in the US for the last ten years.

READING

1 Read the article about a test for people who want to become British citizens. Which of the people 1–8 think the test is a good idea?

2 Read the article again and answer the questions.

1 Which European country already has a test for new citizens?
2 What does Clive Morgan want the government to spend money on?
3 What does Jon Snow think is dead?
4 What has become a dirty word?
5 Where does Claire Rayner come from?
6 What do British people like doing in bars?
7 Who came from Uganda?
8 Who thinks that Britain needs more immigrants?

3 Do you think the test is a good idea? Why or why not?

Are you British enough?

The government has announced that it is to introduce a test about Britain and British culture for people who want to become British citizens. Here are some reactions:

1 I once read that the rock star Malcolm McLaren described being British as 'singing Karaoke in bars, eating Chinese noodles, wearing Prada and Nike, holidaying in Florida and Ibiza …' Why do we need to test that?
(Jared Steele, London nightclub owner)

2 People say they come from Yorkshire, Lancaster, or London, rather than coming from Britain as a whole. There's a certain snottiness in trying to define Britishness. If anybody asked, I would say I am a Londoner and a European.
(Claire Rayner, writer)

3 I think 'Britishness' has died off in my lifetime and nothing has replaced it. When I was a child, Britishness was Winston Churchill and beefeaters. Now it's an irrelevant concept.
(Jon Snow, TV newsreader)

4 Why do we need a test? Most people that I know would fail it. Why don't we welcome immigrants with open arms?
(Penny Porter, Church of England priest)

5 My family is very proud to be British. We came here from Uganda in the 1970s. In those days, they didn't have a test, but I think it's a good idea. People are always asking: What does this country do for me? But a better question is: What can I do for my country? (Amina Patel, shopkeeper)

6 When I think of Britain, I think of the royal family, cricket, warm beer, cheese and cucumber sandwiches and wet weather. Who cares about these things? Why is the government wasting its time and our money on this? They should spend the money on better schools and decent hospitals. (Clive Morgan, rugby player)

7 What's the problem with a nationality test? Why all the fuss? In other countries, like Germany, the United States and Australia, you have to pass a test. Britain shouldn't be any different. (Dieter Krugger, investment analyst)

8 People forget that Britain used to be great. There was a time when we were proud to wear the Union Jack. What happened to all that good old-fashioned patriotism? It's become a dirty word now, but the true British qualities are still important. Of course, we should test them. (S Sullivan, MBE)

GRAMMAR: subject & object questions

Questions

This is the usual word order in questions:

question word	auxiliary	subject	infinitive
What	*does*	*this country*	*do for me?*
Why	*do*	*we*	*need a test?*

Subject questions

When the question word (*who, what, which* or *how many*) is the subject of the question, you do not need an auxiliary verb (*do, does* or *did*) with the present simple and past simple.

subject	verb
Who	*cares about these things?*
How many people	*describe themselves as British?*
What	*happened to patriotism?*

Object questions

If the question word is the object of a question, you use normal question word order with *do, does* or *did*.

object	auxiliary	subject	infinitive
Who	*does*	*he*	*work for?*
What	*did*	*he*	*say?*

> SEE LANGUAGE REFERENCE PAGE 14

1 Look at the questions in Reading exercise 2. Find four subject questions and four object questions.

2 Correct the grammatical mistakes in four of these questions.

1 How many people do live in Scotland?
2 What did happen in 1066?
3 When can the British police arrest you without a reason?
4 What CRE stands for?
5 What number you do dial for the emergency services?
6 Who speaks Cornish?

3 Use the prompts to make questions.

1 *Who became Britain's first woman prime minister in 1979?*

1 Who / become / Britain's first woman prime minister / in 1979?
2 Which British political party / use / blue / as its official colour?
3 Why / the policeman / stand / outside the house / in the photo above?
4 What / happen / on Guy Fawkes' Day?
5 When / women in Britain / vote / in political elections / for the first time?
6 Which / English king / have / six wives?

SPEAKING

1 Work in pairs. Turn to page 126. Choose the correct answer to the questions in Grammar exercises 2 and 3. If you do not know the answer, guess!

2 Now work with a new partner. You are each going to see the answers for one exercise. Tell your partner if his/her answers are correct.

A: Turn to page 130. B: Turn to page 129.

3 Work in groups. Prepare six questions that test knowledge of your own national culture. Use the examples in Grammar exercises 2 and 3 and these topics to help you.

> everyday life   famous people   history
> important places   law   multiculturalism
> politics   regions

4 Work with students from another group. Ask them your test questions.

1c | First impressions

SPEAKING

1 Work in pairs. Discuss these questions.

- When and where was the last time that you met someone new?
- Who was it?
- What was your first impression of them?
- Were your first impressions accurate?

2 Think of five situations when it is important to look good and make a good impression.

3 Explain the meaning of the saying below. Do you agree or disagree? Give examples to explain your opinion.

You can't judge a book by its cover.

LISTENING

1 🔊 1.3–1.5 Listen to three conversations in an office and answer the questions.

1 Look at the picture. Which man do you think Derek is? Why?
2 Which of the women is Avril? How do you know?

2 🔊 1.3–1.5 Listen to the conversations again and say if the sentences are true (T) or false (F).

1 Camilla is the new secretary.
2 Derek is moving to a new office.
3 The first thing Camilla wants to look at is the Accounts Department.
4 Avril says she wants to work for Camilla.
5 Derek thinks Camilla is intelligent and organized.
6 Linda doesn't like Camilla.
7 Camilla is thinking of closing one of the departments in the office.

3 Imagine that you are the new director. What would your first impressions be of the staff in the office?

VOCABULARY: describing people

1 Work in pairs. How many parts of the body can you name?

2 Match the groups of adjectives in column A to the nouns in column B.

A		B	
1	average/muscular/slim	a	eyes
2	bald/round/shaved	b	hair
3	blond/shiny/wavy	c	head
4	dark/narrow/wide	d	nose
5	healthy/pale/tanned	e	complexion
6	pointed/prominent/straight	f	build

3 Write a list of eight famous people. Choose one of the people from your list and describe his/her appearance. Your partner must guess who you are describing.

FUNCTIONAL LANGUAGE: describing people

1 Match the questions 1–3 to the answers a–f.

1 What is she like?
2 What does she look like?
3 What does she like?

a I think she's quite fond of chocolate.
b She seems very calm and organized.
c She's got a rather small, pointed face.
d She's middle-aged with short dark hair.
e She's very intelligent.
f Tea.

2 Work in pairs. Write the names of four people you know. Use the questions in exercise 1 to find out more about the people whose names your partner has written.

A: Who's Mark?
B: He's my brother.
A: What's he like?
B: He's cheerful and funny.

3 Complete the sentences in column A with a phrase from column B.

A		B	
1	She looks	a	a film star. (+ noun)
2	She looks like	b	quite friendly. (+ adjective)
3	She looks as if	c	she is going to a wedding. (+ phrase)

4 Complete the sentences with *like*, *as if* or *–* .

1 He doesn't look _____ very happy.
2 He looks _____ a doctor.
3 He looks _____ about 55.
4 He looks _____ he has just woken up.
5 He looks _____ he wants to be somewhere else.
6 He looks _____ the prime minister.

PRONUNCIATION: intonation (lists)

1 🔘 1.6 Listen to this extract from one of the conversations in Listening exercise 1.

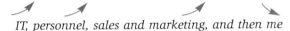

IT, personnel, sales and marketing, and then me

Notice how the voice goes up for each item of the list and then down at the end of the list.

2 Practise reading these lists in the same way.

1 Monday, Tuesday, Wednesday and Thursday
2 who, what, where, when and why
3 Camilla, Derek, Avril, Linda and Dave

3 🔘 1.7 Listen to the recording to check your pronunciation.

4 Work in pairs. Take it in turns to add one more item to the lists below. Repeat the whole list each time.

1 A: Britain, America, Australia and Canada
B: Britain, America, Australia, Canada and Ireland

1 Britain, America, Australia, …
2 eyes, ears, nose, …
3 intelligent, good-looking, kind, …
4 mother, cousin, grandfather, …
5 newspapers, magazines, books, …

GRAMMAR

Stative & dynamic verbs

Some verbs can only be used in the simple form. These are called stative verbs. They often describe emotions, opinions, the senses and states that do not change.

> *I love you.* Not ~~*I am loving you*~~.
> *He seems friendly.* Not ~~*He is seeming friendly*~~.

Here are some common stative verbs:

> *agree   appear   be   believe   belong   contain*
> *dislike   fit   forget   hate   know   last   like*
> *love   matter   mean   need   own   prefer*
> *realize   remember   seem   understand   want*

We can use most verbs in both the simple and the continuous forms. These are called dynamic verbs.

> *The weather **is getting** worse.*
> *It often **snows** in January.*

It is possible for some verbs to be both dynamic and stative if they have two different meanings.

> *He **has** a house in north London.* (have = own)
> *She's **having** a few problems.* (have = experience)

Other common verbs that can be dynamic or stative (with different meanings) include:

be   feel   see   smell   think

Present simple & present continuous

We use the present simple:

- to talk about facts (things that are always true) and permanent situations.
  *She **lives** in a small flat.*

- to talk about habits and actions that happen regularly.
  *She **drives** the kids to school every day.*

We use the present continuous:

- to talk about actions that are happening at the moment of speaking.
  *He's **trying to** explain a problem to them.*

- to talk about temporary situations and activities.
  *She's **going** through a very rebellious phase.*

We can sometimes use both the present simple and the present continuous. Our choice depends on how we see the action.

> *I **live** in Madrid.* (= I think this is permanent.)
> *I'm **living** in Madrid.* (= I think this is temporary.)

See page 64 for information about the present tenses with future meaning.

Subject & object questions

The usual word order in questions is:

	auxiliary verb	subject	verb
Who	*does*	*he*	*work for?*
What	*do*	*you*	*do on New Year's Eve?*
Which party	*did*	*you*	*vote for?*

These questions are called object questions because the question words (*who, what, which party*) are the object of the verb.

In some *Wh-* questions, the question word (*who, what, which* or *how many*) is the subject of the verb. These are called subject questions. With a subject question, we do not need an auxiliary verb (*do, does* or *did*) with the present simple and the past simple.

subject (question word)	verb
Who	*thinks the test is a good idea?*
What	*happens on New Year's Eve?*
Which party	*won the last election?*
How many people	*voted for the government?*

FUNCTIONAL LANGUAGE

Describing people

***What is** she **like**?*
(= We are asking for a general description of the person.)

***What does** she **look like**?*
(= We are asking for a description of the person's appearance.)

***What does** she **like**?*
(= We are asking about the person's preferences or interests.)

	+ adjective *intelligent.*
She looks	*like* + noun *like a doctor.*
	as if/as though + phrase *as if she needs a holiday.*

Some English speakers use *like* instead of *as if/as though*. Many people, however, think this is incorrect.

> *She looks **like** she needs a holiday.*

WORD LIST

See page 125 for a list of abbreviations.

Self-image

consider (sb) + *adj*	/kən'sɪdə/
consider (sb) to be…	/kən'sɪdə tə ˌbiː/
describe (sb) as …	/dɪ'skraɪb ˌəz/
proud to + *infinitive*	/'praʊd ˌtuː/
see (sb) as …	/'siː ˌəz/
think of (sb) as …	/'θɪŋk əv ˌəz/

Physical features

average *adj* **	/'æv(ə)rɪdʒ/
bald *adj*	/bɔːld/
blond *adj*	/blɒnd/
build *n C*	/bɪld/
complexion *n C*	/kəm'plekʃn/
dark *adj* ***	/dɑːk/
healthy *adj* **	/'helθi/
muscular *adj*	/'mʌskjʊlə/
narrow *adj* ***	/'nærəʊ/
pale *adj* **	/peɪl/
pointed *adj*	/'pɔɪntɪd/
prominent *adj*	/'prɒmɪnənt/
round *adj* ***	/raʊnd/
shaved *adj*	/ʃeɪvd/
shiny *adj*	/'ʃaɪni/
slim *adj* **	/slɪm/
straight *adj* **	/streɪt/
tanned *adj*	/tænd/
wavy *adj*	/'weɪvi/
wide *adj* ***	/waɪd/

Other words & phrases

accounts *n pl* **	/ə'kaʊnts/
analyst *n C*	/'ænəlɪst/
approachable *adj*	/ə'prəʊtʃəbl/
arrest *v* **	/ə'rest/
arrogant *adj*	/'ærəgənt/
automatic *n C/adj* *	/ˌɔːtə'mætɪk/
base *n C* ***	/beɪs/
beefeater *n C*	/'biːfˌiːtə/
bite *v* **	/baɪt/
boss *n C* **	/bɒs/
branch *n C* **	/brɑːntʃ/
budget *n C* *	/'bʌdʒɪt/
business-like *adj*	/'bɪznəsˌlaɪk/
button *n C* **	/'bʌtn/
career *n C* **	/kə'rɪə/
cashier *n C*	/kæ'ʃɪə/
challenge *n C* **	/'tʃælɪndʒ/
chaos *n U*	/'keɪɒs/

chew *v* *	/tʃuː/
citizen *n C* **	/'sɪtɪzn/
clever *adj* **	/'klevə/
clip *n C*	/klɪp/
colleague *n C* **	/'kɒliːg/
concept *n C* ***	/'kɒnsept/
cope *v* **	/kəʊp/
courtroom *n C*	/'kɔːtˌruːm/
crossword *n C*	/'krɒsˌwɜːd/
cucumber *n C*	/'kjuːˌkʌmbə/
date *v*	/deɪt/
day-to-day *adj*	/ˌdeɪtə'deɪ/
decent *adj*	/'diːsənt/
define *v* **	/dɪ'faɪn/
dial *v*	/'daɪəl/
diplomacy *n U*	/dɪ'pləʊməsi/
emergency	/ɪ'mɜːdʒənsi ̩
services *n pl*	sɜːvɪsəz/
expense *n C* **	/ɪk'spens/
expert *n C* **	/'ekspɜːt/
eye-opener *n C*	/'aɪ ˌəʊpnə/
fake *v/adj/n C*	/feɪk/
fidget *v*	/'fɪdʒɪt/
fireworks *n pl*	/'faɪəwɜːks/
fit *adj* *	/fɪt/
flatly *adv*	/'flætli/
fuel *n U* **	/'fjuːəl/
fuss *n U*	/fʌs/
get away with (sth) *v*	/get ə'weɪ wɪð/
give (sb) away *v*	/ˌgɪv ə'weɪ/
govern *v* *	/'gʌvn/
head office *n C*	/ˌhed 'ɒfɪs/
headquarters *n pl*	/ˌhed'kwɔːtəz/
hero *n C*	/'hɪərəʊ/
imaginary *adj*	/ɪ'mædʒɪnəri/
immigrant *v*	/'ɪmɪgrənt/
impress *v* **	/ɪm'pres/
instrument *n C* ***	/'ɪnstrʊmənt/
intrigue *v*	/ɪn'triːg/
invade *v*	/ɪn'veɪd/
invasion *n C*	/ɪn'veɪʒn/
investment *n C*	/ɪn'vestmənt/
irrelevant *adj*	/ɪ'reləvənt/
judgement *n C* **	/'dʒʌdʒmənt/
karaoke *n U*	/ˌkærɪ'əʊki/
kid *n C* **	/kɪd/
liar *n C*	/'laɪə/
lie *v/n C* ***	/laɪ/
lifestyle *n C*	/'laɪfˌstaɪl/
likeable *adj*	/'laɪkəbl/
live off (sth/sb) *v*	/'lɪv ɒf/
marketing *n U*	/'mɑːkɪtɪŋ/
mayor *n C*	/meə/

mess around *v*	/mes ə'raʊnd/
modest *adj* *	/'mɒdɪst/
multiculturalism *n U*	/ˌmʌlti ̩ 'kʌltʃələlɪzm/
mum *n C* **	/mʌm/
noodle *n C*	/'nuːdl/
old-age pensioner *n C*	/ˌəʊld eɪdʒ 'penʃ(ə)nə/
palm *n C*	/pɑːm/
parliament *n C* ***	/'pɑːləmənt/
patiently *adv*	/'peɪʃntli/
patriotism *n U*	/'pætrɪəˌtɪzəm; 'peɪtrɪəˌtɪzəm/
personnel *n pl*	/ˌpɜːsə'nel/
phase *n C* *	/feɪz/
pigeon *n C*	/'pɪdʒən/
political *adj* ***	/pə'lɪtɪkl/
politician *n C* **	/ˌpɒlə'tɪʃn/
pretend *v* *	/prɪ'tend/
racism *n U*	/'reɪsɪz(ə)m/
reality TV *n U*	/riːˌæləti tiː'viː/
rebellious *adj*	/rɪ'beljəs/
refugee *n C*	/ˌrefjʊ'dʒiː/
replace *v* ***	/rɪ'pleɪs/
reviewer *n C*	/rɪ'vjuːə/
rhythm *n C* *	/'rɪðəm/
right-wing *adj*	/ˌraɪt'wɪŋ/
royalties *n pl*	/'rɔɪəltɪz/
scary *adj*	/'skeəri/
self-important *adj*	/ˌselfɪm'pɔːtənt/
sincere *adj*	/sɪn'sɪə/
single parent *n C*	/ˌsɪŋgl 'peərənt/
snottiness *n U*	/'snɒtɪnəs/
socialist *adj/n C*	/'səʊʃəlɪst/
soft spot *n C*	/ˌsɒft 'spɒt/
specialize in (sth) *v*	/'speʃəlaɪz ɪn/
spot *v*	/spɒt/
staff *n U* ***	/stɑːf/
stage *n C* ***	/steɪdʒ/
stand for *v*	/'stænd ˌfɔː/
stick to *v*	/'stɪk ˌtuː/
stubborn *adj*	/'stʌbən/
sweaty *adj*	/'sweti/
stumble *v*	/'stʌmbl/
technical *adj* ***	/'teknɪkl/
tell-tale *adj*	/'telˌteɪl/
tension *n U* *	/'tenʃn/
tight *adj* **	/taɪt/
till *n C*	/tɪl/
traditionally *adv*	/trə'dɪʃnəli/
typical *adj* ***	/'tɪpɪkl/
volunteer *n C/v*	/ˌvɒlən'tɪə/
watch out *v*	/ˌwɒtʃ 'aʊt/

2A | Journeys

Lawyer gives up job to cycle around South America

A Spanish lawyer has given up his job and has sold his car to cycle around South America and perform as a clown. Alvaro Neil,
5 also known as 'Biciclown', is cycling his way around South America, performing his clown act free everywhere he goes.

Alvaro, 36, from Asturias in the north of Spain, gave up his job last year when he
10 realized that there was more to life than a nine to five job. 'You only live once and life in an office just isn't life,' he says. So in October last year he set out on his South American adventure.

15 He began his journey in La Paz, Bolivia and so far he has visited six countries (Bolivia, Argentina, Chile, Ecuador, Peru, Colombia) and cycled more than 15,000 kilometres. The journey has
20 already taken him thirteen months, and Venezuela, Brazil, Paraguay and Uruguay lie ahead.

He spends two or three months in each country, but he has never stopped off
25 for more than five days in any one place. Alvaro is getting by on a budget of three dollars a day and has slept in fire stations, police stations and churches, at 4,700 metres in the
30 mountains of Peru and in the dry Atacama Desert of Chile.

He has given about 20 performances to more than 8,000 people. 'My show includes juggling, music, magic,
35 acrobatics and theatre. I perform to the poorest people and my sole purpose is to bring them a little happiness,' says Alvaro. At the end of one performance, a little girl ran up to him from the
40 audience and gave him a big kiss and a hug. This is one of his sweetest memories from the trip so far.

He explains that the trip is a way of bringing together the three things he
45 loves most in life: 'Cycling's in my blood, I'm a born clown and I enjoy helping other people.' He is sponsored by the *Clowns Without Frontiers* organization and
50 his mission is to bring a smile into the lives of the people he runs into on his travels.

SPEAKING

1 Work in pairs. Discuss these questions.

- What do you like and dislike about travelling?
- Who is the most widely-travelled person that you know? Where has he/she been? Why did he/she go there?
- According to an English saying, *travel broadens the mind*. Do you agree? In what ways has travel broadened your mind?

READING

1 Work in pairs. You are going to read an article about a long journey. Look at the photos and headline. Think of two possible answers for each of the questions.

1 Why did the lawyer decide to cycle around South America?
2 Why is he dressed as a clown in the second photo?

Now read the article and find out if you were right.

2 Read the article again. What do the numbers in the box refer to?

36	20	15,000	4,700	3
6	8,000	9 to 5	13	2 or 3

3 Match the highlighted phrasal verbs in the article with the words and phrases 1–6.

1 meets by chance
2 left
3 managing to survive
4 stayed
5 combining
6 started (a journey)

4 Work in pairs. Discuss these questions.

- Would you consider giving up your job or studies to do something like Alvaro did? Why or why not?
- Have you ever wanted to go on a long trip like Alvaro's? Where would you like to go?

GRAMMAR: present perfect & past simple 1

1 Look at the first three paragraphs of the article on page 16 again. Underline all the examples of the present perfect and past simple. Then answer the questions.

1 Which verb form do you use when the time is known?
2 Which verb form do you use when the time is not stated?

2 Choose the correct forms to complete the newspaper article.

From our Dublin Correspondent

The well-known writer and comedian, Tony Hawks, (1) *has accepted / accepted* a bet to hitchhike around Ireland with a fridge. He (2) *has begun / began his* journey in Dublin last week. He (3) *has almost given up / almost gave up* on the first day when his first lift (4) *has taken / took* him only three miles. But since then he (5) *has had / had* better luck. He (6) *has had / had* lifts in vans, cars and trucks, and yesterday he and his fridge (7) *has taken / took* a fishing boat to Tory Island. So if you're driving around in the Sligo area and see a man hitchhiking with a fridge – stop and give him a lift!

3 Complete the questions. Put the verbs in brackets into the present perfect or the past simple.

1 How many countries _____ you _____ (*visit*)?
2 What's the most interesting place you _____ (*be*) to?
3 How many times _____ you _____ (*go*) away last year?
4 Where _____ you _____ (*go*) for your last holiday?
5 What's the furthest you _____ ever _____ (*fly*)?
6 When _____ you _____ (*fly*) for the first time?
7 What's the strangest form of transport you _____ ever _____ (*use*)?
8 _____ you ever _____ (*travel*) on your own?

4 Work in pairs. Ask and answer the questions in exercise 3.

Use the past simple:
- with questions that ask about the time of an event. *When **did** you last **catch** a taxi?*
- to talk about past actions when you know when the event happened. *He **caught** a taxi to the airport yesterday to meet a friend.*
- with certain time expressions, e.g. *yesterday, last week, one night, the last time, when.*

Use the present perfect:
- to talk about past actions when the time is not stated. The event happened in the past, but the time is not important. ***Have** you ever **travelled** alone? I've **travelled** alone on business, but I've never **been** on holiday on my own.*
- with certain time expressions, e.g. *ever, never, already, yet, since, just. I've **just** come back from Dublin.*

> FOR OTHER USES OF THE PRESENT PERFECT, SEE PAGE 74

> SEE LANGUAGE REFERENCE PAGE 24

LISTENING & READING

1 🔊 **1.8–1.10** Listen to three more stories about unusual journeys. Match each journey to two of the photos A–F.

2 🔊 **1.8–1.10** Listen again and answer the questions.

Which journey …

1 was the longest?
2 was for charity?
3 broke a record?
4 was a race against time?
5 had its own website?
6 was made into a TV programme?

3 Read these texts about the three journeys. Find and correct two mistakes in each text.

Hunting the tiger ★★★⯪

Channel 6, 9pm
Tonight's documentary in the *Wildlife on 6* series takes a fascinating look at the animals of Siberia. Award-winning filmmakers, Chiara and Luca Colucci, spent six months in the far east of Russia looking for the rare Siberian tiger. There are only about 300 of these beautiful animals in the wild. With the help of a baby fox cub they found early on the trip, the Coluccis explore the beautiful River Amur region in their search for the tiger. An unforgettable journey and an unforgettable film.

University teachers hitchhike for charity
A group of teachers have hitchhiked the length of Britain to raise money for the charity, Oxfam International. The teachers had to get from Land's End to John O'Groats in less than two days. Only four of the teachers completed the trip in time.

Swedish student wins web competition

21-YEAR-OLD TOMMY KALLSTROM has won this month's Web Travel Site of the Month competition. His winning website contains details of his four-month trip through fifteen European countries on a Vespa that he used to deliver pizzas in his hometown of Uppsala.

4 🔊 **1.8–1.10** Listen again and check your answers.

5 Which journey sounds the most interesting or enjoyable? Why?

VOCABULARY: phrasal verbs

> Phrasal verbs have two parts: a verb and a particle, e.g. *get by,*
> *set out, stop off.*
>
> **Separable phrasal verbs**
> - With some phrasal verbs, the object can come either before or
>   after the particle.
>   *He **sorted out** the problem.*
>   *He **sorted** the problem **out**.*
>
> - If the object is a pronoun, e.g. *him, her, it,* the object always
>   comes before the particle.
>   *He sorted **it out**.* Not ~~He sorted out it~~.
>
> **Inseparable phrasal verbs**
> - With some phrasal verbs, the verb and the particle always
>   come together, so the object always comes after the particle.
>   *They looked after **the bear cub**.*
>   *They looked after **it**.*
>
> ⊙ SEE LANGUAGE REFERENCE PAGE 24

1 Match the phrasal verbs in bold in 1–6 to the definitions a–f.

1 He was able to **sort** the problem **out**.
2 They **came across** the bear near a river.
3 Tizio **got over** his injury.
4 Their friends and families **saw** them **off**.
5 A van **picked** her **up** after only five minutes.
6 The van **dropped** her **off** near the finishing line.

a felt well or happy again after something bad
b found an answer to a problem
c took someone or something in a car
d let someone get out of your car
e met or found by chance
f said goodbye to someone who was going on a journey

2 Which two phrasal verbs in exercise 1 are inseparable?

3 Put *it* in the correct place in the sentences.

*1 I sorted **it** out before I left work.*

1 I sorted out before I left work.
2 I'm sure you'll get over soon.
3 I've never come across before.
4 I've tried to give up many times.
5 Why don't you pick up on your way home?

4 Now think of a noun to replace *it* in each sentence.

1 I sorted the problem out before I left work.

5 Work in pairs. You are going to ask and answer
questions using the phrasal verbs in exercise 1.

A: Turn to page 126.   B: Turn to page 129.

PRONUNCIATION: word linking

1 ⊙ **1.11** We often join two words when an
initial vowel sound follows a final consonant
sound. Look at these examples from the
listening exercise, then listen and repeat.

1 arrived‿in‿Athens
2 gave‿it‿all‿up
3 film‿of‿another‿incredible
4 still‿exist‿in
5 it's‿Alex‿and‿Isabelle
6 part‿of‿a‿group

2 Practise saying the phrases in exercise 1 quickly.

3 ⊙ **1.12** Listen and write the four phrases.

4 Practise saying the phrases. Remember to link
the words.

SPEAKING

1 Think of a film or book you have seen or read
recently that described a long journey. Prepare
to tell a partner about it. Use the questions
below to help you.

- Where was the film/book set?
- Who was going on the journey and why?
- What were the main events?
- Would you like to go on the same journey?
  Why or why not?
- Would you recommend the film/book
  to your partner? Why or why not?

2 Work in pairs.
Tell your partner
about the
film/book.

2B | Down under

SPEAKING

1 Work in groups. Look at the photos on the website below and share all that you know about Australia. Use the ideas in the box to help you.

> sports, film and music personalities
> climate   history   cities   things to do
> animals   well-known sights and landmarks

2 Now prepare a short quiz about Australia. Use your questions to test students from another group.

READING

1 Read the first part of a web diary about a trip round Australia and answer the questions.

1 Who is the author? What does she do?
2 What is she going to do?
3 What is the purpose of her website?

2 Now read the extract from Nerina's web diary and say if the sentences are true (T) or false (F).

1 She didn't see Uluru until the morning after her arrival.
2 Uluru was the most important part of the trip.
3 The trip has not been very interesting.
4 She enjoyed the experience of walking around the Rock.
5 The Rock is very small.
6 She didn't want to have a guide.
7 She spent a whole day at the Rock.

3 Find the adjectives in the web diary that Nerina uses to describe these things.

1 the people that she has met   *incredible*
2 her experiences during the trip
3 the Rock at the start of the day
4 the Anangu caves and sacred art
5 the way that the Rock changes colour

NERINA KLEIN'S TRAVEL WEBLOG

During my 35 years as a travel writer, I've visited more countries than I can count. I've backpacked through Asia, cycled through Europe, driven across
5 Africa, but I've never explored my own home, Australia. So the time has come to put this right. Over the next six weeks, I'm planning to cover as much of the outback as I possibly can in a
10 second-hand four-wheel drive, and I'll be accompanied by my two grandchildren. They, unlike me, want to get to know their own country before they start exploring the rest of
15 the world. What follows is a diary of our travels and adventures. I hope it inspires people to leave the coast and find out what the real Australia is all about.

20 DAY 33 We camped out last night near the best place to watch the sunrise. After a bottle or two of beer and an hour or two of looking at the stars, we turned in and got some sleep before the climax of our six-week trip: our first sight of Uluru (Ayer's Rock).
     In the last five and a half weeks, we've seen and done some amazing things.
25 We've been blinded by the salt lakes of Curara Soak, we've relived history in the goldfields of Kalgoorlie-Boulder, and we've been guests at the campfires of Aboriginal communities. But nothing compares to the spectacular sight of the famous Uluru, shining purple in the light of dawn. Over the years, I've heard plenty of people talk about the wonderful changes in the colour of the Rock, but until you see it yourself,
30 it's impossible to imagine. We were absolutely spellbound.
     We spent a good part of the day walking the 9.4 kilometres around the base of the Rock. It's well worth it. The caves and rock art are fascinating. If you get a chance to join one of the tours given by the Anangu guides, do it. They explain everything about Uluru and all its sacred sites.
35   At sunset, we settled down to watch the Rock turn red against the darkening sky and planned the last leg of our trip – 450 kilometres across the desert to the modern town of Alice Springs. We talked about all the incredible friends we've made during our trip and about the things we're going to miss once we leave the bush behind.

GRAMMAR: present perfect & past simple 2

1 Look at the highlighted phrases in the web diary. Choose the correct phrases to complete the notes.

- They are all expressions that refer to a (1) *specific time in the past / period of time that hasn't finished.*
- The verb form that we use with them is the (2) *present perfect / past simple.*

2 Mark the phrases finished time (F) or unfinished time (U).

in the last few days	last month
last year	up till now
two days ago	during the last two weeks
over the past year	yesterday

3 Complete the text. Put the verbs in brackets into the present perfect or the past simple.

We (1) _____ (*arrive*) in Alice Springs yesterday. It's the biggest town we (2) _____ (*see*) over the last two months. Up till now, we (3) _____ (*camp*) under the stars. Last night, we (4) _____ (*sleep*) in a four-star hotel. We (5) _____ (*have*) a hot bath before we went to bed. We (6) _____ (*not / watch*) TV in the last six weeks.

4 Use the time expressions in exercise 2 and these verbs to make five sentences that are true for you.

> do   eat   go to   have   make   see

I haven't been to a café in the last few days.

5 Make questions from your sentences in exercise 4. Then work in pairs. Ask and answer the questions.

Have you been to a café in the last few days?
No, I haven't. Have you … ?

Use the past simple to talk about actions in the past that happened at a finished time.

> We **camped** out last night.
> At sunset, we **settled** down to watch the Rock turn red.

Use the present perfect to talk about actions in the past that happened in a period of time which is unfinished.

> *During my 35 years as a travel writer, I've visited more countries than I can count.*
> (= She is still a travel writer now.)
>
> *In the last five and a half weeks we've seen and done some amazing things.*
> (= The last five and a half weeks includes now.)

Here are some common expressions to describe unfinished time:

during in over	the last	few months / two years, etc.

> ❯ FOR OTHER USES OF THE PRESENT PERFECT, SEE PAGE 74
> ❯ SEE LANGUAGE REFERENCE PAGE 24

SPEAKING

1 Work in pairs. You are going to plan a journey across your own country. Discuss the topics below and prepare your route.

- from where to where?
- transport: motorbike/car/train/bicycle?
- how long?
- how many stops?
- places to stay?
- things to see/do?

2 Describe your route to the class. Who has the most interesting route?

> *Useful language*
>
> *Our route begins in …*
> *We travel by …*
> *Our first stop is in …*
> *In … we visit the …*

2c | Getting around

SPEAKING & VOCABULARY: verb collocations (travel)

1 Work in pairs. Think about transport in your town and discuss these questions.

- What's the quickest way of travelling round your town?
- What's the most popular form of transport for people going to work?
- What's the best way for a tourist to travel round your city to see the sights?

2 Choose the correct verbs to complete the information from a tourist guide about Edinburgh.

Welcome to Edinburgh

Getting here
By air
From the airport, you can (1) *catch / get out of* the Airport Express (No. 100) bus, which (2) *runs / takes* 25 minutes to the city centre. Alternatively, you can (3) *miss / take* a taxi. The advantage of this is that the taxi driver can (4) *drop / arrive* you wherever you like, but of course it is more expensive than public transport.

By rail
If you (5) *arrive / catch* by train, (6) *drop / get off* at Waverley Station, which is right in the city centre. From there, you can (7) *walk / get on* to most of the major sights.

Getting around
A good way to get to know the city is with a city bus tour. You can buy special tickets for the double-decker buses which allow you to (8) *get in / get on* and off when and where you want. In the evenings, the buses (9) *run / take* late, but if you (10) *get out of / miss* the last one, you can always take a taxi.

3 Work in pairs. Change the information in exercise 2 so that it is true for a city you both know well.

From the airport you can take the metro into the city centre. It takes 40 minutes.

LISTENING

1 🔊 1.13–1.15 Listen to three conversations and match them to the pictures A–C.

A

B

C

2 🔊 1.13–1.15 Listen again and say if the sentences are true (T) or false (F).

1 Avril and Linda both buy return tickets.
2 Avril uses the bus regularly.
3 Dave and Derek are getting a taxi home.
4 Dave and Derek think Camilla has a good sense of humour.
5 Camilla misses the last train home.
6 Camilla gets a taxi from outside the station.

worry about their kids when they're playing in the street and you don't need to lock your door at night.'

Just over twenty years ago, Kirsty founded Paradise
20 Ridge, a cabin park in the heart of the Columbia Mountains, which is now home to 25 families. Each family owns their own small cabin, but they share ownership of the park and the common facilities.'This is a real, living community,' insists Kirsty, 'so residents aren't allowed to
25 use their cabins as a holiday home. They can't come here just for their vacations.'

The heart of the Paradise Ridge community is a large wooden house that stands at the centre of the 25 cabins. Shared meals take place there three times a week and
30 once a month there is a meeting when important decisions are made. 'Residents mustn't miss these meetings,' explains Kirsty, 'because it's important that we all share in the decision-making.' The most important decisions usually concern new residents. Families can sell
35 their homes if they want to leave, but the whole community must vote on new families before they are allowed to join.

'Keeping the community together is hard work,' says Kirsty. 'Everybody has to lend a helping hand and take
40 responsibility for the day-to-day running of the community. That includes doing repairs, looking after the kids, cooking the communal meals or leading one of the monthly meetings.' But it seems that there is no shortage of families who want to join. There are more than seventy
45 on the waiting list.

GRAMMAR: modals of obligation, permission & prohibition (present time)

1 Complete the rules with words and phrases 1–4.

To talk about permission, you use …
To talk about prohibition, you use …
To talk about obligation, you use …
To talk about a lack of obligation, you use …

1 *don't have to* and *don't need to*.
2 *must* and *have to*.
3 *can* and *be allowed to*.
4 *mustn't*, *can't* and *not be allowed to*.

> SEE LANGUAGE REFERENCE PAGE 34

2 Find one example in the article about Paradise Ridge for each of the rules in exercise 1.

3 Complete the house rules with words or phrases from exercise 1. Use your own ideas.

House rules

1 You *don't have to* pay electricity and gas bills.
2 You _____ pay the rent on the first day of the month.
3 You _____ pay for phone calls.
4 You _____ smoke in the kitchen and lounge.
5 You _____ switch off the TV and CD player in the lounge at midnight.
6 You _____ have pets in the house.
7 You _____ do the housework.
8 You _____ have small parties on Saturday nights.
9 Visitors who stay the night _____ help with the housework.
10 Visitors _____ stay for more than three days.

4 Compare your rules with a partner. Whose rules are stricter?

5 Choose a place from the box and write four sentences about it using the words and phrases from exercise 1. Do not mention the name of the place.

church   hospital   library   museum
plane   prison   school   theatre

You aren't allowed to touch anything.
You don't have to go there, but it's usually interesting.
You often have to buy a ticket.
You have to leave your bag outside.

6 Work in pairs. Read your sentences to your partner. He/She must decide which place you are talking about.

7 Do you have to follow any rules where you live? Tell a partner about them.

We aren't allowed to put the rubbish out before 8pm.
We have to pay a monthly charge for the lift and the lights on the stairs.

VOCABULARY: accommodation

1 Look at the photos. Which country do you think this is? What does your town look like from the air?

2 Complete the sentences in column A with a phrase from column B.

A	B
1 Most people in Britain own their homes, but about 30% live	a a house or a **flat** with their friends.
2 Accommodation in British town centres is usually	b in France.
3 It is quite common for young people to share	c in detached or **semi-detached** houses with gardens.
4 British families often prefer to live in the **suburbs**	d in **rented** accommodation.
5 About half a million British people own **holiday homes**	e in **apartment blocks** or rows of old **terraced** houses.

3 Match the words in bold in exercise 2 to the definitions 1–7.

1 two houses joined together
2 houses that are joined together in a line
3 homes that you live in for only part of the year
4 a home that is usually on one floor of a larger building
5 buildings that contain a number of separate flats
6 lived in by someone who pays money to the owner
7 parts of a town that are away from the town centre

4 Change the sentences in exercise 2 so that they are true for your country.

LISTENING

1 Work in pairs. Match the words in the box to the photos A–F. Would you like to live in any of them? Why or why not?

cave   houseboat   lighthouse
mobile home   tree house   windmill

2 🔊 1.21–1.23 Listen to three people talking about their unusual homes. Where do they live? Choose your answers from the box in exercise 1.

3 🔊 1.21–1.23 Listen again and make a note of the best and the worst things about where they live.

4 Match the sentences to the three unusual homes in exercise 2. Then check your answers in tapescripts 1.21–1.23 on page 138.

1 We make dog owners leave their pets in the garden.
2 The local authorities make us move on.
3 We don't let little kids come up on their own.
4 They let us keep pets.
5 The farmers are happy to let us stay on their land.
6 The local people don't let us stay.
7 They don't allow us to have visitors.
8 We don't allow smoking.

GRAMMAR: *make, let & allow*

We can use the verbs *make, let* and *allow* to talk about obligation and permission.

Obligation   *make* + object + infinitive without *to*
Our teacher **makes us do** *a lot of homework.*
(= We must do a lot of homework.)

Permission   *let* + object + infinitive without *to*
The farmer **lets us stay** *on his land.*
(= We can stay on his land.*)

allow + object + *to* + infinitive
They usually **allow us to stay** *overnight.*
(= We can usually stay overnight.)

allow + noun/verb + *-ing*
They **don't allow smoking** *in the living room.*
(= You can't smoke in the living room.)

❯ SEE LANGUAGE REFERENCE PAGE 34

1 Choose the correct verb to complete the sentences.

1 They *let / allow* us to put up our tent wherever we want.
2 They *make / allow* us park our cars in the car park.
3 They *let / allow* us use the washing machine in their kitchen.
4 They *make / let* us come and go when we want.
5 They *make / let* us pay £3 a night.

2 What is being described in exercise 1?

a) a hotel   b) a campsite   c) a holiday flat

3 Use the prompts to make sentences which are true for you.

My	teacher parents boss wife husband boyfriend girlfriend	(doesn't) (don't)	make(s) let(s) allow(s)	me us	(to) …

My boss makes us work late on Fridays.
My girlfriend doesn't let me smoke in her car.

SPEAKING

1 Work in pairs. Discuss these questions.

- Is it common for people to have holiday homes in your country?
- Where are the most popular places to buy a holiday home? Why?
- Do people from abroad buy holiday homes in your country? Which countries do they usually come from?

2 Work in pairs. You are going to design a luxury holiday home. Discuss these questions.

- Where exactly is your holiday home?
- Is it a flat or a house?
- Is it old or new?
- How big is it?
- What facilities has it got? (e.g. garden, swimming pool, private beach …)

3 Talk to other pairs of students. Describe your holiday home and try to persuade them to book a holiday there.

Useful language

I think you'll really like it because …
It's just the thing you're looking for.
It's great for (families/couples/singles).
It's in the most fantastic spot …

3B | Bedrooms

SPEAKING & VOCABULARY: verb collocations (sleep)

1 Complete the sentences with a verb from the box.

fall	feel	go	have	make	set	wake

1 I often find it difficult to _____ up in the morning.
2 I always _____ the bed first thing in the morning.
3 I sometimes _____ a nap after lunch.
4 I sometimes _____ asleep in front of the TV.
5 I often _____ sleepy in the middle of the day.
6 I never _____ to sleep before ten o'clock.
7 I sometimes forget to _____ my alarm clock.

2 Change the sentences in exercise 1 so that they are true for you. Compare your sentences with a partner.

3 Work in pairs. Discuss these questions.

- Do you find it easy to get to sleep?
- What do you do when you can't get to sleep?
- Are you a heavy or a light sleeper?
- Do you usually remember your dreams the next morning?
- Can you remember a recent dream?

READING

1 Look at the photos. What do you know about the people?

2 Read the articles 1–6 and match them to the headings below.

A week in bed	Rules for healthy bedrooms
Going nowhere	Sleeping with strangers
No knives allowed	A king's office

3 Read the articles again and match the phrases a–f with the end of each article.

a and it was never full!
b so he stayed where he was.
c because the green contained arsenic, a poisonous chemical.
d in case they cut themselves.
e where they recorded 'Give Peace a Chance.'
f with 100 people in the room.

6 things you probably didn't know about **beds and bedrooms**

1 **In 19th Century Britain, the Ladies' Sanitary Association published a list of rules for bedrooms. Bedrooms had to be fresh and airy, but not too airy in case people caught a cold. You had to keep cooking smells away from bedrooms, or burn incense to hide the smell. You couldn't put green wallpaper in bedrooms ...**

2 Louis XIV of France was a busy man but he didn't have to worry about getting up in the morning. His valet woke him up at 8.30 and important friends were then allowed to come into his room, where they could watch him wash and have breakfast. On some days when Louis was feeling sleepy, he didn't get up at all and he conducted the day's business from his bed ...

4 Find words in the articles that match the definitions 1–8.

1 a decision by a court of law that someone is guilty of a crime
2 a man who looks after another man's clothes
3 a person who has to leave their country because it is dangerous for them to stay
4 a small hotel
5 a strong complaint or disagreement
6 a substance that gives a strong smell when it is burned
7 large rooms where a lot of people sleep
8 men who live in a religious community away from other people

4 Put the phrases a–f into the gaps 1–6 in the article.

a   and especially the low profile ones
b   (in fact you're more likely to be struck by lightning)
c   buying stocks and shares, for instance
d   in his local pub with his mates
e   When America was recovering from the Civil War
f   that's over £115 million a day

5 How do lotteries work in your country? Do you think that lotteries are a good way to raise money?

GRAMMAR: past simple & past continuous

1 Work in pairs. Look at the sentence from the article below. Then complete the rules with *past simple* or *past continuous*.

> *John **was having** a quiet drink in his local pub when his winning numbers **came up** on the TV.*
>
> Use the _____ for completed past actions.
> Use the _____ for actions that were in progress at a particular time in the past.
>
> You often use the past continuous with the past simple. Use the _____ longer activities. Use the _____ for shorter, completed actions.
>
> *When America **was recovering** from the Civil War, lotteries **helped** pay for more than 50 universities.*

> **SEE LANGUAGE REFERENCE PAGE 44**

2 Complete the two true stories. Put the verbs in brackets into the past simple or the past continuous.

Three friends (1) _____ (*spend*) the weekend in London when they were refused entry at a nightclub because they (2) _____ (*not / wear*) shirts and ties. They (3) _____ (*go*) to an all-night supermarket and (4) _____ (*buy*) some new shirts. While they (5) _____ (*pay*) for the shirts, they (6) _____ (*decide*) to buy a scratchcard and (7) _____ (*win*) £20,000. They (8) _____ (*spend*) the whole night celebrating in the nightclub!

A man (9) _____ (*walk*) under a tree when some bird droppings (10) _____ (*fall*) on his head. As this is supposed to be lucky, he (11) _____ (*decide*) to buy an instant lottery ticket and he (12) _____ (*win*) £24. The following week he (13) _____ (*stand*) under the same tree when the same thing (14) _____ (*happen*) again! So he (15) _____ (*buy*) another lottery ticket and won £444. He now spends time every week standing under that lucky tree, waiting for that little bird.

SPEAKING

1 Work in pairs. Make up a story about a lottery winner by answering the questions below. Then practise telling the story to another pair of students.

- Where and when did he/she buy the ticket(s)?
- How did he/she choose the numbers?
- Where and when did he/she hear about their lottery win?
- What was he/she doing at the time?
- What did he/she do next?

PRONUNCIATION: *was* & *were*

1 🔊 1.31 Listen to the conversation. Are the underlined words pronounced in their strong or weak forms? When do we use the strong forms of these words?

	strong	**weak**
was	/wɒz/	/wəz/
were	/wɜː/	/wə/

A: (1) <u>Was</u> that man standing under the tree again?
B: Yes, he (2) <u>was</u>. He (3) <u>was</u> with a friend this time.
A: What do you think they (4) <u>were</u> doing?
B: I asked them. They said they (5) <u>were</u> waiting for a bird.
A: A bird! I find that hard to believe.
B: They (6) <u>were</u>! They said it (7) <u>was</u> a lucky bird.
A: I knew he (8) <u>was</u> a bit crazy!

2 Work in pairs. Practise the conversation with your partner.

4B | Coincidences

VOCABULARY: *both* & *neither*

Use *both* and *neither* to compare two people or things.
We both have brown hair.
Neither of us has a car.
Jenny and Zoe both live in London.
Neither Jenny nor Zoe has a boyfriend.

Dr Condoleeza Rice,   Julianne Moore,
US Secretary of State   Hollywood actress

1 Look at the photos. Complete the sentences with *both* or *neither*.

1 _____ are very successful.
2 They _____ have brown hair.
3 _____ of them live in the States.
4 _____ of them looks very happy.
5 _____ Condoleeza Rice nor Julianne Moore is poor.
6 _____ Condoleeza Rice and Julianne Moore have university degrees.

2 Look at sentences 5 and 6 in exercise 1 again. Choose the correct words to complete the rules below.

We use a *plural / singular* verb and *and / nor* with **both**.
We use a *plural / singular* verb and *and / nor* with **neither**.

> SEE LANGUAGE REFERENCE PAGE 44

3 Work in pairs. Ask your partner questions and find six things you have in common. Then tell the rest of the class about the things you have in common. Use *both* or *neither* with *we* or *us* in your sentences.

We both have a brother.
Neither of us has visited London.

LISTENING

1 🔘 1.32 Listen to a conversation between Clive, the delivery man, and Linda. Tick the topics a–h they discuss. Which two topics are not discussed?

a a local pub
b a James Bond film
c squash lessons
d the new boss
e their jobs
f where they live
g where they were last night
h children

2 🔘 1.32 Listen again and make a note of the things Linda and Clive have in common.

3 Find these expressions in tapescript 1.32 on pages 139–140 and explain them in your own words.

1 It's worth it.
2 It's a bit out of your way.
3 You're kidding.
4 Small world.
5 No rest for the wicked.

FUNCTIONAL LANGUAGE: talking about similarities & differences

Similarities

So/Neither + auxiliary verb + subject

- Use *so* after a positive sentence and *neither* after a negative.
  I'm very busy at the moment. **So** *am I.*
  I can't drive. **Neither** *can I.*

- Use *do/does/did* if there's no auxiliary.
  I study English on Thursdays. So **do** *I.*
  I started two years ago. So **did** *I.*

- Use *Me, too* and *Me, neither.*
  I like pizzas. **Me, too.**
  I'm not very good at general knowledge. **Me, neither.**

Differences

- Use subject + auxiliary verb, not *so* or *neither.*
  I'm very busy at the moment. **I'm not**.
  I can't speak Chinese. **I can**.

- Use *do/does/did* if there's no auxiliary,
  I didn't go to the meeting yesterday. **I did**.

> SEE LANGUAGE REFERENCE PAGE 44

1 Find and underline five examples of *so/neither* + auxiliary verb + subject in tapescript 1.32 on pages 139–140. For each example, find the verb that corresponds to the auxiliary verb in the response.

So am I. – I'<u>m</u> going tomorrow.

2 Choose the best response to complete the exchanges.

1   A: I didn't like the concert much.
    B: *Neither did I. / Neither didn't I. / Neither I did.*
2   A: I love Beethoven's 5th Symphony.
    B: *I do. / I don't. / Neither do I.*
3   A: I wasn't feeling too well yesterday.
    B: *Neither I was. / Neither was I. / So was I.*
4   A: I work in an office.
    B: *So am I. / So can I. / So do I.*
5   A: I'll have a pepperoni pizza, please.
    B: *So do I. / So have I. / So will I.*
6   A: I'm a very good squash player.
    B: *I'm not. / Neither am I. / So I'm not.*
7   A: I'm sure we've met before.
    B: *I am. / Neither am I. / So am I.*
8   A: I haven't been to the park for ages.
    B: *Me, neither. / Me, too. / Neither I have.*

3 Work in small groups. Take it in turns to respond to the sentences.

1   I like hiphop and rap music.
2   I haven't been on a date for ages.
3   I'm going to be famous one day.
4   I'll probably write a novel when I'm older.
5   I'm never late for anything.
6   I've got several unusual pets, including a snake.
7   I didn't understand maths when I was a kid.
8   I was very popular in my last job/at my last school.

1   A: *I like hiphop and rap music.*
    B: *I don't!*
    C: *Neither do I!*

SPEAKING

1 Work in pairs, A and B. You are going to read a text about two American presidents.

A: Turn to page 127.
B: Turn to page 130.

2 Brigit Harrison and Dorothy Lowe didn't know they were identical twin sisters until they met when they were both 34. Use your imagination to think of at least five coincidences that link them.

They both had the same number of children.

3 🔘 **1.33** Listen and make a note of the coincidences. How many did you guess?

4c | Twists of fate

VOCABULARY: injuries

1 Match the injuries 1–8 to the pictures A–H.

1 He's bleeding.
2 He's got a big bruise.
3 He's got a black eye.
4 He's got a few scratches.
5 He's sprained his wrist.
6 He's suffering from shock.
7 He's twisted his ankle.
8 He's unconscious.

2 Work in pairs. Put the injuries in exercise 1 in order of seriousness. (1 = most serious ➔ 8 = least serious).

3 Work in pairs, A and B.

A: Choose an injury from exercise 1 and explain how it happened.
He was running for the bus when he fell over.

B: Listen to your partner's explanation and decide which injury he/she is talking about.

Then exchange roles.

READING

1 Work in pairs. Discuss these questions.

- Do you know anyone who is particularly unlucky?
- When was the last time that you were unlucky?

2 Work in pairs. Look at the photo and the title of the article. What do you think has happened to make this person 'the world's luckiest man'?

3 Read the article to find out if any of your ideas were correct.

The World's Luckiest Man

Life is going well for music teacher Frane Selak, 74, from the central Croatian town of Petrinja. Selak recently won about $1 million with the first lottery ticket he had bought for 40 years. With the money,
5 **he bought a new house, car and speedboat, and married his girlfriend.**

Selak is lucky to be alive. A few years ago, he was turning a corner in his car in the mountains, when he saw a truck coming straight towards him. His car
10 swerved off the road through the forest for 100 metres, ploughed into a tree and exploded. Fortunately, Selak had jumped out.

4 Read the article again and put these events in the correct order.

☐ He bought a new house.
☐ He had a car accident in the mountains.
☐ He was burnt at a petrol station.
☐ He was hit by a bus.
☐ He was in a plane crash.
☐ He won the lottery.
☐ His bus fell into a river.
☐ His train fell into a river.

5 Find these words in the article and match them to the definitions 1–6.

ploughed into (line 11)	exploded (line 11)
rails (line 15)	corpses (line 17)
haystack (line 23)	sprayed (line 33)

1 crashed into
2 suddenly caught fire with a loud noise
3 threw liquid over something
4 dead bodies
5 the lines that a train runs on
6 large pile of dried grass

But this was not the first of his lucky escapes. Back in 1962, Selak was travelling from Sarajevo to
15 Dubrovnik when the train he was in came off the rails and fell into an icy river. Rescue workers found seventeen corpses in the river, but Selak had swum to safety, suffering only shock, bruises and a broken arm.

20 Then, a year later, he was involved in a plane crash in which nineteen people died. But before the crash, Selak had jumped out of the plane and landed in a haystack. Again, the only injuries were cuts and scratches and the usual shock.

25 His next disaster was a bus accident when four people died. The bus left the road and Selak again found himself in a river. But he was becoming something of an expert at this sort of situation and swam to safety. By this time, said Selak, his friends
30 had stopped visiting him.

Three years later, he lost most of his hair and suffered burns when his car caught fire at a petrol station. The petrol pump was old and had sprayed petrol all over the hot engine of his car. Then, in 1995, he was in
35 hospital again. Another bus had knocked him over.

Selak is philosophical about his fortune. 'I am going to enjoy my life now – I feel like I have been reborn. I know God was watching over me all those years,' he said.

GRAMMAR: past perfect simple

Use the past perfect
- to talk about completed actions in the past that happened *before* other actions in the past.
  *He won the lottery with the first ticket he **had bought** for forty years.*
  (= He bought a ticket and then he won the lottery.)

Make the past perfect
- with ***had/hadn't*** + past participle.

Look at the difference between the past perfect and the past simple.
  *He was in hospital again. He **had had** another accident.*
  (= He had an accident and so he went to hospital.)

  *He was in hospital again where he **had** another accident.*
  (= He had the accident when he was in hospital.)

> SEE LANGUAGE REFERENCE PAGE 44

1 Complete the text. Put the verbs in brackets into the past simple or the past perfect.

In the late 1940s, the members of a church choir in Nebraska (1) _____ (*meet*) every Wednesday at 7.20 to practise their singing. But one day in 1950, it was already 7.25 and the choir (2) _____ (*not / arrive*). They (3) _____ (*be*) fortunate because at that moment a gas explosion (4) _____ (*destroy*) the church. The fifteen members of the choir (5) _____ (*have*) different reasons for being late. Two people (6) _____ (*break*) down in their car. Others (7) _____ (*decide*) to finish some work and another person (8) _____ (*fall*) asleep.

2 Read the two extracts A and B from newspaper stories. Use your imagination to answer the questions.

A

When the ambulance arrived at Mrs Porter's flat, she was lying by the front door crying and in a terrible state. A few minutes later, the paramedics found her two-year-old grandson, Reuben, playing behind a tree in the garden. They couldn't believe he was still alive.

1 Why had the ambulance gone to the flat?
2 Why was Mrs Porter crying?
3 Why couldn't the paramedics believe that the boy was still alive?

B

Hundreds of officers from the Manchester police force began to look for the two men, Martin and Eric Visser. They were surprised to receive a telephone call from the governor of the local prison, saying that he had the two young men.

1 What had the two young men done?
2 How had they got into the prison?
3 Why had they gone there?

3 1.34–1.35 Listen to the recordings to find out if your guesses were correct.

Listening

1 1.36 Listen and match the three bad luck stories 1–3 to the headlines a–c.

a **Mum left out in the cold**

b **Mum pays for expensive joke**

c **Man loses job after mountain top adventure**

2 1.36 Listen again and answer these questions.

Story 1
1 How long was the man stuck on the mountain?
2 How did he survive?
3 Who found him?

Story 2
1 How long did the woman have to wait on the balcony?
2 Why did the woman go out on to the balcony?
3 How old was the little boy?

Story 3
1 How much will the mother have to pay?
2 How did the egg get on the roof of the car?
3 How long did the egg stay there before it was discovered?

3 Have you heard any bad luck stories in the news recently? If so, what were they?

Vocabulary: time linkers

Use *while*, *as* and *when* to show that two actions happen at the same time.
> *A black cat crossed my path **while** / **as** / **when** I was walking down the street.*

Use *the moment*, *as soon as* and *when* to show that one action happens immediately after another action.
> *I crossed the road **the moment** / **as soon as** / **when** I saw the black cat.*

Use *by the time* to show that one action has happened before another.
> *I'd had three different accidents **by the time** I got home.*

> SEE LANGUAGE REFERENCE PAGE 44

1 Look at these extracts from the bad luck stories. One of the three time linkers in italics in each sentence is wrong. Underline it. Then explain why it is wrong.

1 Thomas Milnik found out that he'd lost his job *while / as / after* doctors at the hospital were deciding whether to cut off six of his toes.

2 The 41-year-old hiker was climbing in the Alps *as soon as / when / as* it suddenly started to snow.

3 He was eventually rescued five days later *the moment / after / when* workers at a research station heard his cries for help.

4 A woman had to be rescued by police yesterday *when / after / as soon as* her son locked her out on the balcony.

5 The mother could only watch *as / while / after* her son walked to the sofa, climbed up on to it and then fell asleep.

6 The egg continued to cook until the owner of the car discovered it two hours later. *By the time / When / The moment* he found it, the fried egg had burned into the paint.

2 Complete the article using appropriate time linkers from the language box.

Police arrested two burglars last night (1) _____ they jumped into a police car thinking it was their getaway car.

Police say that the two men had planned to break into two houses on the same street that night. They had arranged to meet a third man on the corner of the street (2) _____ they had finished in the second house.

The policeman who was driving the car, said: 'They only realized it was the wrong car (3) _____ they were actually sitting in the back of it. But (4) _____ they realized it was a police car, it was too late. I'd locked the doors, and they couldn't get out.'

SPEAKING

1 Work as a class. Look at the pictures. They show the start of another bad luck story. Take turns to continue the story one sentence at a time.

A: *Jane was getting ready for an important date.*
B: *She was putting on her make-up when suddenly a black cat jumped onto the table.*
C: *Unfortunately, when the cat jumped on to the table, it smashed the mirror.*
D: *As Jane bent down to pick up the mirror, she banged her head on the table.*

DID YOU KNOW?

1 Work in pairs. Read the information about superstitions and discuss these questions.

Superstitions in Britain

In Britain, there are many superstitions connected with cats. Black cats are good-luck animals, and you should welcome them into your house. A black cat sitting outside your front door means that you will be rich, and you will be very lucky if you see a cat sneeze. However, if a black cat crosses your path, you will have bad luck. The bad luck will go away if you walk backwards or spit on the ground in front of you.

- Which birds or animals in your country are considered to be lucky or unlucky?
- What other superstitions are common?
- How superstitious are you?

GRAMMAR

Past simple & past continuous

We use the past continuous for actions in progress at a particular time in the past. These actions are incomplete.

At nine o'clock last night, he was watching TV.

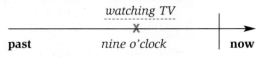

We use the past simple for completed past actions.

*He **decided** to buy a lottery ticket.*

We often use the past continuous and the past simple together. We use the past continuous for longer, 'background' actions and we use the past simple for shorter, completed actions.

*Three friends **were spending** a weekend in London and they **decided** to go to a nightclub.*

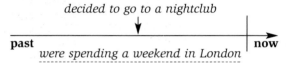

Past continuous

Affirmative
subject + *was/were* + verb + *-ing* ...
Negative
subject + *was/were* + not + verb + *-ing* ...
Question
Was/Were + subject + verb + *-ing*?

Past perfect simple

We use the past perfect to talk about completed actions in the past that happened before other actions in the past.

*Rescuers arrived, but Selak **had swum** to safety.*
(= Selak swam to safety and then rescuers arrived.)

We often use the past perfect and the past simple together to show the order in which two actions took place.

Compare the following pair of sentences:
*He **had married** her when he **won** the lottery.*
(= He married her and then he won the lottery.)
*He **married** her when he **had won** the lottery.*
(= He won the lottery and then he married her.)

Affirmative & Negative			
I/You/He/She/We/They	had hadn't	broken	a leg.
Question			
What	had	I/you/he/she/we/they	done?

Time linkers

We can use *while*, *as* and *when* to show that two actions happen at the same time.

*He was reading a letter **while/as/when** the doctors were deciding what to do next.*
***While/As/When** the doctors were deciding what to do next, he was reading a letter.*

We can use *the moment*, *as soon as* and *when* to show that one action happens immediately after another one.

*The boy fell asleep **the moment/as soon as/when** he climbed onto the sofa.*
***The moment/As soon as/When** the boy climbed onto the sofa, he fell asleep.*

We can use *by the time* to show that one action has happened before another.

*The party had finished **by the time** we arrived.*
***By the time** we arrived, the party had finished.*

FUNCTIONAL LANGUAGE

Talking about similarities & differences

Similarities
We can make short statements that begin with *so* and *neither* to show a similarity or agreement between what we think and a statement made by another person. We use *so* after an affirmative statement, and we use *neither* after a negative statement.

*I'm feeling tired.   **So** am I.*
*She's got a cold.   **So** have I.*
*They won't be happy.   **Neither** will you.*
*He hasn't finished.   **Neither** has she.*

The auxiliary verb in the first statement is repeated in the statement that begins with *so* or *neither*.

If the first statement is in the present simple, the second statement will include *do/don't/does/doesn't*. If the first statement is in the past simple, the second statement will include *did/didn't*.

*I like this place.   **So do** I.*
*I didn't understand.   **Neither did** I.*

It is also possible to use *too* and *neither* after a pronoun.

*He's Canadian.   **Me too.***
*She's not well.   **Me neither.***

Differences

When we want to say the opposite of another statement, we do not use *so* or *neither*. We use a pronoun followed by an auxiliary verb. We stress both the pronoun and the auxiliary verb.

> I can't swim. **I can.**
> I'm not hungry. **I am.**

If the first statement is in the present simple or the past simple, the second statement will include *do/don't/does/doesn't/did/didn't*.

> I don't like hamburgers. I **do!**
> He wants a divorce. She **doesn't**.
> They arrived early. You **didn't!**

Both & neither

We use *both* and *neither* to compare two people or things. The meaning of *both* is positive and the meaning of *neither* is negative.

> **Both** of them have a good job.
> (= He has a good job and she has a good job.)
> **Neither** of them has a good job.
> (= He doesn't have a good job and she doesn't have a good job.)

We use a plural verb when *both* is the subject of the sentence. We normally use a singular verb when *neither* is the subject of a sentence. When we name the two subjects, *both* is used with *and*. *Neither* is used with *nor*.

> Both Ceri and Philip **speak** Spanish.
> Neither Ceri nor Philip **speaks** Slovenian.

Both can be used in two positions in a sentence.

> **Both** of them have children.
> They **both** have children.

WORD LIST

Idioms (taking risks)

a bit of a gamble	/ə ˌbɪt əv ə ˈgæmbl/
a lot at stake	/ə ˌlɒt ət ˈsteɪk/
against the odds	/əˌgenst ði: ˈɒdz/
give (sth) a go	/ˌgɪv ə ˈgəʊ/
it's a lottery	/ˌɪts ə ˈlɒtəri/
play safe	/ˌpleɪ ˈseɪf/
try your luck	/ˌtraɪ jə ˈlʊk/

Injuries

ankle *n C*	/ˈæŋkl/
black eye *n C*	/ˌblæk ˈaɪ/
bleed *v*	/bliːd/
bruise *n C/v*	/bruːz/
burn *n C/v* ***	/bɜːn/
frostbitten *adj*	/ˈfrɒstˌbɪtn/
scratch *n C/v*	/skrætʃ/
shock *n C/v* **	/ʃɒk/
sprain *n c/v*	/spreɪn/
wrist *n C*	/rɪst/
suffer from *v* ***	/ˈsʌfə ˌfrɒm/
twist *v* *	/twɪst/
unconscious *adj*	/ʌnˈkɒnʃəs/

Other words & phrases

according to *prep* ***	/əˈkɔːdɪŋ tuː/
addict *n C*	/ˈædɪkt/
all night *adj*	/ˌɔːl ˈnaɪt/
balcony *n C*	/ˈbælkəni/
bang *v*	/bæŋ/
billion *n C*	/ˈbɪljən/
burglar *n C*	/ˈbɜːglə/
catch fire *v*	/ˌkætʃ ˈfaɪə/
coincidence *n C*	/kəʊˈɪnsɪd(ə)ns/
corpse *n C*	/kɔːps/
critic *n C* *	/ˈkrɪtɪk/
destroy *v* ***	/dɪˈstrɔɪ/
droppings *n pl*	/ˈdrɒpɪŋz/
end up *v*	/ˌend ˈʌp/
explode *v* *	/ɪkˈspləʊd/
explosion *n C* *	/ɪkˈspləʊʒn/
fancy *v*	/ˈfænsi/
fortune *n U* *	/ˈfɔːtʃuːn/
fry *v* *	/fraɪ/
gamble *v*	/ˈgæmbl/
good cause *n C*	/ˌgʊd ˈkɔːz/
governor *n C*	/ˈgʌv(ə)nə/
handful *n C*	/ˈhændfʊl/
have (sth) in common	/ˌhæv ɪn ˈkɒmən/
have (sth) on your mind	/hæv ɒn jə ˈmaɪnd/
haystack *n C*	/ˈheɪˌstæk/
hiker *n C*	/ˈhaɪkə/
horn *n C*	/hɔːn/
icy *adj*	/ˈaɪsi/
identical *adv* *	/aɪˈdentɪkl/
income *n C* ***	/ˈɪnkʌm/
industry *n C* ***	/ˈɪndəstri/
it's (not) worth it	/ɪts nɒt ˈwɜːθ ɪt/
jackpot *n C*	/ˈdʒækpɒt/
jet set *n C*	/ˈdʒet ˌset/
legal *adj* ***	/ˈliːgl/
leisure club *n C*	/ˈleʒə ˌklʌb/
lightning *n U*	/ˈlaɪtnɪŋ/
liquid *n C/U* ***	/ˈlɪkwɪd/
local *adj/n C* *	/ˈləʊkl/
lucky break *n C*	/ˌlʌki ˈbreɪk/
make-up *n U*	/ˈmeɪk ˌʌp/
mate *n C*	/meɪt/
oven *n C* *	/ˈʌvn/
parachute *n C/v*	/ˈpærəˌʃuːt/
paramedic *n C*	/ˌpærəˈmedɪk/
parental *adj*	/pəˈrentl/
pepperoni *n U*	/ˌpepəˈrəʊni/
petrol station *n C*	/ˈpetrəl ˌsteɪʃn/
philosophical *adj*	/ˌfɪləˈsɒfɪkl/
pile *n C* *	/paɪl/
plough into *v*	/ˌplaʊ ˈɪntuː/
profile *n C*	/ˈprəʊfaɪl/
pupil *n C* ***	/ˈpjuːpl/
quick-fix *adj*	/ˌkwɪkˈfɪks/
rail *n C* **	/reɪl/
reduce *v* ***	/rɪˈdjuːs/
regular *n C/adj* ***	/ˈregjʊlə/
regularly *adv* **	/ˈregjʊləli/
scream *n C/v* *	/skriːm/
siren *n C*	/ˈsaɪrən/
smash *v* *	/smæʃ/
snake *n C*	/sneɪk/
sneeze *v*	/sniːz/
solution *n C* **	/səˈluːʃn/
solve *v* **	/sɒlv/
speedboat *n C*	/ˈspiːdˌbəʊt/
spit *v*	/spɪt/
spray *v/n C/U*	/spreɪ/
squash *n U*	/skwɒʃ/
superstition *n C*	/ˌsuːpəˈstɪʃn/
survive *v* ***	/səˈvaɪv/
symphony *n C*	/ˈsɪmfəni/
tempt *v*	/tempt/
throughout *prep* *	/θruːˈaʊt/
toddler *n C*	/ˈtɒdlə/
toe *n C* *	/təʊ/
turnover *n U*	/ˈtɜːnəʊvə/
twin *n C/adj* *	/twɪn/
twist of fate	/ˌtwɪst əv ˈfeɪt/
warehouse *n C*	/ˈweəhaʊs/
wave *v* **	/weɪv/
wicked *adj*	/ˈwɪkɪd/
you're kidding	/jɔː ˈkɪdɪŋ/

5A | Hard sell

VOCABULARY: adjectives (advertising)

1 Think of three different brand names that you know for each of the products below.

Which are your favourite brands for these products? Why?

2 Match the adjectives in the box to the products in exercise 1. Can you think of any other adjectives to describe them?

> comfortable   delicious   efficient   fashionable   fresh
> healthy   popular   reliable   strong   stylish

3 Think of another product and write six adjectives to describe it. Read your adjectives to the class. Can they guess what the product is?

READING

1 Look at this list of products that are often advertised with children in mind. How many more items can you add to it?

breakfast cereals, computer games, fast food, sweets …

Can you remember seeing any advertisements for these products? How did the advertisements appeal to children?

2 Read the article and answer the questions.

1 What is more important for American advertisers – the money that children spend now, or the money they will spend in the future?
2 How many different ways of catching children's attention are mentioned in the text?
3 Why is classroom advertising 'here to stay'?

CATCH THEM YOUNG

Y OU WANT CHILDREN to learn languages, compute skills, play the piano or become good, honest citize Any educationalist will tell you the simple answe catch them young. You want children to buy your produc
5 and to develop brand loyalty? The answer is the same.

In 1997, children in America spent or influenced the spendi of $500 billion and the figure is certainly much higher no But far more important to the advertisers is what they will spend when they are adults. 'The kids we're reaching are
10 consumers in training,' said Joseph Fenton of Donnelly Marketing.

Kids spend 20% of their lives in school, so it is no surprise to find advertisers turning their attention to the classroom. What is rather more surprising is to learn how far advertisers
15 have already gone.

- Over half of American students receive free covers for their text books with adverts for snacks and breakfast cereals.
- Many teachers use educational materials that are paid
20   for by big business – mathematics worksheets with Disney characters, for example.
- Students who do better than others in their studies are given vouchers for free pizzas, burgers and French fries.
- Many school cafeterias serve and advertise brand name
25   food. Schools also sell advertising space in school corridors and toilets, on the side of the school bus and school websites.
- Probably the least popular form of classroom advertising is Channel One. Eight million American teenagers have
30   to watch a twelve-minute programme every day. This contains ten minutes of news and two minutes of commercials.

Not everyone is happy with the growth of classroo advertising, but it is almost certainly here to stay. The bigge
35 problem facing most schools in America is a shortage of cas Taxpayers don't want to pay more and other fund-raising programmes don't raise enough money. 'Advertising is not just the best way to raise money,' said one school head. 'It's the only way.'

3 Read the article again and complete the end of each line where it has been torn.

4 Is it right to advertise to young children? Why or why not?

GRAMMAR: comparatives 1

Use comparatives to compare two things or people.

*The figure is **higher than** in 1997.*
*Advertisers have **bigger** budgets **than** they used to have.*
*Brand names are **more expensive than** other products.*

Make negative comparisons with *less + adjective + than.*

*Classroom advertising is **less common** in Europe **than** in the States.*

Make the difference between the two things bigger or smaller with a modifier before the comparative adjective. For big differences use *much, a lot, far.* For small differences, use *a little, slightly, a bit.*

*The figure is **much higher** now than in 1997.*
*Advertisements are **slightly longer** than they used to be.*

Use superlatives to compare more than two things or people.

***The biggest** problem for schools is cash.*
*Children are one of **the most important** markets for advertisers.*

Make negative comparisons with *the least + adjective.*

***The least popular** form of advertising is Channel One.*

⊙ SEE LANGUAGE REFERENCE PAGE 54

1 Write the comparative and superlative forms of the adjectives in the box.

bad   big   good   happy   healthy   strong   surprising

2 Complete the sentences. Put the words in brackets into positive or negative comparative or superlative forms. Remember that you may also need to include *than* or *the*.

1 I usually buy famous brand names because they are a lot _____ (*reliable*) other brands.
2 I always do my shopping at _____ (*cheap*) shops in town.
3 I prefer to go shopping during the week when it is _____ (*busy*) the weekend.
4 I think that _____ (*good*) time to go shopping is during the sales.
5 Small shops are often a bit _____ (*expensive*) big supermarkets, but they are much _____ (*interesting*).

3 Work in pairs. Think of three shops in your town. Make comparative and superlative sentences about them using the prompts.

cheap/expensive   stylish/old-fashioned
popular/crowded   bad/good quality
bad/good service   wide range of goods
friendly staff   easy to get to

4 Compare your ideas with another pair of students.

SPEAKING

1 Work in small groups. Read the information.

You work for an advertising agency. A company that produces a fizzy mineral water called *Life* has hired you to create an advertisement. It wants to sell the water to young people (16–25) as an alternative to cola and other fizzy drinks. It has decided to advertise on TV. The advertising slogan will be 'Natural and Healthy'.

2 Plan your advertisement. Follow the steps below.

• Make a list of seven images you associate with the words 'natural' and 'healthy'.
• Choose one image from your list that is fashionable and will appeal to young people.
• Choose the kind of music you want to use.
• Decide whether you want to use a famous personality.
• Decide when would be the best time to show the advert on TV (before or after which programme).

3 Present your advertisement to the class.

LISTENING

1 Work in pairs. Discuss these questions.

- Do you ever get emails, letters or phone calls from people who want to sell you something? If yes, do you ever reply? Why or why not?
- Do you think this kind of selling is a good idea? Explain your reasons.

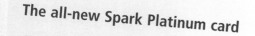

The all-new Spark Platinum card

Spark Platinum

40009 9908 4443 1234

VALID FROM 01 05
MR A N OTHER
EXPIRES END 10 07
VISA

Low interest rate – only 5.5%
High credit limit – borrow up to £15,000
Six months' free credit
Reward points for every £500 you spend

Apply for your card now

Mr Thomas Jones
491 Western Avenue
Greenford

The red seal of approval

2 Look at the advertising envelope. Find words or phrases that match the definitions 1–3.

1 a period of time when you don't pay extra for borrowing money
2 the maximum amount of money that you can borrow
3 the money (percentage) that you pay when you borrow money from a bank

3 🔘 1.37 Listen to a telephone conversation and say if the sentences are true (T) or false (F)? Explain your answers.

1 The salesman is doing a market research survey.
2 Mr Jones wants the salesman to send him lots of credit cards.

4 🔘 1.37 Listen to the conversation again. Find five differences between the credit card that the salesman describes and the credit card on the envelope.

GRAMMAR: comparatives 2

Use *the same as, as* + adjective *as* … or *similar to* to say that two things are the same, or almost the same.
*This credit card is **the same as** that one.*
*This credit card is **as good as** that one.*
*His name is **similar to** mine.*

Use *different from* or *not as* + adjective *as* … to talk about the differences between two things.
*This credit card is **different from** that one.*
*The Platinum Card is **not as good as** the Gold Card.*
(= The Gold Card is better.)

▶ SEE LANGUAGE REFERENCE PAGE 54

1 Find and correct six grammatical mistakes in the text.

Yes, sir, this is slightly different as the Mark V. It looks same, but this one is black and white. The black and white sets are not as popular colour these days. If you've ever watched television in colour, you'll know that it isn't the same thing at all. Of course, it's not expensive as the colour set. However, it's certainly as reliable the Mark V, and you'll see that the style is similar the colour set.

2 Rewrite the sentences using the prompts so that they keep the same meaning.

1 *Whizzo* is better than any other washing powder.
No other washing powder <u>is as good as Whizzo</u>.
2 *Whizzo* is different from other washing powders.
Whizzo isn't _____.
3 *Whizzo* washes whiter than all other washing powders.
Other washing powders don't _____.
4 *Whizzo* is the most popular washing powder.
Other washing powders aren't_____.
5 *Whizzo* is cheaper than other washing powders.
Whizzo isn't _____.

FUNCTIONAL LANGUAGE: on the phone

1 How many phone expressions can you make from the words in the boxes below?

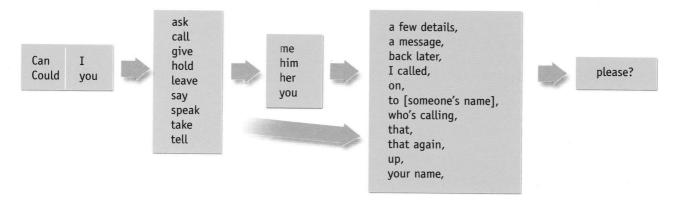

| Can | I |
| Could | you |

| ask |
| call |
| give |
| hold |
| leave |
| say |
| speak |
| take |
| tell |

| me |
| him |
| her |
| you |

| a few details, |
| a message, |
| back later, |
| I called, |
| on, |
| to [someone's name], |
| who's calling, |
| that, |
| that again, |
| up, |
| your name, |

| please? |

Can I leave her a message, please?
Could you say that again, please?

2 What questions from exercise 1 could you ask to get these replies?

1 Yes, the name's Bond. James Bond.
2 Yes, of course. I'll just get a pen and some paper.
3 Yes, I'll tell him as soon as he gets back.
4 Yes, but I don't think she'll be in the office until tomorrow morning.
5 Yes, OK. In about half an hour. Is that OK?
6 Yes, I'm sorry. It's a bad line, I think.

3 🔘 1.42 Listen to the recording to check your answers.

Roleplay

4 Work in pairs, A and B. You are going to act out a telephone conversation with an office supplies company.

A: Phone the office supplies company and place an order for some stationery.

B: You work for the office supplies company. Answer the phone and use the order form in Listening exercise 2 to take the order.

Then exchange roles.

DID YOU KNOW?

1 Work in pairs. Read the information about offices in London and answer the questions below.

The most expensive offices in the world are in London's Mayfair and Park Lane districts – and these are also the most expensive properties in the game of Monopoly. Prices are almost twice as high as in the most popular parts of New York and Hong Kong. Besides having the most expensive offices and hotels, this part of London is close to the main shopping streets and some of the city's most fashionable squares.

• Where are most of the offices in your town? What is that part of town like?
• Which is the best part of your town to work in?

GRAMMAR

Comparatives

We use comparatives to compare two things or people. We use *than* to join the two things we are comparing.

> The supermarkets are cheaper **than** my local shops.
> Famous brand names are often more expensive **than** other brands.

We can make negative comparisons with *less +* adjective + *than*.

> Orange juice is **less popular than** fizzy drinks.

We can make the difference between two things bigger or smaller with a modifier before the comparative adjective. With big differences we use *much, a lot, far* and with small differences we use *a little, slightly, a bit.*

> Digital cameras are **much** more powerful these days.
> The shop now has a **slightly** wider range of goods.

We use superlatives to compare more than two things or people. We put *the* before the superlative adjective.

> She buys **the** cheapest clothes she can find.
> It's **the** most fashionable brand at the moment.

We can make negative superlatives with *the least +* adjective.

> Which shop is **the least friendly**?

With short adjectives, we usually add *-er/-est.*

| fresh | fresher | the freshest |
| cheap | cheaper | the cheapest |

When an adjective ends in *-e*, we add *-r/-est.*

| wide | wider | the widest |
| late | later | the latest |

When an adjective ends in *-y* after a consonant, we change the *-y* to *-ier/-iest.*

| easy | easier | the easiest |
| busy | busier | the busiest |

When an adjective with one syllable ends with a consonant after a vowel, we double the consonant.

| big | bigger | the biggest |
| hot | hotter | the hottest |

With longer adjectives, we add *more/the most.*

| important | more important | the most important |
| reliable | more reliable | the most reliable |

Some adjectives have irregular comparative and superlative forms.

good	better	the best
bad	worse	the worst
far	further	the furthest

If we want to say that two things are the same, or almost the same, we can use the following structures:

1 *the same as*
  Her trainers are **the same as** mine.

2 *as +* adjective + *as*
  Her trainers are **as old-fashioned as** mine.

3 *similar to*
  Her trainers are **similar** to mine.

If we want to talk about the differences between two things or people, we can use the following structures:

1 *different from*
  Her trainers **are different from** mine.

2 *not as +* adjective + *as*
  Her trainers **are not as nice as** mine.
  (= My trainers are nicer.)

Comparing nouns

We can use comparative and superlative forms with nouns as well as adjectives.

We use *more +* noun + *than* to compare two things or people.

> In the US, there are **more classroom advertisements than** in Europe.

We use *less/fewer +* noun to make negative comparisons. We use *less* with uncountable nouns and *fewer* with plural (countable) nouns.

> He does **less work** than his boss.
> The company wants everybody to take **fewer days** off.

We use *the most/the least/the fewest +* noun to compare more than two things or people. We use *the least* with uncountable nouns and *the fewest* with plural (countable) nouns.

> Who has **the most experience**?
> Of all the people in the office, she spends **the least time** behind her desk.
> Her department gets **the fewest complaints**.

FUNCTIONAL LANGUAGE
On the phone

Can/Could I …
  ask who's calling?
  ask your name?
  call (you) back later?
  give him/her a message?
  leave a message?
  speak to (name)?
  take a few details?
  take a message?
  take your name?

Can/Could you …
  call (me) back later?
  give him/her a message?
  give me a few details?
  give me your name?
  hold on?
  say that again?
  speak up?
  take a message?
  tell him/her who's calling?
  tell him/her I called?

WORD LIST
Adjectives

comfortable **	/ˈkʌmftəbl/
crowded *	/ˈkraʊdɪd/
delicious *	/dɪˈlɪʃəs/
efficient **	/ɪˈfɪʃnt/
fashionable **	/ˈfæʃnəbl/
fresh ***	/freʃ/
healthy **	/ˈhelθi/
popular ***	/ˈpɒpjʊlə/
reliable *	/rɪˈlaɪəbl/
strong ***	/strɒŋ/
stylish	/ˈstaɪlɪʃ/

Negative prefixes (adjectives)

dishonest	/dɪsˈɒnɪst/
disloyal	/dɪsˈlɔɪəl/
dissatisfied	/dɪsˈsætɪsfaɪd/
impatient *	/ɪmˈpeɪʃnt/
impolite	/ˌɪmpəˈlaɪt/
impossible ***	/ɪmˈpɒsəbl/
improbable	/ɪmˈprɒbəbl/
inaccurate	/ɪnˈækjʊrət/
inconvenient	/ˌɪnkənˈviːnɪənt/
incorrect	/ˌɪnkəˈrekt/

unbelievable	/ˌʌnbɪˈliːvəbl/
unemployed *	/ˌʌnɪmˈplɔɪd/
unhappy **	/ʌnˈhæpi/
unlucky	/ʌnˈlʌki/
unprepared	/ˌʌnprɪˈpeəd/
unsuccessful	/ˌʌnsəkˈsesfl/

Office activities

do	a report
	some photocopying
	the filing

make	a phone call
	a report
	a photocopy
	the coffee

| receive | an email |
| | a phone call |

| send | an email |
| | a report |

| write | an email |
| | a report |

Office supplies

biro *n C*	/ˈbaɪrəʊ/
drawing pin *n C*	/ˈdrɔːɪŋ ˌpɪn/
filing cabinet *n C*	/ˈfaɪlɪŋ ˌkæbɪnət/
highlighter (pen) *n C*	/ˈhaɪˌlaɪtə (ˌpen)/
in tray *n C*	/ˈɪntreɪ/
ink cartridge *n C*	/ˈɪŋk ˌkɑːtrɪdʒ/
mouse mat *n C*	/ˈmaʊs ˌmæt/
notepad *n C*	/ˈnəʊt ˌpæd/
paperclip *n C*	/ˈpeɪpə ˌklɪp/
pencil sharpener *n C*	/ˈpensl ˌʃɑːp(ə)nə/
Post-its® *n pl*	/ˈpəʊstɪts/
stapler *n C*	/ˈsteɪplə/
Tipp-Ex® *n U*	/ˈtɪpeks/

Other words & phrases

advertiser *n C*	/ˈædvəˌtaɪzə/
annoying *adj* *	/əˈnɔɪɪŋ/
appeal *v* *	/əˈpiːl/
approval *n U* *	/əˈpruːvl/
bankrupt *adj/v*	/ˈbæŋkrʌpt/
big business *n C*	/ˌbɪg ˈbɪznəs/
blank *adj*	/blæŋk/
bossy *adj*	/ˈbɒsi/
brand *n C* *	/brænd/
bully *n C*	/ˈbʊli/
call round *v*	/ˌkɔːl ˈraʊnd/
catch (sb's) attention	/ˌkætʃ əˈtenʃn/
cereal *n C/U*	/ˈsɪərɪəl/
client *n C*	/ˈklaɪənt/

code *n C* **	/kəʊd/
commercial *n C*	/kəˈmɜːʃl/
compliment *n C*	/ˈkɒmplɪmənt/
consumer *n C* **	/kənˈsjuːmə/
corridor *n C* **	/ˈkɒrɪˌdɔː/
cover *n C* ***	/ˈkʌvə/
credit limit *n C*	/ˈkredɪt ˌlɪmɪt/
crisis *n C* **	/ˈkraɪsɪs/
cutback *n C*	/ˈkʌtbæk/
digital *adj* *	/ˈdɪdʒɪtl/
district *n C* ***	/ˈdɪstrɪkt/
double *v/adj* **	/ˈdʌbl/
educational *adj* **	/ˌedjʊˈkeɪʃn(ə)l/
educationalist *n C*	/ˌedjʊˈkeɪʃn(ə)lɪst/
energy *n U* ***	/ˈenədʒi/
enthusiastic *adj* *	/ɪnˌθjuːzɪˈæstɪk/
existing *adj* ***	/ɪgˈzɪstɪŋ/
fizzy *adj*	/ˈfɪzi/
flirt *n C/v*	/flɜːt/
fund-raising *n U*	/ˈfʌndˌreɪzɪŋ/
get rid of (sth/sb) *v*	/get ˈrɪd əv/
growth *n U* ***	/grəʊθ/
influence *v* ***	/ˈɪnfluəns/
interest rate *n C*	/ˈɪntrəst ˌreɪt/
joker *n C*	/ˈdʒəʊkə/
laser *n C*	/ˈleɪzə/
loyalty *n U*	/ˈlɔɪəlti/
market research *n U*	/ˌmɑːkɪt rɪˈsɜːtʃ/
maternity leave *n U*	/məˈtɜːnəti ˌliːv/
mood *n C* **	/muːd/
ordinary *adj* ***	/ˈɔːdn(ə)ri/
percentage *n C* *	/pəˈsentɪdʒ/
platinum *n U*	/ˈplætɪnəm/
procedure *n C* *	/prəˈsiːdʒə/
process *v* *	/ˈprəʊses/
property *n C/U* ***	/ˈprɒpəti/
rent *v* *	/rent/
repetitive *adj*	/rɪˈpetətɪv/
seal *n C*	/siːl/
secret *n C/adj* **	/ˈsiːkrət/
shortage *n C* *	/ˈʃɔːtɪdʒ/
slogan *n C*	/ˈsləʊgən/
snack *n C*	/snæk/
stationery *n U*	/ˈsteɪʃn(ə)ri/
survey *n C* **	/ˈsɜːveɪ/
sweet *n C*	/swiːt/
task *n C* ***	/tɑːsk/
taxpayer *n C*	/ˈtæksˌpeɪə/
terrible *adj* **	/ˈterəbl/
trainee *n C*	/ˌtreɪˈniː/
transfer *v* **	/ˈtrænsfɜː/
urgent *adj* *	/ˈɜːdʒ(ə)nt/
voucher *n C*	/ˈvaʊtʃə/
washing powder *n U*	/ˈwɒʃɪŋ ˌpaʊdə/
workaholic *n C*	/ˌwɜːkəˈhɒlɪk/

6A | Summer holiday

VOCABULARY: holidays 1

1 Choose the correct word or phrase to complete the collocations 1–8.

1 arrive *at the resort / a flight*
2 book *a flight / your way around*
3 check out of *the hotel / some holiday brochures*
4 choose *a destination / the packing*
5 do *the packing / the resort*
6 find *a deposit / your way around*
7 pay *a destination / a deposit*
8 pick up *the hotel / some holiday brochures*

2 What is the most logical order to do the things in exercise 1?

3 Work in pairs. Tell your partner about your last holiday. Use as many expressions as you can from exercise 1.

We chose our destination from a travel brochure. Then we …

READING

1 Read the questionnaire and answer each question for yourself.

2 Work in pairs and compare your answers. Do you have similar attitudes to travelling? Read your results on page 127 and see if you agree.

3 Find words or phrases in the questionnaire that match the definitions 1–8.

1 reading something to find specific information
2 happen unexpectedly or without planning it
3 a cheap holiday because you're booking late
4 do something after you've intended to do it for a long time
5 not take a lot of luggage
6 not prepare a long time ahead
7 made yourself comfortable
8 someone who looks after you when you're on holiday

4 Have you already decided what you're doing for your next holiday? Tell your partner about your plans.

Travel questionnaire

What kind of holiday person are you?

1 It's the end of February and lots of people are already planning their summer holidays. What about you?

a) I've already decided that I'm going back to the same place as last year and the year before.
b) I've just picked up some brochures from the travel agent and I'm going to spend the weekend looking through them and deciding where I want to go.
c) I really don't know yet. I fancy somewhere different, but I don't really care where. I know something will turn up, maybe a last-minute bargain or an invitation from a friend.

2 You've decided where to go and the next step is to book a flight. What are you going to do?

a) I'm picking my ticket up from the travel agent's tomorrow.
b) I'm planning to have a look for some cheap flights on the internet tonight.
c) It's too early to decide yet, I'll probably get round to it in a week or two.

3 When do you usually do your packing?

a) I've already started doing some shopping. I always like to get everything ready at least a day or two before I leave.
b) I'm going to do it all the night before. I know what I need to take already and I'm going shopping tomorrow to buy sunscreen and some film for my camera.
c) I'll probably do it the morning before I leave. It usually only takes about half an hour. I always travel light.

GRAMMAR: future 1 (future plans)

1 Look at question 5 of the questionnaire again and underline the future verb forms. Which verb form:

a) describes an intention?
b) suggests that no definite plans have been made yet?
c) suggests that a firm arrangement has already been made?

4 When do you plan get to the airport?

a) A taxi's picking me up first thing in the morning. I want to check in at least two and a half hours before my flight leaves.

b) I'd like to check in about an hour to an hour and half before my flight leaves.

c) I'll probably get there just in time – I always leave things till the last minute.

5 You've just settled into your hotel. What are you going to do first?

a) I'm meeting the travel rep and the other new arrivals for a welcome cocktail in the bar.

b) I'm going to find the tourist information centre and ask about where I can hire a car.

c) I don't know yet. I'll just wait and see what there is on offer.

2 Choose the best verb forms to complete the conversation.

A: Hello, we were on the same flight, I think.

B: Yes, we were sitting just behind you. How long (1) *will you stay / are you staying?*

A: We're here for two weeks. And you?

B: We're not too sure. (2) *We're going to stay / We'll stay* for a couple of days and then (3) *we're deciding / we'll decide* if we want to move on. Have you made any plans for tomorrow?

A: Yes, we've hired a car, (4) *we're picking it up / we'll pick it up* in the morning and (5) *we'll drive / we're going to drive* around the island. We want to find the best beaches. What about you?

B: We haven't made any plans yet. We'll probably wait to see what the weather's like tomorrow and then (6) *we're making up / we'll make up* our minds!

A: Well, there's plenty of room in our car if you fancy coming along. (7) *We'll leave / We're leaving* at 9.30, straight after breakfast.

B: OK, thanks. That sounds like a good idea. We'll let you know tomorrow.

3 Work in pairs. Write the three options for the last two questions in the quiz.

6 You know you should send some postcards. When are you going to write them?

7 It's your last day. Your plane leaves at 7.30 this evening. What are you going to do?

4 Find out if any of your classmates are doing anything special this evening / tomorrow / at the weekend.

Use *be going to* + infinitive to talk about intentions: things you definitely want to do, but you haven't made firm arrangements for yet.
We're going to book some tickets on the Internet this evening.
(= This is what we intend to do, but we haven't done it yet.)

Use the present continuous to talk about things you've already decided to do and made some arrangements for.
We're meeting at the pizza house at 8.30.
(= We've already spoken to our friends and arranged a time and a place to meet.)

Use *will* + infinitive
• to talk about the future when you haven't made any plans or arrangements.
• with *probably, possibly* or *perhaps.*
We haven't made any plans yet, we'll probably decide what to do when the others arrive tomorrow.

▶ SEE LANGUAGE REFERENCE PAGE 64

SPEAKING

Roleplay

1 Work in groups of three, A–C. It's your first morning in a hotel and you are sharing a breakfast table with some other guests. Find out what their plans are for the day.

A: Turn to page 127.
B: Turn to page 129.
C: Turn to page 134.

VOCABULARY: holidays 2

1 Read the information. Match the resorts to the photos A and B.

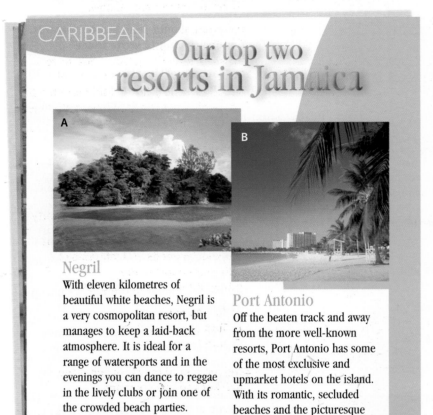

CARIBBEAN

Our top two resorts in Jamaica

Negril

With eleven kilometres of beautiful white beaches, Negril is a very cosmopolitan resort, but manages to keep a laid-back atmosphere. It is ideal for a range of watersports and in the evenings you can dance to reggae in the lively clubs or join one of the crowded beach parties. Exotic, fun and completely unforgettable!

Port Antonio

Off the beaten track and away from the more well-known resorts, Port Antonio has some of the most exclusive and upmarket hotels on the island. With its romantic, secluded beaches and the picturesque scenery of the Blue Mountains, this is an area that you will never want to leave.

2 Read the information again and say if the sentences are true (T) or false (F). Then underline the adjectives in the texts that helped you find each answer.

1 There are people from many different countries in Negril.
2 Negril has a very relaxed atmosphere.
3 The clubs in Negril are quiet and boring.
4 You will find Negril very similar to your home town.
5 Port Antonio is far from the places that people usually visit.
6 Port Antonio has cheap hotels.
7 The beaches in Port Antonio are all very crowded.
8 The Blue Mountains are very pretty.

3 Work in pairs. Discuss these questions.

• Would you prefer to go to Negril or Port Antonio? Why?
• What sort of holiday destination do you like? Use the adjectives in the texts about Negril and Porto Antonio to describe it.

Buenos Aires is ideal for a range of cultural and fun activities. You can dance tango in La Boca or visit exclusive restaurants in Recoleta.

58

LISTENING

1 A radio reporter at Heathrow Airport asked six tourists the question: What are you most looking forward to on your holiday? Here are some of the things they mentioned. Which ones do you think were mentioned by men (M) and which by women (W)?

• the football
• the weather
• the nightlife
• romantic walks along the beach
• the shopping
• the beautiful women

2 🔊 1.43–1.48 Listen to the interviews to check your answers in exercise 1.

3 🔊 1.43–1.48 Listen again and answer these questions for each person.

1 Where are they going?
2 How long are they staying?

4 🔊 1.43–1.48 Match the extracts a–f to the speakers 1–6. Then listen again to check your answers.

a There won't be much time to do anything else.
b That's definitely going to be the highlight of the four days.
c We're planning to visit every one.
d It looks like it's going to be wet and cold here.
e We're going to spend all of it.
f We'll have plenty of time to catch up on our sleep when we get back home.

5 What do you most look forward to when you go on holiday?

GRAMMAR: future 2 (predictions)

Use both *will* and *be going to* + infinitive to make predictions about the future.

> That**'ll** definitely be the highlight of the trip.
> That's definitely **going to be** the highlight of the trip.

Use *be going to* when you have present evidence for the prediction.

> It**'s going to be** hot today. (= The skies are blue and it's already 25°C at nine o'clock in the morning.)
> You**'re going to be** late. (= The class is about to start and you're still at home.)

Note that often the two forms have a very similar meaning.

⊙ SEE LANGUAGE REFERENCE PAGE 64

1 Look at the pictures. Make two different predictions about what's going to happen next in each one.

A

B

2 ⊙ 1.49–1.50 Listen to the two conversations. Were any of the predictions you made in exercise 1 correct?

3 Work in pairs. Look at the ideas in the box and predict five things for your partner.

> career   personal life   ten years from now
> money   tomorrow   friends   exams   travel

4 Tell your partner what your predictions are. Does he/she think they are possible?

SPEAKING

1 Work in groups of three, A–C. Read the information below.

You work for a travel agency that specializes in 'made-to-measure' holidays for small groups. You have been asked to arrange a two-week summer holiday for a family group who are celebrating the grandparents' golden wedding anniversary.

2 Decide on the following things.
- destination
- accommodation
- possible activities and excursions
- facilities for the golden wedding party

You will find more information about the special needs and interests of different people in the group at the back of the book.

A: Turn to page 127.
B: Turn to page 128.
C: Turn to page 132.

3 Tell the rest of the class about the holiday you have planned.

Useful language

We've decided to … because …
We're going to arrange some …
They won't want to …
They'll probably be interested in …
They'd like to … so we're going to …

4 Now discuss the holidays in your groups.
- Which holiday is:
  a) the most expensive?
  b) the most relaxing?
  c) the most fun?
- Which holiday do you think the family will choose?
- Which holiday would you enjoy most?

6B | Perfect day

SPEAKING

1 Work in pairs. Discuss these questions.

- Do you often go out for the day? Where do you usually go?
- Where's the best place to go for a day out in your area?

2 With your partner make a list of the five most important things for a good day out.

good weather, a nice restaurant ...

READING

1 Read the article and match the headings to the excursions A–D.

1 Time travel   3 Bird's-eye view
2 Sports day   4 Song and dance

2 Read the article again and match the comments 1–8 to the excursions A–D.

1 Great fun, but I fell in twice and the sea was freezing!
2 I was very nervous at first, but the pilot was very kind and he took us to some amazing places.
3 In one place, there was a brilliant harp player. I bought the CD.
4 Ireland's history is so fascinating. We learnt so much.
5 It was my first time on a horse, but it certainly won't be my last!
6 The guide made it really interesting with his funny stories about Irish heroes.
7 The scenery was absolutely fantastic and we'll never forget the sight of the seal cubs.
8 We loved it so much that we decided to stay until the very end. We had to get a taxi back to our hotel.

3 Which excursion A–D should these people choose to go on? Explain your reasons.

1 a young couple on their honeymoon
2 a businessman who wants to impress a customer
3 a group of four retired holidaymakers from Florida
4 two students from a Dublin language school who want to celebrate their last weekend in Ireland
5 a family with two teenage children
6 a delegation of European politicians on a cultural visit

4 Work in pairs. Discuss these questions.

- Which day trip would you choose to go on?
- What do you think the people in exercise 3 would like to see and do in your area?

EMERALD TOURS

Discover the best of Ireland in a day. We've put together an unbeatable selection of one-day excursions from Dublin.

CALL NOW TO MAKE YOUR RESERVATION

A Those of you who've had enough of sightseeing will love this action-packed day. In the morning, you can experience the thrills of rock climbing under the guidance of an experienced instructor. After lunch, there's sea-kayaking in Dublin Bay. To round the day off, there's a visit to the National Aquatic Centre, Europe's largest indoor waterworld. Or if you've had enough of water sports, our guide will take you for a pony ride along the sandy beaches of the Bay.

B For a taste of Ireland's ancient past, this excursion takes you to the magical area north of Dublin. As the sun sets, the highlight of the day will be a guided tour of the World Heritage Site of Newgrange, surrounded by its giant standing stones that are nearly 5,000 years old. Before we take you back into the depths of time, we will see the Hill of Tara, home of the ancient kings of Ireland, before the arrival of Christianity. This memorable day will begin with a visit to Slane Abbey where Saint Patrick brought the message of the Bible in the early 5th century.

C Ireland's west coast is one of the most beautiful and dramatic places on earth, and the ideal way to see it is from the air. In our brand new six-seater helicopter, you will first see the incredible lakes, mountains and rivers of Connemara. After you've had lunch in the pretty fishing village of Clifden, you'll be back in the air for breathtaking views of the wild Aran Islands. Don't forget to bring a camera with a zoom lens for once-in-a-lifetime shots of the seal colony.

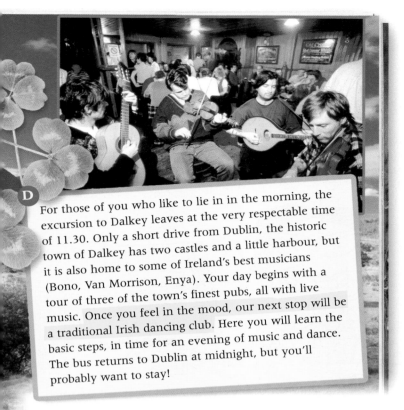

D For those of you who like to lie in in the morning, the excursion to Dalkey leaves at the very respectable time of 11.30. Only a short drive from Dublin, the historic town of Dalkey has two castles and a little harbour, but it is also home to some of Ireland's best musicians (Bono, Van Morrison, Enya). Your day begins with a tour of three of the town's finest pubs, all with live music. Once you feel in the mood, our next stop will be a traditional Irish dancing club. Here you will learn the basic steps, in time for an evening of music and dance. The bus returns to Dublin at midnight, but you'll probably want to stay!

GRAMMAR: present tenses in future time clauses

1 Look at the highlighted sentences in the text and answer the questions below.

a Do the sentences refer to the present or the future?

b Which two verb forms are used after the expressions *if, after, before* and *once*?

c Which verb form is used in the other part of the sentence?

2 Complete the text. Put the verbs in brackets into the correct tense.

KING'S PARK HOLIDAY VILLAGE

Thank you for booking your weekend away at King's Park. When we (1) _____ (*receive*) your payment, we (2) _____ (*send*) you a brochure with details of all our fantastic offers. If you (3) _____ (*want*) to hire a bicycle during your stay, please let us know and we (4) _____ (*make*) sure it's waiting for you on your arrival. Once you (5) _____ (*settle*) into your cabin, one of our guides (6) _____ (*come*) over to see that everything is to your liking. And as soon as you (7) _____ (*have*) a chance to have a look around, our reception staff (8) _____ (*be*) more than happy to take your bookings for dinner and your choice of evening entertainment. If there (9) _____ (*be*) anything else you need during your stay (morning newspapers, extra bedding, food or drink in your cabin), just let the staff know and they (10) _____ (*help*) you out as soon as they can.

3 Complete the sentences so that they are true for you.

1 I _____ as soon as I get some free time.
2 When I've done this exercise, I _____.
3 I _____ before I go to bed tonight.
4 Once I've _____, I _____.
5 I _____ as soon as I _____.

4 Compare your sentences with a partner.

> Use a present tense to talk about future time after conjunctions like *if, when, after, before, as soon as* and *once*. You often use *will* in the main clause of the sentence.
> **He'll get** in touch with you **as soon as he arrives**.
>
> Use the present perfect if you want to emphasize that the future action will have finished.
> **Once I've finished** this, **I'll give** you a call.

▶ SEE LANGUAGE REFERENCE PAGE 64

DID YOU KNOW?

1 Work in pairs. Read the information and discuss these questions.

In 2005, the city of Cork became the second Irish town (after Dublin) to become a European Capital of Culture. Visitors in search of culture can see the sculptures in the Crawford Gallery, go to a concert at the Opera House, take part in the Jazz and Blues festival, or simply find a bar in one of the historic streets and listen to some traditional Irish music. The most famous tourist attraction, however, is the Blarney Stone (just outside Cork). According to tradition, people who kiss the stone will become talkative and eloquent.

- What are the 'cultural capitals' of your country?
- What can you do in these cities?
- Which of these cities have you visited and what did you do there?

6c | Travel plans

SPEAKING

1 Work in pairs. Read the title of this best-selling book and the comment below. Then discuss the questions.

Men usually prefer to get the information they need from a guide book or the internet. Women usually prefer to ask somebody.

- Do you agree with the title of the book and the comment?
- Do you know anyone who proves that the title and comment are right or wrong?

2 Discuss these questions with your partner.

- When was the last time you needed to find out some information?
- How did you find it?
- Was it difficult to find?

LISTENING

1 🔘 **1.51** You are going to listen to Avril enquiring about a long-distance flight. Write three questions you think she and the travel agent will ask each other. Then listen to the conversation and see if your questions are answered.

2 🔘 **1.51** Listen again and complete the form.

T&A TRAVEL ➡

Flight enquiry

Customer: *Avril Goodman*

Destination: _____

Option 1:	airline _____	cost _____
Option 2:	airline _____	cost _____
Option 3:	airline _____	cost _____

3 Work in pairs. Are the sentences true (T) or false (F)?

1 Avril knows the travel agent quite well.
2 She wants to book a flight for Derek.
3 Derek knows the dates when he wants to fly.
4 The cost is more important than the flight time.
5 There isn't a big difference in cost between direct and indirect flights.
6 Only one airline flies direct.
7 Avril gets all the information she wants.

4 🔘 **1.51** Listen again to check your answers.

FUNCTIONAL LANGUAGE: indirect questions

Use indirect questions when you are making polite enquiries. Direct questions can sometimes sound impolite.

Begin indirect questions with introduction + *if* or question word + indirect question.
> ***Do you know*** *if he wants to go direct?*

Here are some more common introductions to indirect questions:
I wonder …
I'd like to know …
Could you tell me … ?
Do you think you could tell me … ?

Note that the word order in an indirect question is the normal affirmative sentence word order (subject + verb).
> *Can you tell me how long that takes?*
> Not … how long does that take?

❯ SEE LANGUAGE REFERENCE PAGE 64

1 Look at tapescript 1.51 on pages 143–144 and find seven examples of indirect questions.

2 Change the questions below into indirect questions. Use different introductions.

1 Where can I buy an American or English newspaper?
2 How many cinemas are there in the town?
3 What time do banks open in the morning?
4 Is there an internet café in the city centre?
5 Which restaurant is the best in town?
6 Are there any non-smoking restaurants near here?

3 Work in pairs. Look at the questions you made in exercise 2. Decide what you would say if a tourist asked you these questions about your city.

VOCABULARY: collocations with *sound*
PRONUNCIATION: word stress

1 🔘 **1.52** Listen to three short extracts from Avril's conversation with the travel agent and tick the endings you hear.

1 That doesn't sound   a) much fun.
                          b) too bad.
                          c) very interesting.

2 Does that sound   a) all right?
                          b) like a good idea?
                          c) OK?

3 That sounds   a) fun.
                          b) great.
                         c) lovely.

2 Mark the adjectives positive (P) or negative (N).

1	amazing	5	fantastic
2	awful	6	horrible
3	dreadful	7	superb
4	excellent	8	terrible

3 Put the adjectives from exercise 2 under the correct stress pattern in the table.

• ●	● •	• ● •	● • •
_____	_____	*amazing*	_____
_____	_____	_____	_____
		_____	_____

4 🔘 **1.53** Listen to the exchanges and make a note of the intonation on the adjectives. Does it go up or down on the stressed sylable?

5 Tell your partner about three things that you have done today / that you did last week / that you are going to do at the weekend.

Your partner must respond using an expression with *sound*. Use an expression from the exercises above or choose a word from the box.

boring   different   enjoyable   exciting
fascinating   nice   painful   wonderful

A: Last week I had toothache so I went to the dentist and he took out the tooth.
B: That sounds painful!

GRAMMAR

Future 1 (plans)

We use *going to* + infinitive to talk about future plans and intentions. These are things that we definitely want to do, but we haven't made firm arrangements yet.

> *We're going to get some brochures tomorrow.*

> **Affirmative & Negative**
> *They're going to hire a car.*
> *He's going to visit his parents.*
>
> **Question**
> *What is she going to do next?*

We use the present continuous to talk about things we have already decided to do and made arrangements for.

> *We're getting the two o'clock flight from Heathrow.*
> (= We've already bought the tickets.)

We tend not to use *going to* + infinitive with the verbs *go* and *come*. We prefer to use the present continuous.

> *They're going to Corfu next summer.*
> *What time are you coming?*

We use *will* + infinitive to talk about the future when we haven't made any plans or arrangements. This is often used with *probably, possibly* or *perhaps*.

> *We haven't made any plans yet, we'll probably decide what to do when the others arrive tomorrow.*

Future 2 (predictions)

We can use both *will* and *going to* + infinitive to make predictions about the future.

> *You'll really enjoy the trip.*
> *You're really going to enjoy the trip.*

We use *going to* + infinitive when we have present evidence for the prediction.

> *It's going to rain later this morning.*
> (There are black clouds in the sky.)
> *I'm not going to finish this today.*
> (I still have a lot of work and it's already late.)

In many situations, it is possible to use both *will* and *going to*.

Present tenses in future time clauses

We use a present tense to talk about future time after conjunctions like *if, when, after, before, as soon as* and *once*. We often use *will* in the main clause of the sentence.

> *As soon as everybody gets here, the coach will leave.*
> *We will have lunch after we get to Dalkey.*

Sentences which include *if*, a present tense to talk about future and *will* in the main clause are often described as *first conditional* sentences.

We use the present perfect if we want to emphasize completion of a future action.

> *Once we have seen the castle, we'll visit some of the pubs.*

FUNCTIONAL LANGUAGE

Indirect questions

We use indirect questions when we want to make polite enquiries. Indirect questions usually sound more polite than direct questions.

> *I'd like to know if I can buy a return ticket.*
> *Could you tell me if this is the right train for Dublin?*
> *Do you know what time the next train leaves?*
> *Can you tell me where the station is, please?*

Indirect questions begin with an introduction.

> *Do you know … ?*
> *Can you tell me … ?*
> *Could you tell me … ?*
> *Do you think you could tell me … ?*
> *I wonder …*
> *I'd like to know …*

For yes/no questions, we use *if* (or *whether*) after the introduction.

In the second part of an indirect question (after the introduction), we use normal affirmative sentence word order (subject + verb).

> *Can you tell me what time it arrives?*
> Not *Can you tell me what time does it arrive?*

WORD LIST
Holidays

action-packed *adj*	/ˌækʃənˈpækt/
airline *n C* *	/ˈeəlaɪn/
beach *n C* **	/biːtʃ/
bedding *n U*	/ˈbedɪŋ/
brochure *n C*	/ˈbrəʊʃə/
capital *n C* ***	/ˈkæpɪtl/
check out of *v*	/ˌtʃek ˈaʊt əv/
cosmopolitan *adj*	/ˌkɒzməˈpɒlɪtən/
deposit *n C* *	/dɪˈpɒzɪt/
destination *n C* *	/ˌdestɪˈneɪʃn/
exclusive *adj*	/ɪkˈskluːsɪv/
excursion *n C*	/ɪkˈskɜːʃn/
exotic *adj*	/ɪgˈzɒtɪk/
find your way around	/ˌfaɪnd jə ˌweɪ əˈraʊnd/
flight *n C* ***	/flaɪt/
fun *adj*	/fʌn/
guided tour *n C*	/ˌgaɪdɪd ˌtʊə/
laid-back *adj*	/ˌleɪdˈbæk/
off the beaten track	/ˌɒf ðə ˌbiːtn ˈtræk/
packing *n U*	/ˈpækɪŋ/
postcard *n C*	/ˈpəʊstˌkɑːd/
picturesque *adj*	/ˌpɪktʃəˈresk/
resort *n C*	/rɪˈzɔːt/
romantic *adj*	/rəʊˈmæntɪk/
sandy *adj*	/ˈsændi/
secluded *adj*	/sɪˈkluːdɪd/
sightseeing *n U*	/ˈsaɪtˌsiːɪŋ/
sunscreen *n U*	/ˈsʌnˌskriːn/
tourist attraction *n C*	/ˈtʊərɪst əˌtrækʃn/
travel agent *n C*	/ˈtrævl ˌeɪdʒənt/
travel rep *n C*	/ˈtrævl ˌrep/
upmarket *adj*	/ˌʌpˈmɑːkɪt/

Other words & phrases

abbey *n C*	/ˈæbi/
amazing *adj* *	/əˈmeɪzɪŋ/
ancient *adj* **	/ˈeɪnʃənt/
awful *adj* **	/ˈɔːfl/
babysitter *n C*	/ˈbeɪbɪˌsɪtə/
bargain *n C*	/ˈbɑːgɪn/
battery *n C* *	/ˈbæt(ə)ri/
bay *n C*	/beɪ/
bird's-eye view *n C*	/ˌbɜːdzaɪ ˈvjuː/
boring *adj* **	/ˈbɔːrɪŋ/
brand new *adj*	/ˌbrænd ˈnjuː/
breathtaking *adj*	/ˈbreθteɪkɪŋ/
cabin *n C*	/ˈkæbɪn/
cocktail *n C*	/ˈkɒkteɪl/
colony *n C*	/ˈkɒləni/
congratulations *n pl*	/kənˌgrætʃʊˈleɪʃənz/
delegation *n C*	/ˌdeləˈgeɪʃn/
depth *n C* ***	/depθ/
discreet *adj*	/dɪsˈkriːt/
dramatic *adj* *	/drəˈmætɪk/
dreadful *adj*	/ˈdredfl/
eloquent *adj*	/ˈeləkwənt/
enjoyable *adj*	/ɪnˈdʒɔɪəbl/
excellent *adj* ***	/ˈeksələnt/
exhausted *adj*	/ɪgˈzɔːstɪd/
fantastic *adj*	/fænˈtæstɪk/
fascinating *adj* *	/ˈfæsɪneɪtɪŋ/
fate *n U* *	/feɪt/
flexibility *n U*	/ˌfleksəˈbɪlɪti/
get round to (sth)	/get ˈraʊnd tə/
giant *adj/n C*	/ˈdʒaɪənt/
goalkeeper *n C*	/ˈgəʊlˌkiːpə/
gorgeous *adj*	/ˈgɔːdʒəs/
guidance *n U*	/ˈgaɪdəns/
harbour *n C*	/ˈhɑːbə/
harp *n C*	/hɑːp/
heritage *n U*	/ˈherɪtɪdʒ/
highlight *n C*	/ˈhaɪˌlaɪt/
hill *n C* ***	/hɪl/
horrible *adj* *	/ˈhɒrəbl/
hyper-organised *adj*	/ˌhaɪpəˈɔːgənaɪzd/
in particular	/ˌɪn pəˈtɪkjʊlə/
in person	/ˌɪn ˈpɜːsn/
indoor *adj*	/ˈɪndɔː/
instructor *n C*	/ɪnˈstrʌktə/
kayak *n C*	/ˈkaɪæk/
knock out *n C*	/ˈnɒk ˌaʊt/
last minute *adj*	/ˌlɑːst ˈmɪnɪt/
lens *n C*	/lenz/
make sure *v*	/ˌmeɪk ˈʃʊə/ ˈʃɔː/
make up your mind	/ˌmeɪk ʌp jə ˈmaɪnd/
memorable *adj*	/ˈmem(ə)rəbl/
option *n C* ***	/ˈɒpʃn/
painful *adj* *	/ˈpeɪnfl/

pilot *n C* *	/ˈpaɪlət/
pony *n C*	/ˈpəʊni/
reckon *v* *	/ˈrekən/
relatively *adv* ***	/ˈrelətɪvli/
respectable *adj*	/rɪˈspektəbəl/
rock-climbing *n U*	/ˌrɒkˈklaɪmɪŋ/
round (sth) off *v*	/ˌraʊnd ˈɒf/
rush *v* **	/rʌʃ/
saint *n C*	/seɪnt/
sculpture *n C*	/ˈskʌlptʃə/
seal *n C*	/siːl/
settle into *v*	/ˌsetl ˈɪntuː/
shot *n C* ***	/ʃɒt/
shy *adj* *	/ʃaɪ/
site *n C* ***	/saɪt/
step *n C* ***	/step/
stop off *n C/v*	/ˌstɒp ˈɒf/
stunning *adj*	/ˈstʌnɪŋ/
superb *adj*	/sʊˈpɜːb/
talkative *adj*	/ˈtɔːkətɪv/
terrible *adj* **	/ˈterəbl/
thrill *n C/v*	/θrɪl/
unbeatable *adj*	/ʌnˈbiːtəbl/
unexpectedly *adv*	/ˌʌnɪkˈspektɪdli/
up in the air	/ˌʌp ɪn ðiː ˈeə/
via *prep* *	/ˈvaɪə/
wind surfing *n U*	/ˈwɪn(d) sɜːfɪŋ/
wonderful *adj* **	/ˈwʌndəfl/
zoom *v*	/zuːm/

7A | Life changes

Vocabulary: phrasal verbs with *live*

1 Complete the sentences with words from the box.

for off on out of through up to

1 I love travelling and I'm quite happy living _____ a suitcase.
2 I don't need much money to live _____ – just enough for food and basics.
3 I can't understand people who live _____ their work – there are more important things in life.
4 You haven't really lived if you haven't lived _____ difficult times.
5 I want to live my own life. I'm not interested in living _____ my parents' expectations.
6 There's no point working if you can live _____ social security.

2 Work in pairs. Do you agree or disagree with the sentences in exercise 1?

Reading

1 Read the article below about a woman who has moved from the city to the country. Answer these questions.

1 What was Zoe doing before she moved?
2 Why did she move?
3 Is she happy with her decision? Why or why not?

2 Read the article again and put the phrases a–g in the gaps 1–7.

a and I just didn't feel like looking for another job
b and a busy social life of expensive restaurants and late-night clubs
c and she blushed with embarrassment
d and I knew I wanted to stay
e and one of Kathy's wonderful dinners
f and says she has no regrets
g and she has learnt to drive a tractor

3 Work in pairs. Discuss these questions.

● Zoe says that she has no regrets. Do you think that she will have any regrets later?
● Are you happy with your lifestyle? Why or why not?
● Would you like to make a radical change to your lifestyle? What kind of change?

Redundancy was the best thing that ever happened to me

Like many of her colleagues, Zoe Chambers lived for her work. She was a successful PR consultant and life was going well –
5 she had a great job, a beautiful flat on London's fashionable King's Road (1) _____. Then, the unthinkable happened. One evening in June last year, she received a text message
10 telling her she was out of work. Suddenly, as she put it, life was 'hell'.

'The first two weeks were the most difficult to live through,' she said. 'After everything I'd done for the
15 company, they fired me by text! I was so angry (2) _____. I hated everything about the city and my life.'

Then, Zoe received an invitation from an old schoolfriend, Kathy, to come
20 and stay. Kathy and her husband, Huw, had just bought a farm in north-west Wales. Zoe jumped at the chance to spend a weekend away from London, and now, ten months
25 later, she is still on the farm.

'The moment I arrived at Kathy's farm, I loved it (3) _____,' said Zoe. 'Everything about my past life suddenly seemed superficial. When I
30 asked Kathy if I could work for her, she refused to take me seriously at first. She told me how much farm hands get paid (4) _____.'

Zoe has been working on the farm
35 since October of last year (5) _____. 'It's a hard life, physically very tiring,' she says. 'In London I was stressed and often mentally exhausted. But this is a
40 good, healthy tiredness. Here, all I need to put me in a good mood is a hot bath (6) _____.'

After almost six months on the farm, Zoe says she has never felt bored.
45 Every day brings a new experience. Kathy has been teaching her how to ride a horse (7) _____. Since Christmas, she has been helping with the lambing – watching a lamb being
50 born is incredible, she says, 'It's one of the most moving experiences I've ever had. I could never go back to city life now. Redundancy is the best thing that has ever happened to me!'

GRAMMAR: present perfect continuous 1

Use the present perfect continuous
- to talk about actions which started in the past and are still in progress now.
  I've been living here for six months. (= I still live here.)

- often with time expressions and *for* or *since*. Use *for* + time expression to talk about the length of time the action has been taking place. Use *since* + time expression to talk about the starting point of the action.
  for ten years, for a long time, for the last six months, …
  since I left London, since last September, since last Saturday …

- in questions with *How long … ?*
  *How long **have** you **been waiting**?*

Make the present perfect continuous with *have/has + been + verb + -ing*.
  *I've **been working** here for over six months.*
  *He's **been working** here since he was a boy.*

Use the present perfect simple (not the continuous) with stative verbs.
  *I've **been** here since last autumn. Not ~~I've been being here~~.*

> FOR MORE INFORMATION ABOUT STATIVE VERBS AND CONTINUOUS VERB FORMS, SEE PAGE 14

> SEE LANGUAGE REFERENCE PAGE 74

1 Complete the text. Put the verbs in brackets into the present perfect continuous.

Dave is a violinist. He (1) _____ (*study*) music for the last ten years and last year he moved to London to look for work. Dave (2) _____ (*live*) in London for five months now and while he is looking for a job with one of the London orchestras, he (3) _____ (*work*) as a waiter in an Italian restaurant. One of his colleagues in the restaurant (4) _____ (*also / look*) for a job as a violinist and for the past two months they (5) _____ (*play*) their violins for the customers in the restaurant. Their concerts (6) _____ (*get*) a lot of attention in the local press and they (7) _____ (*receive*) requests to perform in restaurants all over the city. Could this be the beginning of a new career?

2 Look at the time expressions in the box. Which ones can we use with *for* and which ones with *since*? Mark the expressions *for* (F) and *since* (S).

a long time	I left school
last summer	about three hours
I started work	the last two weeks
1996	ages
	as long as I can remember

3 Find three mistakes in the sentences and correct them. Explain why the verbs are incorrect.

1 I haven't been understanding any of your explanation.
2 How long have you been studying English?
3 How long have you been knowing your best friend?
4 How long have you been being in the classroom?
5 How long have you been doing this lesson?

4 Work in pairs. Answer questions 2–5 in exercise 3 using expressions with *for* or *since*.

5 Choose five of the expressions in exercise 2 and write sentences that are true for you, or a member of your family, using the present perfect continuous.

My dad's been collecting jazz CDs for as long as I can remember.

VOCABULARY: metaphor

1 🔊 1.54 Listen to a poem from *The Lord of the Rings* by JRR Tolkien. What is it about?

> The Road goes ever on and on
> Down from the door where it began.
> Now far ahead the Road has gone,
> And I must follow, if I can,
> Pursuing¹ it with eager² feet,
> Until it joins some larger way
> Where many paths and errands³ meet.

1 following   2 with enthusiasm   3 things you must do

2 The sentences below contain metaphors of life as a journey. Translate them into your own language.

1 Her life **took an unexpected turn**.
2 Her life was **at a crossroads**.
3 She and her husband **went their separate ways**.
4 She **embarked** on a new stage of her life.
5 She felt that it was time to **move on**.
6 She realized that there was **no turning back**.
7 She wanted to **take a new direction**.
8 Suddenly, her life **took off**.

3 Complete the text with the phrases in bold in exercise 2.

JK Rowling was born in Bristol on July 31st, 1965. After graduating from Exeter University, she worked as a translator and researcher for Amnesty International in London. But she wanted to (1) _____ and she moved to Portugal. There she (2) _____ on a new career as an English teacher and fell in love with a Portuguese journalist. But their marriage ended in divorce and the couple (3) _____. Rowling suddenly found herself (4) _____. Should she stay in Portugal and continue teaching or return to the UK? She decided that it was time to (5) _____. She went back to Edinburgh with her baby daughter and that's where her life (6) _____. For years, she had had an idea for a book and she now completed *Harry Potter and the Philosopher's Stone*. The book (7) _____ immediately and when Hollywood bought the film rights to Harry Potter, there was (8) _____.

4 🔊 1.55 Listen to the recording to check your answers.

5 Work in pairs. Discuss these questions.

- Do you know anyone whose life has taken an unexpected turn?
- Have you ever made a decision and felt that there was no turning back?
- Have you ever felt that you were at a crossroads in your life?
- Have you ever wanted to take a new direction in life? What did you do?

LISTENING

1 🔊 1.56 Listen to an interview with a man whose life has taken a new direction. Answer the questions.

1 How has his life changed?
2 How has this changed his day-to-day life?

2 🔊 1.56 Listen again and answer the questions.

1 Why did he decide to leave his job?
2 Why didn't his wife leave her job?
3 Why did he feel guilty about going to work?
4 How long has he been looking after Ben?
5 Does he enjoy his new lifestyle?
6 Is it an easy lifestyle?
7 Would he like to go back to work one day?

3 Find these expressions in tapescript 1.56 on pages 144–145. Explain what the words in italics refer to.

1 *It* didn't make much sense.
2 We were missing out on *it* all.
3 Neither of us was there to see *it*.
4 *It* all turns into a game.
5 *That's* great.

4 Would you be happy as a 'stay at home' parent? Why or why not?

Speaking

1 Work in pairs. Look at the list of life-changing events below and discuss these questions.

- Which are the three most important changes?
- Which is the most difficult decision to make?
- Which is the easiest change to deal with? Which is the most stressful?
- Have you had to make any of these changes in your life? If yes, what difficulties (if any) did you face?

2 Imagine that you have just made a big life change. Use your imagination or choose one of the ideas on page 127. Write your answers to the questions in note form.

- What change have you just made?
- Why did you decide to make this change?
- How long have you been doing what you are now doing?
- What difficulties did you face at the beginning?
- Are you happy with the change?
- Are there any aspects you particularly enjoy? Are there any that you really don't like?
- How long do you think you'll continue with this new lifestyle?

3 Work in pairs. Interview your partner about their life change. Find out as much as you can about their new lifestyle.

Useful language

I think the most difficult thing was …
I really didn't know what to expect …
At first I was excited/nervous/unsure …
It took me some time to …
From the start I really enjoyed/loved/hated …
It's the best thing I've ever done!
I'd recommend it to anyone!

Did you know?

1 Work in pairs. Read the information and discuss these questions.

From a legal point of view, life in England and Wales begins at the age of ten. The law says that children from ten upwards can understand the consequences of their actions. The next big birthday is at sixteen, when you can leave school, get a job and pay tax and smoke. You can also leave home and get married (if your parents agree). At seventeen, you can drive or ride a small motorbike. At eighteen, you can get married without your parents' permission and you can finally vote. You can also buy alcohol, play the National Lottery and get a tattoo.

- Are these ages the same or different in your country?
- What do you think the various minimum legal ages should be?

7B | Happy birthday

SPEAKING & VOCABULARY: life stages

1 Match the sentences 1–7 to the pictures a–g.

1 He retired many years ago and lives in a home for the **elderly**.
2 He's a **pensioner** now, but he's still very active.
3 He's a **toddler**.
4 He's a typical **adolescent**.
5 She's **middle-aged**, probably in her late forties or early fifties.
6 She's still a **teenager**, but she's very adult in some ways.
7 She's **thirty something** and she's got two young children.

2 Use the words in bold in exercise 1 to make sentences about people you know. Talk about these people with a partner.

3 Work in pairs. Discuss these questions.

- Which stage of life do you associate with the following adjectives: wise, rebellious, overworked, lively, irresponsible, happy, bored?
- Which stage are you in at the moment? What are the advantages and disadvantages of being your age?
- Which stage are you most looking forward to? Why?

READING

1 You are going to read an article about a woman who is celebrating her 110th birthday. Answer the questions.

1 How do you think she's going to celebrate her birthday?
2 In what way has the world changed since she was a young girl? What do you think are the changes that have shocked her most?

2 Read the article and compare your ideas to the information in the article. Has Maria led a happy life?

Maria prepares to celebrate her 110th birthday

Maria Pettigrew says the odd drop of sherry in the evening has helped her live so long.

Scotland's oldest woman, who has ⁵lived in three centuries, is today celebrating her 110th birthday. Maria Pettigrew explains that her recipe for a long life is a simple diet, not smoking and the odd drop of sherry in the evenings.

¹⁰ Her friends and family have been preparing a special party for her at the hospital where she lives. She wants to look good for her birthday and she has been putting together a special outfit for the occasion. Speaking from the hospital, she said: 'My nurse has taken me out ¹⁵shopping a couple of times, once to buy shoes and once to order a new wedding ring, because this one is getting a bit loose.'

Maria was born one of four children in Liberton, Edinburgh, to policeman Andrew Scougall and mother ²⁰Helen. She left school at fourteen to work on a farm, where she met the two loves of her life. At nineteen, she married one of them, farm worker William McCardle. Her secret admirer, Tom Pettigrew, was heartbroken and he left for Australia to set up a new home.

²⁵Shortly after the First World, War William died in a flu epidemic. Maria brought up their three children on her own until thirteen years later when Tom returned from Melbourne. He confessed his secret love to Maria and the pair were married for 42 years.

³⁰Maria says: 'I've only had two boyfriends and they were both decent men. Two happy marriages – what more could a woman ask for?'

Maria keeps in good health, although her eyesight is beginning to fail. She lived in her own home, doing her ³⁵own cooking and housework until five years ago, when she moved to the hospital.

Maria was born before telephones, televisions and washing machines were invented. Of all the changes she has lived through she says that 'the most extraordinary ⁴⁰thing I ever saw was a motor car. I had never seen one before. I was so shocked I fell in a ditch.'

Maria has six grandchildren and fourteen great-grandchildren and they have all been helping with the preparations for the party. Maria is sure she will enjoy ⁴⁵sharing her birthday cake with her children, grandchildren and the rest of her family and friends today. Though no doubt they'll have to help her blow out all those candles!

3 Read the article again and put the topics in the correct order.

☐ Maria's childhood
☐ her two husbands
☐ Maria's secret for a long life
☐ Maria's health
☐ the changes that Maria has seen
☐ preparations for her birthday party

4 Work in pairs, A and B. Test your partner's memory.

A: Turn to page 128. Ask your partner the questions.
B: Turn to page 131. Ask your partner the questions.

5 Would you like to live to be 110 years old? Why or why not?

GRAMMAR: present perfect continuous 2

Use the present perfect continuous
- to talk about an action that has been in progress recently. The action may or may not still be in progress.
  They've **been planning** the party for weeks.
  They've **been decorating** the living room.

- to emphasize an action, or the duration of an action.
  They've **been writing** invitations all day.

Use the present perfect simple (not the continuous)
- to talk about the result of an action.
  They've **written** more than a hundred invitations.

- to talk about single, completed actions.
  They've **ordered** a special birthday cake.
  She's **bought** a new pair of shoes.

⊙ FOR MORE INFORMATION ABOUT THE PRESENT PERFECT SIMPLE, SEE PAGE 24

⊙ SEE LANGUAGE REFERENCE PAGE 74

1 Complete the text. Put the verbs in brackets into the present perfect simple or continuous.

It's my mum and dad's golden wedding anniversary next weekend. We (1) _____ (arrange) a surprise party for them for the last three months. We (2) _____ (book) a room in a local hotel and we (3) _____ (order) an enormous cake with a photo of their wedding on top. We (4) _____ (work) hard trying to get in touch with friends and family from all over the world and so far we (5) _____ (receive) more than 50 replies to our invitations. Mum and Dad suspect that we (6) _____ (plan) something special, but they don't really know what. I know that Mum (7) _____ (think) very carefully about their outfits. She (8) _____ (buy) a new dress and she (9) _____ (persuade) my dad that he needs a new suit.

2 Work in pairs. Look at the picture. Write as many sentences as possible to say what the people have been doing recently.

They've been preparing food for the party.

SPEAKING

1 Work in two groups, A and B. You are going to talk about the changes that have taken place in your lifetime.

Group A: Look at the questions on page 128.
Group B: Look at the questions on page 131.

2 Use your notes and the Useful language to help you report back to the class on your discussion.

Useful language

Our group has been discussing …
We spent a lot of time talking about …
We think that the biggest changes have been …
We agreed that the …
We thought it was particularly interesting that …

7c | Dilemmas

SPEAKING

1 Read the three situations. Who has the most difficult decision to make?

At a Crossroads

Briony is a single mother with two young children. At work, she is offered promotion, but the new job will involve a lot of travelling – sometimes she will need to be away from home for two weeks at a time. Her parents have offered to look after the children when she is away, but Briony is not sure if she should accept the promotion.

Eighteen-year-old Steve receives two letters. In the first, there is an offer of a place at a top university. He has won a scholarship and all his fees will be paid. In the second letter, he receives an offer of a professional contract with a top London football club. He can't do both.

Pilar (Mexican) and David (British) live in Mexico. She is a successful doctor, but David is unhappy. He cannot speak very good Spanish, he can't find a good job and he wants to return to England, where he hopes to return to his career as a journalist. Pilar wants her husband to be happy, but she doesn't want to leave her family, friends and career in Mexico.

2 Work in pairs. Discuss these questions.

- What advice would you give the three people in exercise 1?
- Have you ever had an important or difficult decision to make? What was it?

LISTENING

1 🔘 1.57 Listen to a conversation between Dave and Derek. Explain why Derek is looking worried.

2 🔘 1.57 Listen to the conversation again and complete the sentences about the conversation with one word.

1 Derek received some _____ news this morning.
2 Dave already knows about the _____ in Japan.
3 Derek hasn't decided if he's going to _____ it.
4 He thinks that two _____ is a long time.
5 Dave's _____ used to live in Japan.
6 Dave thinks that Derek and _____ are more than good friends.
7 Derek is worried that Avril will say _____.
8 Dave thinks that Derek should _____ the job.

3 Find these phrases in tapescript 1.57 on page 145 and explain them in your own words.

1 It didn't take much to put two and two together.
2 You've got to be joking!
3 Stop dithering!

4 What do you think Derek should do? Tell the rest of the class.

FUNCTIONAL LANGUAGE: giving advice

1 ⊙ 1.57 Listen to the conversation between Derek and Dave again. Complete the sentences in column A with a phrase from column B.

A		B	
1	I think you should	a	asking her what she'd do.
2	Why don't you	b	give him a ring?
3	What you need to do is	c	go for it.
4	Have you thought about	d	talk to her first thing in the morning.
5	If I were you, I'd	e	talk to someone about it.
6	Have you tried	f	talking to Avril?
7	There's no harm in	g	talking to Camilla?

2 Find these responses in tapescript 1.57 on page 145. What advice is Derek reacting to in each case?

1 Of course, you're right.
2 Do you really think that's a good idea?
3 I wouldn't want to do that.
4 Well, yes, maybe, but …
5 Oh no, I couldn't.
6 I hadn't thought of that.
7 I suppose I could give it a go.

3 Rearrange the words to make six pieces of advice.

1 her dinner take why out to you don't ?
2 wants she harm asking no what there's her in .
3 flowers were I'd her get you if some I .
4 weekend to away need what do take her you is for the .
5 should theatre her the some get I tickets think you for .
6 gift thought voucher giving have her you about a ?

4 Read the advice in exercise 3 again. What do you think has happened? Why is the person giving this advice?

Roleplay

5 Work in pairs, A and B. Act out the roleplay.

A: You want some advice about a problem. Turn to page 128.
B: You want to help your friend with a problem. Turn to page 133.

6 Now exchange roles.

A: Turn to page 130.   B: Turn to page 132.

VOCABULARY: exclamations with *what*

1 Match the comments 1–8 with an appropriate response a–h.

1 I thought it was something serious, but the doctor said it was nothing really.
2 … and then he said that Slovakia was the capital of the Czech Republic!
3 You'll never guess what! For the first time in my life, he bought me some flowers!
4 Mum! Look, I've got tomato ketchup all over my T-shirt. And on my trousers, too.
5 I thought we were going to win, but the other team scored a goal in the last minute.
6 So, she's lost her job, her husband's left her and now she's broken her leg!
7 There was no hot water this morning, so I couldn't have a shower.
8 I can't remember his address. Oh, I know, I'll see if it's in the phone book.

a	What a good idea!	e	What a relief!
b	What a mess!	f	What a shame!
c	What a nightmare!	g	What a surprise!
d	What a nuisance!	h	What an idiot!

2 Work in pairs. Think of four situations in which somebody would say these things.

• What a day!   • What a waste of time!
• What a night!   • What bad luck!

PRONUNCIATION: intonation (feelings)

1 ⊙ 1.58 Listen to this extract from Derek and Dave's conversation. Choose the best explanation of the word *what* in the extract.

1 I didn't hear you very well.
2 I'm really angry with you.
3 I'm really surprised.

2 ⊙ 1.59 Now listen to these three words. Match each word with a feeling from the box.

1 hello   2 right   3 yes

> anger   surprise   happiness
> boredom   interest

3 Practise saying the words in exercise 2 with as many different feelings as you can.

GRAMMAR

Present perfect continuous

We can use the present perfect continuous to talk about actions which started in the past and are still in progress now.

> *I've **been studying** geography for two years.*
> (= I'm still studying geography.)

To describe the period of time between the start of the action and now, we can use *for* and *since*. We use *for* + an expression that describes the length of time.

> ***for** five years/a long time/the last two years/three weeks*

We use *since* + an expression that refers to the time when the action started.

> ***since** two o'clock/last year/2002/I met you*

We use *how long* ... in questions to ask about the length of time.

> ***How long** have you been living here?*

We also use the present perfect continuous to talk about an action that has been in progress recently. The action may or may not still be in progress.

> *She's **been getting** ready for the party.*
> *They've **been swimming** in the river.*

We use the present perfect continuous to emphasize the action itself, or the duration of the action. However, we use the present perfect simple (not the continuous) to talk about the result of the action.

> *She's **been writing** letters.*
> (Here the speaker is interested in the action of writing.)

> *She's **written** 50 letters.*
> (Here the speaker is interested in the result of the action – the number of letters that have been completed.)

We also use the present perfect simple (not the continuous) to talk about single, completed actions.

> *She's **chosen** a new outfit.*
> *They've **booked** a holiday.*

Affirmative & Negative

I/You/We/They	've haven't	been working.
He/She	's hasn't	

Question

What	have	I you/we/they	been doing?
	has	he/she	

We use the present perfect simple (not the continuous) with stative verbs.

> *I've **been** here since last autumn.*
> Not ~~I've been being here~~.

For more information about stative verbs and continuous verb forms, see unit 1 (Language reference page 14).

For more information about the present perfect simple see unit 2 (Language reference page 24).

FUNCTIONAL LANGUAGE

Giving advice

Have you thought about + -ing form?
Have you tried + -ing form?
I think you should + infinitive
If I were you, I'd + infinitive
There's no harm in + -ing form
What you need to do is + infinitive
Why don't you + infinitive?

WORD LIST

Phrasal verbs with *live*

live for (sth)	/lɪv fə/
live off (sth/sb)	/lɪv ɒf/
live on (sth)	/lɪv ɒn/
live out of (sth)	/lɪv aʊt əv/
live through (sth)	/lɪv θruː/
live up to (sth)	/lɪv ʌp tə/

Metaphor

an unexpected turn	/ən ˌʌnɪkˌspektɪd ˈtɜːn/
at a crossroads	/ˌæt ə ˈkrɒsrəʊdz/
embark on a new stage of life	/ɪmˈbɑːk ɒn ə ˌnjuːˌsteɪdʒ əv ˈlaɪf/
go their separate ways	/ˌgəʊ ðeə seprət ˈweɪz/
her life took off	/hɜː ˌlaɪf tʊk ˈɒf/
move on	/ˌmuːv ˈɒn/
no turning back	/ˌnəʊ tɜːnɪŋ ˈbæk/
take a new direction	/ˌteɪk ə ˌnjuː dɪˈrekʃn/

Life stages

adolescent *adj/n C*	/ˌædəˈlesnt/
adult *adj/n C* ***	/ˈædʌlt; əˈdʌlt/
elderly *adj* **	/ˈeldəli/
in your early/late forties	/ˌɪn jɔː ˌɜːli/leɪt ˈfɔːtiz/
middle-aged *adj*	/ˌmɪdlˈeɪdʒd/
pensioner *n C*	/ˈpenʃ(ə)nə/
retired *adj*	/rɪˈtaɪəd/
teenager *n C* *	/ˈtiːneɪdʒə/
toddler *n C*	/ˈtɒdlə/

Exclamations with *what*

What a good idea!	/ˌwɒt ə ˌgʊd aɪˈdɪə/
What a day!	/ˌwɒt ə ˈdaɪ/
What a mess!	/ˌwɒt ə ˈmes/
What a night!	/ˌwɒt ə ˈnaɪt/
What a nightmare!	/ˌwɒt ə ˈnaɪtˌmeə/
What a nuisance!	/ˌwɒt ə ˈnjuːsəns/
What a relief!	/ˌwɒt ə rɪˈliːf/
What a shame!	/ˌwɒt ə ˈʃeɪm/
What a surprise!	/ˌwɒt ə səˈpraɪz/
What a waste of time!	/ˌwɒt ə ˌweɪst əv ˈtaɪm/
What bad luck!	/ˌwɒt ˌbæd ˈlʌk/
What an idiot!	/ˌwɒt ən ˈɪdiət/

Other words & phrases

admirer *n C*	/ədˈmaɪərə/
anniversary *n C*	/ˌænɪˈvɜːs(ə)ri/
appreciate *v* **	/əˈpriːʃieɪt/
aspect *n C* **	/ˈæspekt/
blow out *v*	/ˌbləʊ ˈaʊt/
blush *v*	/blʌʃ/
cheers	/tʃɪəz/
childcare *n U*	/ˈtʃaɪldkeə/
compete *v* **	/kəmˈpiːt/
confess *v*	/kənˈfes/
consequence *n C* ***	/ˈkɒnsɪkwəns/
consultancy *n C*	/kənˈsʌltənsi/
consultant *n C*	/kənˈsʌltənt/
contract *n C* ***	/ˈkɒntrækt/
ditch *n C*	/dɪtʃ/
dither *v*	/ˈdɪðə/
drop *n C* *	/drɒp/
eager *adj*	/ˈiːgə/
embarrassment *n U*	/ɪmˈbærəsmənt/
epidemic *n C*	/ˌepɪˈdemɪk/
errand *n C*	/ˈerənd/
expectation *n C* **	/ˌekspekˈteɪʃn/
eyesight *n U*	/ˈaɪˌsaɪt/
farm hand *n C*	/ˈfɑːm ˌhænd/
fire *v* **	/ˈfaɪə/
flu *n U*	/fluː/
get in touch with (sb)	/ˌget ɪn ˈtʌtʃ wɪð/
graduate *v/n C* *	/ˈgrædʒueɪt/ (*v*); /ˈgrædʒuːət/ (*n*)
guilty *adj* **	/ˈgɪlti/
heartbroken *adj*	/ˈhɑːtˌbrəʊkən/
hell *n U*	/hel/
invitation *n C* **	/ˌɪnvɪˈteɪʃn/
irresponsible *adj*	/ˌɪrɪˈspɒnsəbl/
jealous *adj* *	/ˈdʒeləs/
ketchup *n U*	/ˈketʃʌp/
lamb *n C*	/læm/
loose *adj* *	/luːs/
make sense	/ˌmeɪk ˈsens/
miss out on (sth) *v*	/ˌmɪs ˈaʊt ɒn/
moving *adj*	/ˈmuːvɪŋ/
nappy *n C*	/ˈnæpi/
newsreader *n C*	/ˈnjuːzˌriːdə/
nursery *n C*	/ˈnɜːs(ə)ri/
occasion *n C* ***	/əˈkeɪʒn/
odd *adj* **	/ɒd/
orchestra *n C* *	/ˈɔːkɪstrə/
outfit *n C*	/ˈaʊtˌfɪt/
over-worked *adj*	/ˌəʊvəˈwɜːkt/
physically *adv*	/ˈfɪzɪkli/
playgroup *n C*	/ˈpleɪˌgruːp/
PR (public relations) *n pl*	/ˌpiːˈɒː (ˌpʌblɪk rɪˈleɪʃənz)/
promotion *n C/U* *	/prəˈməʊʃn/
pursue *v* *	/pəˈsjuː/
put two and two together	/ˌpʊt ˌtuː ən ˌtuː təˈgeðə/
radical *adj*	/ˈrædɪkl/
redundancy *n C*	/rɪˈdʌndənsi/
regret *n C/v* **	/rɪˈgret/
scholarship *n C*	/ˈskɒləʃɪp/
set up *v*	/ˌset ˈʌp/
sherry *n U*	/ˈʃeri/
social security *n U*	/ˌsəʊʃl sɪˈkjʊərəti/
stressful *adj*	/ˈstresfl/
superficial *adj*	/ˌsuːpəˈfɪʃl/
take (sth/sb) seriously	/ˌteɪk ˈsɪəriəsli/
tattoo *n C*	/tæˈtuː/
tiredness *n U*	/ˈtaɪədnəs/
travel expenses *n pl*	/ˈtrævl ɪkˌspensəz/
tropical *adj*	/ˈtrɒpɪkl/
unsure *adj*	/ʌnˈʃɔː/
unthinkable *adj*	/ʌnˈθɪŋkəbl/
violinist *n C*	/ˌvaɪəˈlɪnɪst/

8A | Breaking news

VOCABULARY: newspapers

1 Complete the text with words from the box.

> articles   circulation   daily   features   right-wing   headline
> journalists   news coverage   quality newspapers

The best-selling (1) _____ newspaper in the UK is *The Sun*, with a
(2) _____ of many millions. Its front page has a large (3) _____ and
photo, but there is not much news. Inside, you find (4) _____ about
pop stars and other celebrities, details of TV programmes, sports news,
games, crosswords and competitions.

Readers who want to know what is happening in the world choose one
of the (5) _____ and *The Daily Telegraph* is the most popular. It has
(6) _____ all over the world and, as well as its (7) _____, it contains
special (8) _____ on subjects such as gardening, motoring and travel.
It is widely accepted that it is a (9) _____ newspaper and it supports
the Conservative party.

2 Work in pairs. Discuss these questions.

- What are the most popular quality newspapers in your country?
- Which paper do you think has the best international news coverage?
  What about local news?
- Are there any daily newspapers like *The Sun*?
- Which newspapers are considered right-wing or left-wing?
- Which newspaper do you read? How often?
- What kind of articles do you find most interesting?

LISTENING

1 🔘 2.1 Listen to an interview with
a journalist, Colin Ashley. Put the
topics in the correct order.

☐ his advice to other journalists
☐ his attitude towards America
☐ his new book
☐ his work for television

2 Match the questions 1–6 to the
answers a–f.

1 What is his new book about?
2 Where do the ideas in Colin's book
  come from?
3 Where does Colin come from?
4 What was his last book about?
5 Where does Colin have a lot of
  friends?
6 Who does he not want to work for?

a The World Bank.
b Australia.
c Some TV channels.
d Joseph E Stiglitz.
e The Pentagon.
f Wall Street.

3 🔘 2.1 Listen to the interview again
to check your answers.

4 Find these sentences in tapescript
2.1 on page 146. Explain what the
words in italics refer to.

1 Most of the time, *it* does the
  complete opposite.
2 I'm not the first person to say *it*.
3 I wouldn't say *that*.
4 The one before *that*.
5 I'd love to do *more*.

GRAMMAR: *would*

> Use *would* + infinitive
> - to give an opinion about hypothetical future situations.
>   *I'd never **work** for CNN.*
>   *It **would be** great to have more money.*
>
> - to ask for and offer advice or suggestions.
>   *What **would** you **say** to someone who wants to become a journalist?*
>
> - with *like, love, prefer* etc. to express preferences.
>   *I'd **love** to do more TV work.*
>
> ❯ SEE LANGUAGE REFERENCE PAGE 84

1 Replace *'d* in the sentences with *would* or *had*.

1 I'd already read two of his books.
2 I'd hate to do that.
3 I'd never forgive myself.
4 I'd never speak to you again.
5 You'd never heard of him?
6 You'd regret it.

2 Complete the conversation with verbs from the box.

> be (x2) hate like love (x2) mind prefer

A: Would you (1) _____ to be a journalist?
B: I wouldn't (2) _____, but I'd (3) _____ to be a photographer.
A: What? A news photographer?
B: Yes, I'd (4) _____ that.
A: You mean working for one of the big newspapers?
B: Yes, that would (5) _____ really nice.
A: Personally, I'd (6) _____ it! Being away from home all the time, travelling to countries at war, …
B: Oh, I'd (7) _____ to. It would (8) _____ really interesting.

3 💿 2.2 Listen to the recording to check your answers.

4 Work in pairs. Discuss these questions.

- As a journalist, which country would you like to work in?
- Who would you like to interview?
- What questions would you ask?
- Would you prefer to work for a newspaper or for TV?
- Is there anywhere in the world where you would never work?

SPEAKING

1 Work in two groups, A and B.

You work for the editorial team of a popular newspaper. You must choose one main story and one secondary story for the front page of the newspaper.

- Choose stories that will make people buy your newspaper and explain the reasons for your choice.
- Decide what kind of photograph you want to use on the front page.
- Write headlines for the stories that you choose.

Group A: Turn to page 128 for a list of possible stories.
Group B: Turn to page 130 for a list of possible stories.

2 Work in new groups that contain students from Group A and Group B. Compare the ideas from exercise 1 and decide together which stories you will use.

DID YOU KNOW?

1 Work in pairs. Read the information about newspapers and discuss these questions.

Seven out of ten Australian daily newspapers are owned by News Corporation, a company that was founded by Rupert Murdoch. In Britain, the company controls about a third of the national newspapers, including *The Sun* and *The Times*, and also owns BSkyB, a cable TV company. In the US, News Corporation controls the Fox cable TV networks, 20th Century Fox studios, 35 local TV stations and the *New York Post*. In Asia, the company owns Star Television.

- Who owns the newspapers and TV stations in your country?
- Which TV station do you think gives the best news coverage in your country?

READING

1 Work in pairs. Discuss these questions.

- When was the last big demonstration in your town? What was it about?
- Have you ever been on a demonstration? What was it about?
- For what reasons would you go on a demonstration?

2 Match the headlines a–g to the newspaper articles 1–5. There are two headlines you do not need.

a Dads stop cars
b Health workers refuse to go back to work
c Jail protest continues
d Pie man strikes again
e Police stop anti-war demonstration
f Prison officers demand pay rise
g Strip protest

3 The last sentence of each article is missing. Match the sentences a–g to the articles 1–5. There are two sentences you do not need.

a 'Cream is too good for him.'
b He has refused to eat food for three days.
c He said that the protest was the result of overcrowding.
d The men failed to deliver their heart-shaped message, but said they were happy with the protest.
e Leaders of UNISON, the nurses' union, are meeting employers again later today.
f Protesters said this was not true.
g The protest ended with hot protesters cooling off in the Cibeles fountain.

4 Find words in the articles that match the definitions 1–7.

1 used to describe someone who thinks he/she is very important
2 people who suffer from the actions of other people
3 not wearing any clothes
4 a protest where people stop working
5 places where legal decisions are taken
6 discussions where people try to agree something
7 a man who speaks for other people

5 Which of the protests in the newspaper articles do you sympathize with most? Which is the best form of protest?

1

BILL GATES, the president of Microsoft, has been hit in the face with a cream pie during a visit to Brussels. The attack was the work of Noel Godin. For the last 30 years, Godin says he 'has been sending the suits of our most pompous public figures to the dry cleaner's.' Godin chooses his victims carefully. 'I would never attack George W. Bush,' he says.

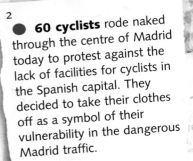

2 **60 cyclists** rode naked through the centre of Madrid today to protest against the lack of facilities for cyclists in the Spanish capital. They decided to take their clothes off as a symbol of their vulnerability in the dangerous Madrid traffic.

3 Over 5,000 Scottish nurses have entered the second week of a strike. The nurses are demanding better pay. Maggie Hunter, a nurse with eighteen years' experience told our reporter: 'My annual salary is £13,500 and the starting salary is £10,000. How would you feel if you were living on that kind of money?'

4 Traffic in London came to a stop earlier today as a group of Elvis Presley look-alikes danced to the London family courts – or 'Heartbreak Hotel', as they call it. The men, all divorced fathers, were protesting at being refused access to their children. In a statement to the press, one of the men said: 'If we had courts that were fair to men, we would be able to see our children. But they only think about the mothers.'

5 **After a day of negotiations**, four of the prisoners in the rooftop protest at Wealstun prison have come down. But a group of twenty prisoners are still refusing to move. A spokesman for the prisoners said: 'If we had decent living conditions, this wouldn't be necessary.' Colin Moses, of the Prison Officers' Association agreed that there was a problem at the jail.

GRAMMAR: unreal conditions 1

Use a conditional clause beginning with *if* to imagine impossible or improbable situations in the present or in the future.

Note that you use a past tense in the conditional clause.

> If we **had** decent living conditions, this wouldn't be necessary.
> (=but we don't have decent living conditions)
> If we **had** courts that were fair to men, we would be able to see our children.
> (= but we don't have courts that are fair to men)

Use *would ('d)* + infinitive to talk about the consequence or the result of the imagined situation.

> How **would** you **feel** if you were living on that kind of money?

> SEE LANGUAGE REFERENCE PAGE 84

1 Put *if* in the correct place in the sentences.

1 Conditions would be better there were fewer prisoners.
2 Godin wouldn't throw cream pies at these people they were less pompous.
3 He had the chance he would attack the British prime minister.
4 Courts were fairer to men it wouldn't happen.
5 Maggie didn't like her job she wouldn't do it.
6 She would be happier she earned more money.

2 Complete the questions. Put the verbs in brackets into the correct tense.

1 What _____ (*you / do*) if someone _____ (*throw*) a cream pie in your face?
2 _____ (*you / go*) on strike if you _____ (*be*) unhappy about something at work?
3 How _____ (*you / feel*) if you _____ (*not / paid*) a reasonable salary?
4 If you _____ (*meet*) the leader of your country, what _____ (*you / say*)?
5 If you _____ (*be*) able to change three things in the world, what _____ (*you / do*)?

3 Work in pairs. Ask and answer the questions in exercise 2.

PRONUNCIATION: /ʊ/ & /uː/

1 Mark the words in the box short /ʊ/ (S) or long /uː/ (L).

book *S*	choose *L*	few	food	foot	good
group	moved	pull	put	stood	suit
took	true	two	whose	would	

2 2.3 Listen to the recording to check your answers.

3 Complete the poem with the words in the box.

clue	could	do	good	Hood

A man who was called Robin _____
Went on demos* whenever he _____.
He hadn't a _____
What he wanted to _____,
But he felt it was doing him _____.

* demos = demonstrations

4 2.4 Listen to the recording to check your answers. Then practise saying the poem.

SPEAKING

1 Look at the three newspaper headlines and say what you think the stories are about.

> New road will cut journey times by 12 minutes

> **Local residents promise to fight new road**

> **New road endangers wildlife says report**

2 Work in groups of three. Read the stories and share the information with the other students in your group.

A: Turn to page 128.
B: Turn to page 131.
C: Turn to page 134.

3 Discuss these questions in your groups.

- What would you do if you lived in one of the houses that will be destroyed?
- What would be the best form of protest?
- How would you encourage other people to join your protest?

4 Compare your ideas with the ideas of other groups. Decide whose ideas are best.

8B | Speeding

SPEAKING & VOCABULARY: compound nouns (driving)

1 Who are better drivers – men or women? Why?

2 Complete the compound nouns in the phrases 1–8 with a word from the box.

belt	licence	lights	limit
phone	street	way	zone

1 driving a car 20 kph over the speed _____
2 driving a car while you are using a mobile _____
3 driving a car without a driving _____
4 driving a car without a seat_____
5 driving the wrong way down a one-way _____
6 driving very slowly in the fast lane of a motor_____
7 not stopping at the traffic _____ when they are red
8 parking your car in a no-parking ____

3 Work in pairs. Choose the three most serious actions from exercise 2. What should the punishment for these actions be?

4 What annoys you most about other drivers? What kind of driver are you?

LISTENING

1 🔊 2.5–2.6 Listen to two conversations between Linda and Clive. Then describe what is happening in the two pictures A and B.

2 🔊 2.5–2.6 Listen to the conversations again and complete the sentences with Linda (L) or Clive (C).

1 __C__ can't keep a promise.
2 _____ had pizza for dinner yesterday.
3 _____ has a lot of work to do.
4 _____ has to go to the police station.
5 _____ is going to rent a video.
6 _____ is worried about having problems at work.
7 _____ was driving too fast.
8 _____ went shopping at lunchtime.

3 Work in pairs. Student A, imagine that you are Linda. You are talking to a friend. Tell your partner the story of what happened to you today. Begin like this:

I had a really bad day …

Then Student B, imagine that you are Clive.

FUNCTIONAL LANGUAGE: offers

1 Complete the offers from the conversations in Listening exercise 1 with a verb from the box.

can	'll	let	like	shall	want

1 _____ I get three or four pizzas?
2 I _____ get some pizzas on the way, if you like.
3 _____ me go and get you one.
4 Do you _____ me to get a video for the kids to watch?
5 Would you _____ me to pick up the children after work?
6 _____ I do anything for you?

2 Look at tapescripts 2.5–2.6 on pages 146–147. Match the responses a–f to the offers 1–6 in exercise 1.

a Thanks.
b That's really kind of you.
c No, that's all right, thanks.
d No, it's OK, thank you.
e Yes, that would be lovely.
f No, I'll manage, thanks.

3 How many different ways can you offer to help in the following situations? Tell the rest of the class your ideas.

1 A friend's car has broken down. It will probably take a week to repair.
2 A friend has broken a leg. He will not be able to walk for a long time.
3 A friend has lost a bag on the metro. It contained money, credit cards, ID card and mobile phone.
4 A friend is going away for two weeks and will not be able to attend English classes.
5 A friend is organizing a huge party for 100 people.
6 A friend is moving house and is feeling very stressed.
7 A friend is going to have a baby next week.

4 Work in pairs. Choose three situations from exercise 3. Act out a conversation for each situation.

SPEAKING

1 Work in pairs. Imagine a world without cars and make a list of the advantages and disadvantages.

Advantages	Disadvantages
less pollution	*many things would take a lot longer*

2 Discuss these questions with your partner.

- Do you think that governments should do more to discourage people from driving? Why or why not?
- What could governments do to encourage people to drive less?

8c | Bank robbers

SPEAKING

1 Work in pairs. Discuss these questions.

- How many different films can you think of in which a robbery takes place?
- What are the titles of these films in your language?
  Ocean's Eleven   The Italian Job   The Pink Panther
- What can you remember about these films?

Bonnie and Clyde

One of the most famous gangster movies of all time, *Bonnie and Clyde*, won two Oscars. The film, starring Warren Beatty and Faye Dunaway, tells the story of two young gangsters in 1920s America.

2 Work in pairs, A and B. Read the information about Bonnie and Clyde above. Then practise reading the dialogue from the film.
A: Turn to page 129. B: Turn to page 132.

3 What do you think happens next? Continue the dialogue with your partner.

VOCABULARY: law & order

1 Complete the article with words from the box.

> guilty judge police prison stolen thieves

The robbery happened at ten o'clock and more than £10,000 was (1) _____. There were many **witnesses** who saw it happen – both customers and bank staff. The (2) _____ also had other **evidence** – a bag that the (3) _____ had left behind. It did not take them long to **arrest** the criminals. The **trial** began two months later in the High **Court**. The **jury** found the men (4) _____ and the (5) _____ **sentenced** the men to ten years in (6) _____.

2 Match the words in bold in exercise 1 to the definitions 1–7.

1 a place where legal decisions are taken
2 to catch (a thief)
3 information that helps to show who is responsible for a crime
4 a group of ordinary members of the public who decide if a person is guilty or innocent
5 people who see a crime
6 gave a punishment
7 the process of deciding if a person is guilty

READING

1 Read the newspaper article on the next page and think of a headline for it.

2 Read the article again and answer the questions.

1 Why did the judge have to speak to the jury?
2 Why did the judge say that the robbery was not a joke?
3 Why did the robbers go into a toy shop?
4 Why did they go into a launderette?
5 Why did Michael fall over?
6 Why did no one reply to Laurence's demands?
7 Why did Laurence fall over?
8 When did the police arrest the brothers?

3 Do you agree with the judge's sentence? Why or why not?

E arlier today, a judge at the Central Criminal Court sentenced two men to twelve years in prison for attempting to rob a branch of the Chelmsford Savings Bank. During the trial, the
5 judge repeatedly had to ask members of the jury to stop laughing as they listened to the evidence. In his summing-up, the judge said that the robbery was not funny, but he described the men as pathetic. He continued, 'If everything had gone
10 according to plan, this would have been no joke.' He told the jury to find the men guilty.

In January of this year, the two men, brothers Michael (63) and Laurence Parsons (59), took the bus into Chelmsford town centre. They got off just
15 outside the bank but left their bag, containing masks and an old Webley revolver, on the bus. Not wanting to abandon their plans, the men went into a toy shop opposite the bank and bought two clown masks and a toy gun.

20 The masks were too small and the men had difficulty seeing where they were going. Wearing their masks, they crossed the road, ran into the launderette next to the bank and shouted, 'This is a stick-up!' Surprised customers laughed and
25 suggested that they try next door.

At the second attempt, the men found the bank. Witnesses described how Michael slipped and fell on the polished floor as the two men ran into the bank. Meanwhile, his brother went up to a counter,
30 not realizing that it was unattended, pointed his gun and demanded £5,000. Surprised customers laughed as Laurence repeated his demand. Getting no reply, he decided to give up the attempt, but tripped and fell over his brother who was still on
35 the floor.

Later in the day, the men received treatment in hospital for their injuries. They explained what had happened to the doctors, who then called the police. At first, the police refused to believe the men's
40 story, but arrested them the following day when the missing bag was found.

GRAMMAR: unreal conditions 2

Use a conditional clause beginning with *if* to imagine situations in the past which are the opposite of what actually happened. Note that you use *had* + past participle in the conditional clause.

*If everything **had gone** according to plan, …*
(= but things didn't go according to plan)
*If they **hadn't left** their bag on the bus, …*
(= but they left their bag on the bus)

Use *would* ('d) + have + past participle to talk about the consequence or the result of the imagined situation.

*If they had had their own masks, they **would have seen** what they were doing.*

> SEE LANGUAGE REFERENCE PAGE 84

1 These sentences all refer to the past. Put the verbs in brackets into the correct tense.

1 The sentence _____ (*be*) longer if they _____ (*steal*) any money.
2 If the toy shop _____ (*be*) closed, they _____ (*go*) home.
3 If he _____ (*not / run*) into the bank, he _____ (*not / fall*) over.
4 The customers _____ (*be*) frightened if they _____ (*think*) it was a real robbery.
5 The police _____ (*not / believe*) them if they _____ (*not / find*) the missing bag.

2 Read the story. Write five sentences about the story with *if* and the past perfect.

If the owners had been at home, the thief wouldn't have broken into the house.

One evening, a thief broke into a house in the village of Lachelle. The owners were not there because they had gone to visit some friends. The thief had not eaten all day and was extremely hungry. He found a packet of biscuits in the kitchen and ate them. He then felt thirsty and, finding a bottle of champagne in the fridge, drank that. He now felt sleepy and he decided to have a little rest before robbing the house. Unfortunately, he didn't wake up and the owners of the house found him on their bed when they returned. He was still asleep when the police arrived.

3 Think of five important events in your life. Imagine what would have happened if these events hadn't taken place. Tell a partner.

If I hadn't got married, I wouldn't have had any children.

GRAMMAR

Would

We use *would* + infinitive to give an opinion about hypothetical present and future situations.

> It **would be** nice to have a pay rise.
> They**'d** probably **say** no.
> I **wouldn't go** there for a holiday.

We use *would* + infinitive to ask for and offer advice or suggestions.

> What **would** you **do** in my situation?
> I**'d** probably **tell** her the truth.

We use *would* with *like, love, prefer* and *hate* to express preferences.

> **Would** you **prefer** to have coffee or tea?
> I**'d love** to be a journalist.

Unreal conditions

We can talk about impossible or improbable (hypothetical) situations in a conditional clause that begins with *if*.

When we want to refer to a hypothetical situation in present or future time, we use a past tense in the conditional clause.

> If she **had** a car, ...
> (= but she doesn't/won't have a car)
> If I **were*** the president of the USA, ...
> (= but I'm not/won't be the president of the USA)

* With the verb *be*, we can use *were* for *I/she/he/it* in a conditional clause.

We use *would* + infinitive in the main clause of the sentence to talk about the consequence or result of the hypothetical situation.

> If she had a car, she **would drive** to work.
> She **would drive** to work if she had a car.
> If I were the president of the USA, I**'d do** things very differently.

These sentences are sometimes called second conditional sentences.

Compare the following pair of sentences:

> If you listened, you **would understand**.
> (The condition here is hypothetical. The speaker is saying that you don't or you won't listen.)
> If you listen, you**'ll understand**.
> (The condition here is real. The speaker is saying that it is possible that you will listen.)

Unreal conditions in the past

When we want to refer to a hypothetical situation in the past, we use the past perfect (*had* + past participle) in the conditional clause. These clauses express the opposite of what actually happened.

> If you **had listened** to me, ...
> (= but you didn't listen to me)
> If he **hadn't missed** the train, ...
> (= but he missed the train)

We use *would* + *have* + past participle in the main clause of the sentence to talk about the consequence or result of the hypothetical situation.

> If you had listened to me, you **would've understood**.
> You **would've understood** if you'd listened to me.
> If he hadn't missed the train, he **would have been** on time.

These sentences are sometimes called third conditional sentences.

FUNCTIONAL LANGUAGE

Making offers

Can I + infinitive ... *for you?*
Do you want me to + infinitive ... ?
I'll + infinitive ..., *if you like.*
Let me + infinitive ...
Shall I + infinitive ... ?
Would you like me to + infinitive ... ?

Responding to offers

Thank you.
Thanks.
That's (really) kind of you.
That would be nice/lovely.

No, I'll manage, thanks.
No, it's/that's OK, thank you.
No, that's all right, thanks.

WORD LIST
Newspapers

article *n C* ***	/ˈɑːtɪkl/
circulation *n U*	/ˌsɜːkjʊˈleɪʃn/
daily *adj/n C* **	/ˈdeɪli/
feature *n C/v* ***	/ˈfiːtʃə/
headline *n C*	/ˈhedlaɪn/
journalist *n C* **	/ˈdʒɜːnəlɪst/
left wing *adj*	/ˌleft ˈwɪŋ/
news coverage *n U*	/ˈnjuːz ˌkʌv(ə)rɪdʒ/
press *n U* ***	/pres/
quality	/ˌkwɒləti/
newspaper *n C*	/ˈnjuːzpeɪpə/
right wing *adj*	/ˌraɪt ˈwɪŋ/

Compound nouns (driving)

childminder *n C*	/ˈtʃaɪldˌmaɪndə/
credit card *n C*	/ˈkredɪt ˌkɑːd/
driving licence *n C*	/ˈdraɪvɪŋ ˌlaɪsəns/
ID card *n C*	/aɪˈdiː ˌkɑːd/
mobile phone *n C*	/ˌməʊbaɪl ˈfəʊn/
motorway *n C*	/ˈməʊtəˌweɪ/
no-parking zone *n C*	/ˌnəʊˈpɑːkɪŋ ˌzəʊn/
one-way street *n C*	/ˌwʌnweɪ ˈstriːt/
police station *n C*	/pəˈliːs ˌsteɪʃn/
seatbelt *n C*	/ˈsiːtbelt/
speed limit *n C*	/ˈspiːd ˌlɪmɪt/
traffic lights *n C*	/ˈtræfɪk ˌlaɪts/

Law and order

arrest *v* **	/əˈrest/
clue *n C* *	/kluː/
court *n C* ***	/kɔːt/
crime *n C/U* ***	/kraɪm/
criminal *n C* **	/ˈkrɪmɪnl/
evidence *n U* ***	/ˈevɪdəns/
gangster *n C*	/ˈgæŋstə/
guilty *adj* **	/ˈgɪlti/
innocent *adj* *	/ˈɪnəsənt/
judge *n C* **	/dʒʌdʒ/
jury *n C* **	/ˈdʒʊəri/
mask *n C*	/mɑːsk/
punishment *n C* *	/ˈpʌnɪʃmənt/
revolver *n C*	/rɪˈvɒlvə/
rob *v*	/rɒb/
robber *n C*	/ˈrɒbə/
robbery *n C*	/ˈrɒbəri/
sentence *v*	/ˈsentəns/
stick-up *n C*	/ˈstɪkʌp/
trial *n C* **	/ˈtraɪəl/
violent *adj* ***	/ˈvaɪələnt/
witness *n C* *	/ˈwɪtnəs/

Other words & phrases

abandon *v* *	/əˈbændən/
access *n U* **	/ˈækses/
annual *adj* **	/ˈænjuəl/
attitude *n C* ***	/ˈætɪˌtjuːd/
best-selling *adj*	/ˌbestˈselɪŋ/
biscuit *n C*	/ˈbɪskɪt/
bomb *n C* *	/bɒm/
cable *n C*	/ˈkeɪbl/
cheerful *adj*	/ˈtʃɪəfl/
corporation *n C*	/ˌkɔːpəˈreɪʃn/
cream *n U* **	/kriːm/
cyclist *n C*	/ˈsaɪklɪst/
demand *v* ***	/dɪˈmɑːnd/
demonstration *n C* **	/ˌdemənˈstreɪʃn/
divorced *adj* *	/dɪˈvɔːst/
engineering *n U* *	/ˌendʒɪˈnɪərɪŋ/
facilities *n pl* ***	/fəˈsɪlətɪz/
flan *n C/U*	/flæn/
fountain *n C*	/ˈfaʊntɪn/
globalization *n U*	/ˌgləʊbəlaɪˈzeɪʃn/
investigative *adj*	/ɪnˈvestɪgətɪv/
lane *n C* **	/leɪn/
launderette *n C*	/ˌlɔːndəˈret/
link *v* ***	/lɪŋk/
living conditions *n pl*	/ˈlɪvɪŋ kənˌdɪʃənz/
look-alike *n C*	/ˈlʊkəˌlaɪk/
movie *n C* *	/ˈmuːvi/
naked *adj* *	/ˈneɪkɪd/
negotiation *n C*	/nɪˌgəʊʃiˈeɪʃn/
network *n C* **	/ˈnetwɜːk/
overcrowding *n U*	/ˌəʊvəˈkraʊdɪŋ/
pathetic *adj*	/pəˈθetɪk/
pie *n C/U*	/paɪ/
point *v* ***	/pɔɪnt/
pompous *adj*	/ˈpɒmpəs/
public figure *n C*	/ˌpʌblɪk ˈfɪgə/
publish *v* ***	/ˈpʌblɪʃ/
reasonable *adj* **	/ˈriːznəbl/
roof *n C* ***	/ruːf/
salary *n C* *	/ˈsæl(ə)ri/
schedule *n C* *	/ˈʃedjuːl/
scribble *v*	/ˈskrɪbl/
slip *v* **	/slɪp/
statement *n C* ***	/ˈsteɪtmənt/
strike *n C/v* **	/straɪk/
strip *v*	/strɪp/
studio *n C* **	/ˈstjuːdɪəʊ/
summing-up *n C*	/ˌsʌmɪŋˈʌp/
symbol *n C* *	/ˈsɪmbl/
sympathize *v*	/ˈsɪmpəˌθaɪz/
thriller *n C*	/ˈθrɪlə/
toy *n C* **	/tɔɪ/
traffic *n U* ***	/ˈtræfɪk/
treatment *n U/C* ***	/ˈtriːtmənt/

valley *n C* *	/ˈvæli/
valuable *adj* **	/ˈvæljʊbl/
value *n C* ***	/ˈvæljuː/
vulnerability *n C*	/ˌvʌln(ə)rəˈbɪləti/
war *n C* ***	/wɔː/
write-off *n C*	/ˈraɪtˌɒf/

9A | Shops & shoppers

VOCABULARY: containers

1 Look at the photo of the shopping basket and complete the phrases 1–8 with a word or phrase from the box.

cat food   jam   lemonade   margarine
milk   mineral water   nappies   tissues

1 a bottle of _____   5 a jar of _____
2 a box of _____   6 a packet of _____
3 a can of _____   7 a tin of _____
4 a carton of _____   8 a tub of _____

2 Think of two more items that can go in each of the containers in exercise 1.

3 What can you tell about this family from the items in their shopping basket?

They've got a baby because there are nappies in the basket.

4 Work in pairs. Discuss these questions.

- How many of the things in the shopping basket do you (or your family) buy regularly?
- Which five items are always in your shopping basket?

PRONUNCIATION: *of*

1 ⊙ 2.7 Listen to a phone conversation. Complete the phrases with the name of the container.

1 some _____ of beer
2 a _____ of carrot soup
3 a _____ of cranberry juice
4 a _____ of jam
5 a couple of _____ of peanuts
6 a _____ of tuna

2 ⊙ 2.7 Listen again. What do you notice about the pronunciation of *of*?

3 ⊙ 2.8 Listen to the complete shopping list and repeat. Then close your book and repeat the list from memory.

4 Turn to page 134. You have one minute to remember all the objects on the page.

5 Work in pairs. Take turns to remember and say as many of the objects from page 134 as you can.

Checking out the CHECK OUT

The eighteenth-century French writer, Brillat-Savarin, wrote that we are what we eat. But in the consumer world of the twenty-first century, it is perhaps truer to say we are what we buy.

5 Every year, in order to find out more about who we are, the National Office of Statistics draws up a list of the typical contents of the nation's shopping basket. The list is designed to analyze the nation's buying habits as accurately as possible. Every year they remove any items that are becoming less
10 popular and replace them with new products.

In this year's basket they have included: a carton of low-fat milk, a bottle of mineral water, a tub of olive oil based-margarine, a bag of pre-washed salad leaves and some free-range chicken. The basket does not contain a box of matches
15 (apparently we prefer lighters), a bottle of gin (it seems that we've become a nation of vodka drinkers) or a packet of cheese slices (which were very popular a few years ago).

Changes in the basket show that traditional British foods, like bread and butter or bacon and eggs and a cup of tea, which

READING

1 Read the first two paragraphs of the article. Answer the questions.

1 What is the 'nation's shopping basket'?
2 What is its purpose?
3 How often do the contents change?

2 Work in pairs. Read the rest of the article and make lists of the following things.

1 typical products in the nation's 'basket of goods' at present
2 products that have been added to the basket in the last ten to twenty years
3 any changes in British eating habits

3 Discuss these questions with your partner.

- What are the differences between the typical British shopping basket and a typical basket in your country?
- Have eating habits in your country changed in the last twenty years?
- What do you think will be in a typical shopping basket in twenty years' time?

20 used to be so popular, are being replaced by a more Mediterranean diet. Twenty years ago very few households included olive oil or fresh pasta on their shopping lists.

Now they are among the top ten most likely items on the Great British shopping list. Ten years ago very few families
25 bought bottled mineral water to drink at home – they thought it was a luxury item. But, influenced by holidays in other European countries, we're now buying so much that it has taken over from more traditional drinks such as lemonade. And it would seem that the typical British consumer is also
30 spending more money on organic fruit and vegetables, vegetarian burgers and decaffeinated coffee. At the same time, less healthy food items have been crossed off the list.

So it seems that Britain as a nation is looking more to its European neighbours and thinking more about its health. The
35 next time you're in the supermarket, take a quick look at the contents of your trolley and see if you're a part of modern Britain.

GRAMMAR: articles & determiners

1 Choose the correct words to complete the text.

(1) *A / The* nation's shopping basket not only contains items of (2) *the / –* food. It also includes (3) *any / –* electronic and household goods. Here are (4) *some / –* new items that have appeared recently: DVD players, digital cameras, CDs bought over (5) *the /an* internet. Have you bought (6) *any / –* of these items recently? I'm sure you have. And what about (7) *the / any* products that are falling out of favour? When was the last time you bought (8) *the / an* exercise bike or (9) *the / a* typewriter? (10) *Some / A* quick look at anyone's birthday wish list shows their lack of (11) *the / –* popularity.

2 Correct the six grammatical mistakes in the conversation.

A: Do you ever buy the traditional British food items?
B: No, I don't think I know some traditional British foods.
A: Oh, come on! The packet of English tea bags? Any jar of marmalade? Some crackers?
B: Crackers?
A: Yes, a biscuits that we eat with cheese. Or some Cadbury's chocolate?
B: Sorry, I've never bought any of these things.
A: You should. Any British food is really nice.

3 🔘 2.9 Listen to the recording to check your answers.

Use *the*
- to refer to something because you have already mentioned it or it is defined by the context of the sentence.
  ***The** basket will include …*
  (= the basket I was talking about earlier)
- to refer to something when it's the only one in the context.
  ***The** nation's shopping basket …*
  (= we know which nation we're talking about)

Use zero article to talk about things in general.
Very few households bought fresh pasta.

Use *a/an*
- to talk about things in general.
  ***a** more Mediterranean diet*
- to introduce new information or to refer to something for the first time.
  *The Office of National Statistics draws up **a** list.*
- to refer to one of a group of things.
  *It seems that Britain as **a** nation …*

Use *some* and *any* to describe an unspecified number or quantity. Note that *some* is common in positive sentences, and *any* in negative sentences and questions.
  *a bag of salad leaves and **some** chicken*
  *There isn't **any** gin in the shopping basket.*

Use *any* in positive sentences to show that the quantity is not important.
  *They remove **any** items that are becoming less popular.*

▶ SEE LANGUAGE REFERENCE PAGE 94

VOCABULARY: shopping

1 Match the words in the box to the categories 1–3.

> shop assistant   shopping centre/mall   window-shopping
> shoplifter   corner shop   discount shop   online shopping
> high street shopping   shopaholic

1 people   2 types of shopping   3 places to go shopping

2 Complete the quiz with a word or phrase from exercise 1.

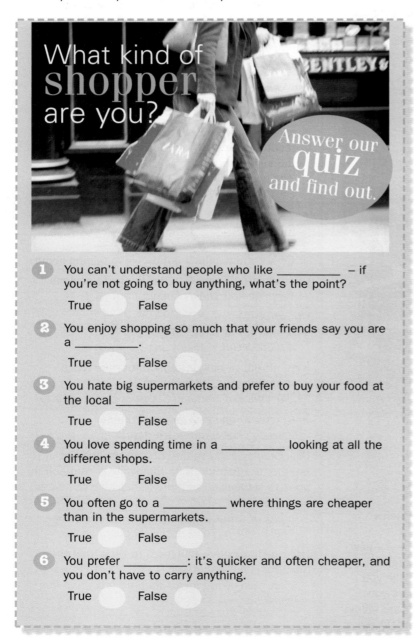

What kind of **shopper** are you?

Answer our *quiz* and find out.

1 You can't understand people who like _____ – if you're not going to buy anything, what's the point?

   True   False

2 You enjoy shopping so much that your friends say you are a _____.

   True   False

3 You hate big supermarkets and prefer to buy your food at the local _____.

   True   False

4 You love spending time in a _____ looking at all the different shops.

   True   False

5 You often go to a _____ where things are cheaper than in the supermarkets.

   True   False

6 You prefer _____: it's quicker and often cheaper, and you don't have to carry anything.

   True   False

3 Which of the sentences in exercise 2 are true for you? Compare your answers with a partner.

LISTENING

1 🔘 2.10 Listen to an interview with Katy, a shopaholic. Which of the questions does the interviewer not ask?

1 Are you really an addict?
2 When do you usually go shopping?
3 Is there an ideal time to go shopping?
4 Where do you most like shopping?
5 Do you travel a lot?
6 How much do you usually spend a week?
7 What's your favourite country for shopping?
8 What do you most enjoy shopping for?
9 When did you last go shopping?
10 What did you buy?

2 🔘 2.10 Listen again and make notes on Katy's answers.

3 Work in pairs, A and B. Make up a short conversation between Katy and one of her friends who wants to give her some advice about her shopping addiction.

   A: You are Katy.
   B: You are one of Katy's friends.

GRAMMAR: quantifiers 1

1 Add one word to each sentence.

                                    his
1 My brother spends most of ʌ money on presents for his new girlfriend.

2 All friends prefer shopping to doing sport.

3 None them actually enjoys going shopping.

4 My mum spends most her free time on the internet finding new shopping sites.

5 Last week I spent all money on a really expensive bottle of champagne for my boss.

6 My boyfriend never likes any of clothes I buy for him.

7 Some the best shops in town are down the little side streets.

2 🔘 2.11 Listen to the recording to check your answers.

3 Complete the sentences so that they are true for your town. Use *some, many, most, all, any, none* or *no* with or without *of* as appropriate.

1 *Most of* the big shopping centres are on the outskirts of town.
2 _____ people prefer to drive to the big supermarkets to do their shopping.
3 _____ the shops in the town centre sell tourist souvenirs.
4 _____ shops in the centre have private parking facilities.
5 _____ smaller shops have had to close because they can't compete with the big malls.
6 _____ the people you meet can tell you that the town centre has changed a lot in the last ten years.
7 And _____ them will say that they are happy with the changes.

Use *some, any, many, most* and *all* with or without *of*.

some any many most all	of	the + noun my/his, etc. + noun them/us, etc.

Most of the time I go out of my way …
Many of my good friends think I'm an addict.
All of them seem to agree.

some any many most	+ noun
all	+ the/my/his, etc. + noun

Some people complain that they're boring.
Most countries are good for something.
All the shops look alike.

Always use *of* when *none* is followed by a noun or a pronoun.

none of	the + noun my/his/her, etc. + noun us/them, etc.

None of the shops in the centre …
Not *None shops in the centre …*

Use *no* followed by a noun without an article or a possessive adjective.
No country I know is better than Italy.

> SEE LANGUAGE REFERENCE PAGE 94

SPEAKING

1 Work in three groups, A–C. Read the information.

The local council is planning to develop a new shopping area in your town. They want the area to include cinemas, cafés, an arts centre and a sports centre.

2 Prepare a proposal for the new shopping area. Your proposal must cover the following points:

- exact location and reasons for choosing this location
- parking and transport arrangements
- parks and green areas
- leisure facilities (sports, cinema, concerts, exhibitions, etc.)

Group A: Turn to page 131.
Group B: Turn to page 132.
Group C: Turn to page 134.

3 Work in new groups of three or more. Each group must include at least one student from groups A, B and C in exercise 1. Explain your proposal to your partners and decide together on a joint proposal for the shopping centre.

4 Present your proposal to the class.

Useful language

First of all, we'll talk about …
Then, we'll move on to consider …
We have decided to …
We propose to …
We believe that it is important that …
In conclusion we'd like to say that …

9B | E-shopping

READING

1 Read the situations a–e and look at the website. Decide which link you would click on for each.

a This is your first visit to the site. You don't want anything now, but you want to find out what's on offer.

b A friend has told you this site has very cheap DVDs and you want to find out how much it costs to get the *Lord of the Rings* trilogy.

c You have ordered a shirt and a pair of jeans from the site, but they haven't arrived.

d You've just ordered some CDs for a friend's birthday. You want to send them to your friend's address with a special birthday greeting.

e You're a music fan who is looking for cheap price CDs.

2 Turn to page 133. Read the descriptions and match them to stores in the mall.

3 Read the descriptions again (both the one on this page and the three on page 133). Answer the questions.

1 Which stores offer discount prices on selected items?

2 Which store is running a special prize competition?

3 Which store specializes in presents, both traditional and unconventional?

4 Which store offers a special advice service?

5 Which stores claim to cater for all age groups?

6 Which store regularly features products associated with a famous person?

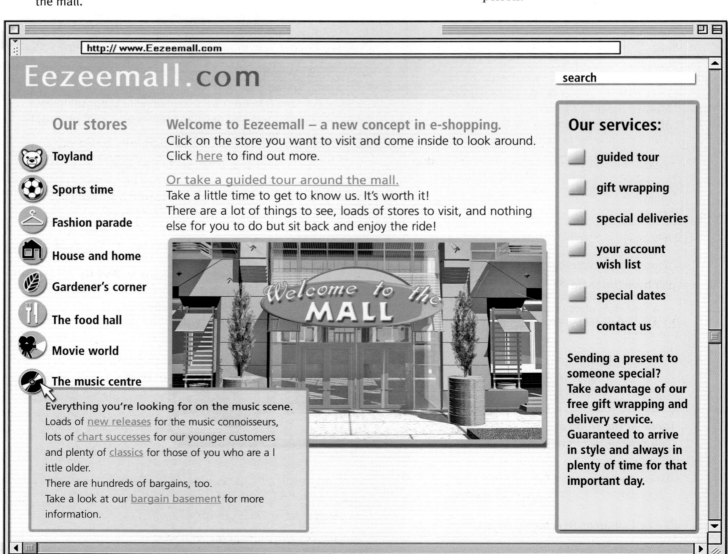

http:// www.Eezeemall.com

Eezeemall.com

search

Our stores

- Toyland
- Sports time
- Fashion parade
- House and home
- Gardener's corner
- The food hall
- Movie world
- The music centre

Welcome to Eezeemall – a new concept in e-shopping.
Click on the store you want to visit and come inside to look around.
Click here to find out more.

Or take a guided tour around the mall.
Take a little time to get to know us. It's worth it!
There are a lot of things to see, loads of stores to visit, and nothing else for you to do but sit back and enjoy the ride!

Welcome to the MALL

Everything you're looking for on the music scene.
Loads of new releases for the music connoisseurs, lots of chart successes for our younger customers and plenty of classics for those of you who are a little older.
There are hundreds of bargains, too.
Take a look at our bargain basement for more information.

Our services:

- guided tour
- gift wrapping
- special deliveries
- your account wish list
- special dates
- contact us

Sending a present to someone special? Take advantage of our free gift wrapping and delivery service. Guaranteed to arrive in style and always in plenty of time for that important day.

VOCABULARY: collocations with *take*

1 Complete the texts with a word or phrase from the box.

> our word   your breath   a look
> a little time   our advice   advantage

1 Take _____ at our summer sales. You're sure to find something to wear on that special occasion!
2 Looking for something to read on the beach? Take _____ for it – you've come to the right place.
3 Take _____ of our special offer – running this week only. 50% off all frozen products.
4 Can't find that special present? Take _____, buy a gift voucher! Let your friends choose from our huge range of new releases and all-time classics, films and video games!
5 Enjoy the atmosphere of our historic towns, relax on our spectacular beaches and let the beauty of the landscape take _____ away.
6 Take _____ out of your busy day to look after yourself. Work out at the gym, take it easy in the Jacuzzi, or play a friendly game of tennis. We've got exactly what you need.

2 What products are the texts trying to sell?

3 Write a short advert for another popular product. Include at least one phrase with *take*. Your classmates must guess what the product is.

GRAMMAR: quantifiers 2

1 Work in pairs. Decide whether the sentences in each pair have the same (S) or different (D) meaning.

1 a A few sites offer free gift wrapping.
  b A couple of sites offer free gift wrapping.
2 a The government is doing little to protect e-shoppers against credit card fraud.
  b The government is doing enough to protect e-shoppers against credit card fraud.
3 a People spend too much money on clothes.
  b People spend plenty of money on clothes.
4 a Not many web sites offer such a wide range of goods.
  b Few web sites offer such a wide range of goods.
5 a Most internet users spend a little time window shopping online.
  b Most internet users don't spend a lot of time window shopping online.

2 Put these quantifiers in the table: *few, too many, lots of, loads of, little, much, plenty of, enough, too much*. Then choose the correct option to complete the rules.

countable	uncountable	both
not many	*not much*	*a lot of*

Use *few* and *little* without *a* with a *negative / positive* meaning. (*few* = not many; *little* = not much)
*The government is doing **little** to protect e-shoppers.*

Use *enough* when you mean that the quantity is *sufficient / more than sufficient* for the purpose.
*We've got **enough** for two, but not for three.*

Use *plenty* when you mean that the quantity is *sufficient / more than sufficient* for the purpose.
*We've got **plenty** of time to get to the station. There's no need to hurry.*

Use *too much* and *too many* (of something) when you mean that this is a *good / bad* thing.
*Ugh! There's **too much** salt in this soup!*

> ● SEE LANGUAGE REFERENCE PAGE 94

3 Complete the sentences so that they are true for you. Choose a positive or negative verb and add a quantifier.

1 I *spend / don't spend* _____ money on clothes.
2 I *know / don't know* _____ people who hate shopping.
3 I *buy / don't buy* _____ books every year.
4 I *have / don't have* _____ time to shop online.
5 There *are / aren't* _____ online shops for young people.

4 Compare your sentences with a partner. How similar are your shopping habits?

SPEAKING

1 Work in groups. You are going to prepare a quiz to find out if your classmates are cybernauts or technophobes. Use the prompts below to help you prepare questions for the quiz.

Do you know what ... ?   Have you ever used ... ?
How often do you ... ?   Would you like to ... ?
When did you first ... ?   How important is ... ?

2 Work in pairs. Interview a student from another group. After the quiz, give them a score out of 10 (1 = total technophobe → 10 = absolute cybernaut).

Does your partner agree with your score?

9c | Telephone bills

SPEAKING

1 Have you ever bought one of the products shown in this advertisement? Why or why not?

2 Work in pairs. Think of a fascia, a logo and ring tone for three of your classmates. Do they agree with your choices?

LISTENING

1 🔘 **2.12–2.14** Listen to three conversations. In each conversation, someone is unhappy. What is each person unhappy about?

2 Can you remember who said the following phrases?

Conversation 2: Derek (Dk) / Dave (D)
5 What a cheek! As if we had the time!
6 I've had nothing but problems with it.
7 I think we can make an exception.

Conversation 1: Camilla (C) / Derek (Dk)
1 There's something I wanted to talk to you about. *C*
2 I'll ask her to sort them out.
3 I didn't know we had any customers in Japan.
4 I'll speak to you again at the end of the day.

Conversation 3: Dave (D) / Service assistant (S)
8 I'm not too sure.
9 I take your point.
10 I'm not sure what to suggest.

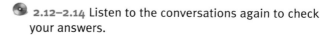 🔘 **2.12–2.14** Listen to the conversations again to check your answers.

FUNCTIONAL LANGUAGE: complaints

1 💿 2.12–2.14 Listen to the conversations again and complete the extracts.

Conversation 1
1 I'm _____ finding anything.
2 Could you _____ to have a look at them?
3 I'm afraid that's _____ enough.
4 I'll see _____ this afternoon.

Conversation 2
5 It's just not on, I mean it's totally _____.

Conversation 3
6 I've got a _____ my phone.
7 I'm sorry, sir. What seems to be _____?
8 I think there's _____ the power.
9 The phone doesn't _____.
10 Could I _____ the manager?
11 I'd like a _____.
12 I want to have my _____.

2 Match the sentences in exercise 1 with the four groups a–d.

a Explaining the problem (4 sentences)
b Saying what you want (4 sentences)
c Expressing dissatisfaction (2 sentences)
d Responding to a complaint (2 sentences)

3 Work in pairs. Think of one more sentence for each group a–d in exercise 2.

Roleplay

4 Work in pairs. You are going to act out a conversation where someone makes a complaint. Choose one of the situations below. Prepare and perform the roleplay.

1 You have recently opened an account with an internet service provider (ISP). Every time you log on to the net, your computer crashes. Telephone the ISP to complain.
2 You ordered some DVDs from a website. After four weeks, they still have not arrived. You have received no replies to your emails. Telephone the company to complain.
3 You bought an expensive digital camera from a local shop to take on holiday with you. It didn't work. You couldn't even switch it on. You return from your holiday and go back to the shop to complain.

VOCABULARY: prepositional phrases

1 Complete the sentences with an appropriate preposition.

1 Do you ever meet friends in the street _____ chance?
2 Have you ever telephoned the wrong number _____ mistake?
3 At what time of the day are you most often _____ a hurry?
4 Have you ever solved a problem _____ accident?
5 What organizations have information about you _____ file?
6 Have you ever been _____ danger of losing your job?
7 Do you ever leave your bedroom _____ a mess?
8 Have you ever been _____ trouble at school?

💿 2.15 Listen to the recording to check your answers.

2 Work in pairs. Choose five questions to ask your partner.

DID YOU KNOW?

1 Work in pairs. Read the information about phone boxes in the UK and discuss these questions.

The red phone box has been a traditional symbol of Britain for over 80 years. But now, they are disappearing from the British landscape, mostly because of an increase in the use of mobile phones.

At their peak, there were more than 140,000 red phone boxes throughout the country. Today, there are fewer than 60,000 of them in use. Most of these are modern in style and do not look like the traditional box which was first introduced in 1924.

The red boxes were owned by British Telecom (BT), the biggest phone company in the UK. BT used to be a government company and had a monopoly. However, in 1984 it became a private company and other phone companies were allowed to compete with it. Now there are a lot of telephone companies operating in the UK, including supermarket chains like Tesco.

- How many phone companies are there in your country?
- Which is the most popular?
- What advice would you give to someone who wants to have a mobile phone account in your country?

GRAMMAR

Articles, determiners & quantifiers

We use the definite article, *the*

- to refer to something or someone because we have already mentioned it, or it is defined by the context of the sentence.

  The Office of Statistics draws up a list of goods. **The** *list is designed to reflect the nation's buying habits.*

- to refer to something or someone when it's the only one in the context.

  In **the** *consumer world of* **the** *twenty-first century …*

We use the zero article with uncountable or plural nouns to talk about things in general.

> *They replace them with* **Ø** *new products.*
> *We prefer* **Ø** *lighters.*

We use the indefinite article, *a* or *an*

- to talk about things in general (with singular nouns).

  The basket does not contain **a** *box of matches.*

- to introduce new information or to refer to something for the first time (with singular countable nouns).

  The Office of Statistics draws up **a** *list of goods.*

- to refer to one of a group of things.

  … to see if you're **a** *part of modern Britain.*

We use the determiners *some* and *any* to describe an unspecified number or quantity (with uncountable and plural nouns).

> *We should get* **some** *mineral water.*
> **Some** *families are spending more on organic food.*

Some is common in positive sentences. In negative sentences and questions, *any* is more common.

> *It does not contain* **any** *luxury goods like caviar.*
> *Have you bought* **any** *coffee recently?*

We can also use *any* in positive sentences to show that the quantity is not important.

> *If you see* **any** *special offers at the shops, let me know.*
> (= it doesn't matter how many/which special offers)

We can use the quantifiers *some, any, many, most* and *all* in two different ways: with or without *of*.

with *of*		
some any many most all	of	the + noun my/his/her/etc. + noun them/us/you

> **Some of** *the shops are very expensive.*
> *I don't know* **any of** *your friends.*

without *of*	
some any many most all	+ noun + *the* + noun

> **Some people** *hate shopping.*
> *Are there* **any shops** *that sell souvenirs?*

We use *none* to talk about no amount or quantity of something. When *none* is followed by a noun or pronoun, we always use *of*.

none of	the + noun my/his/her/etc. + noun them/us/you

> **None of the shops** *are open.*
> Not ~~none shops are open~~ …
> **None of my friends** *smoke.*
> **None of them** *has time to help you.*

When *none* is the subject of a sentence, it is used with an affirmative verb. The verb can be singular or plural.

We use *no* followed by a noun without an article or a possessive adjective.

> *There were* **no** *parking facilities.*
> **No** *website is better for cheap flights.*

Quantifiers that can be used with both plural countable nouns and uncountable nouns:
a lot of, lots of, enough, not enough, plenty of

Enough means the quantity is sufficient for the purpose.

> *Do we have* **enough** *money to go out for a meal?*
> *I think you've probably had* **enough** *time.*

Plenty of means the quantity is more than sufficient for the purpose.

> *You've got* **plenty of** *time to catch the train.*
> *There's* **plenty of** *room for everybody.*

quantifiers with plural countable nouns	quantifiers with uncountable nouns
many	—
not many	not much
too many	too much
a few	a little
few	little

We do not usually use *much* in affirmative sentences in modern English. We use *a lot of/lots* of instead.

> *They gave us* **a lot of** *advice.*
> Not ~~They gave us much advice.~~

GRAMMAR: modals of speculation 2 (present time)

Use a modal verb + *be* + verb + *-ing* to make guesses or speculations about actions in progress now.

sure ↑ less sure ↓ sure	subject	*must* *might* (*not*) *may* (*not*) *could* *can't*	*be* + verb + *-ing*

Someone **might be watching** you.
You **must be joking**.
Could he **be telling** the truth?

> SEE LANGUAGE REFERENCE PAGE 104

1 Find four examples of modal verbs followed by *be* + verb + *-ing* in tapescript 2.19 on pages 149–150.

2 ◉ 2.20 Listen to the recording. You will hear seven different actions from the story of *The Da Vinci Code*. After each action, say what you think Robert Langdon is doing. Use a modal verb of speculation and the ideas below to help you.

He might be hiding his gun.

- escaping from the police in the Louvre
- hiding his gun
- looking for a key in a desk
- looking for information in a library
- looking for information on the internet
- reading about himself in a newspaper
- trying to open a locked door
- typing a letter to his girlfriend
- walking around an old church

3 Think of four people you know. What do you think they are doing now? Write two sentences with modals of deduction for each person.

My friend Pete could be presenting sales figures in a meeting.
He can't be sitting at home.

DID YOU KNOW?

1 Work in pairs. Read the information and discuss the questions.

Glastonbury

Glastonbury, a town in the south-west of England, is a magical and mysterious place. There are many legends and myths about it. A large number of people believe that one of the followers of Jesus Christ, a man called Joseph of Arimathea, brought the Holy Grail (the cup that Christ used at the Last Supper) to England, and buried it at Glastonbury. They also say that he built the first church in England in Glastonbury. Archaeological research shows that there may have been an early Christian church in the town.

There is also a connection with King Arthur and his knights of the Round Table, who spent their lives looking for the Grail. In the 12th Century, some monks announced that they had found King Arthur's grave at Glastonbury, along with a stone. On the stone there was some writing that said, 'Here lies Arthur, king.'

- Are there any magical or mysterious places in your country?
- What stories are associated with these places?

10B | Mysteries

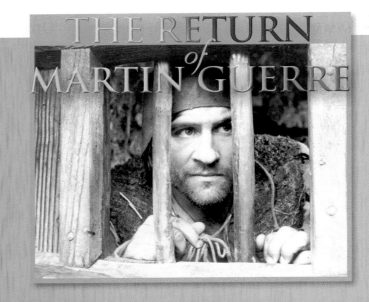

READING

1 The film *The Return of Martin Guerre* tells the story of a man who is not what he seems. Even his wife did not know the truth about him. What do you think the truth was?

2 Read the story of Martin Guerre and put the paragraphs in order. Was your guess in exercise 1 correct?

3 Read the story again. Complete the sentences 1–7 with the phrases a–g.

1 This is the story of a man who suddenly
2 Years later, another man
3 Almost everybody in the family
4 However, the man's uncle
5 In the end, the real Martin Guerre
6 Everybody now
7 The second man

a believes that it is the man who left.
b is killed for his crime.
c knows the truth.
d leaves his wife and child without any explanation.
e returns home from the war.
f suspects that something is wrong.
g takes his place.

4 Could Bertrande really have believed that Arnaud was her husband? Why or why not?

A Pierre accused Martin of being an imposter. Martin was arrested and went to court. At the trial, Bertrande supported her husband. She refused to believe that he was someone else. Arnaud du Tilh convinced the judges that he was telling the truth. The case seemed to be closed when the real Martin Guerre dramatically returned. He had one leg and he had been a soldier. He and du Tilh had been friends in the army.

B There was no news of him until, eight years later, a man arrived in Artigat who claimed to be Martin. His appearance was similar to Martin's, but there were a number of differences. However, he managed to convince Bertrande, his uncle and his four sisters that he was the real Martin Guerre. He moved in with Bertrande and they had two more children. It seems that this time the marriage was much happier.

C When Bertrande also agreed that the man with one leg was her real husband, du Tilh finally admitted his crime. The judges decided that he deserved to die and, four days later, he was hanged in front of the Guerre's family house. The case was solved, but one question remained. How could Bertrande have believed that du Tilh was her husband? Martin Guerre thought that his wife must have known the truth and he never forgave her.

D Martin Guerre was fourteen years old when he got married to Bertrande de Rols, whose family also lived in the village of Artigat in the south of France. It was not a happy marriage, but after eight years, they had a son, Sanxi. Then, when Sanxi was only a few months old, Martin suddenly disappeared. The reasons for his disappearance are not clear, but it is thought that he may have had an argument with his father.

E After a few years, Martin's uncle, Pierre, began to suspect the new Martin. The two men argued about money and Pierre even tried to kill him. Bertrande saved Martin's life. Pierre also met a soldier who said that Martin's real name was Arnaud du Tilh. Arnaud had pretended to be Martin because he wanted to get his money. The real Martin Guerre had lost a leg in the war.

GRAMMAR: modals of speculation (past time)

Use a modal verb + *have* + past participle to make guesses or to speculate about the past.

sure ↑ less sure ↓ sure	subject	*must* *might* (*not*) *may* (*not*) *could* *can't* *couldn't*	have	past participle (*had, known, seen, said, etc.*)

He **may have had** an argument with his father.
She **must have known** the truth.
How **could** she **have believed** him?

⊙ SEE LANGUAGE REFERENCE PAGE 104

1 Match the sentences 1–6 to one of the newspaper headlines a–d.

  a **Politician's clothes found on beach**

  b **Police find box of snakes on highway**

  c ALIEN ATTACKS TEACHER

  d Six people see monster in Chinese mountains

1 I'm sure they didn't come from a zoo.
2 Someone definitely left them there.
3 It's possible that they attacked someone.
4 Maybe they fell off the back of a lorry.
5 Perhaps they weren't dangerous.
6 There's a possibility that someone intended to pick them up later.

2 Rewrite the sentences in exercise 1 beginning with the words given below and a modal verb.

1 *They can't have come from a zoo.*

1 They …		4 They …
2 Someone …		5 They …
3 They …		6 Someone …

3 Now make deductions about the other headlines.

It can't have been an alien!
It might have been someone dressed as an alien.

4 ⊙ 2.21–2.24 Listen to the recordings to find out what really happened.

VOCABULARY: verbs followed by infinitive

1 These words are highlighted in the story about Martin Guerre. Underline the words and the two words that follow them in the story.

began   claimed   deserved   managed
pretended   refused   seemed   tried

2 Work in pairs. Complete the text with words from the box in exercise 1.

Before their wedding, Nicola's husband (1) *seemed* to be normal in every way. But afterwards, he (2) _____ to act very strangely. He often came home late from work and he (3) _____ to say where he had been. Nicola (4) _____ not to mind, but she was very worried. She (5) _____ to speak to him, but he never explained why he was late. Then, one day at dinner, he suddenly (6) _____ to be an alien. He said that all humans were bad and (7) _____ to die. He was very excited, but Nicola (8) _____ to calm him down. But the next morning, her husband had gone and she never saw him again.

SPEAKING

1 Work in groups, A and B. You are going to work out the answer to a mystery.

Group A: Read the information below. Find out more information by asking the students in Group B questions. They can only answer *Yes, Sort of, No* or *Not exactly*.

A woman went to the shops and bought a new pair of shoes. Later that day, she went to work and died. How did she die?

After every eight questions, discuss what you have learnt with the other members of your group.

Group B: Turn to page 132. Read the explanation of the situation and answer the questions the students in group A ask you. You can only answer *Yes, Sort of, No* or *Not exactly.*

2 Now exchange roles.

Group B: Try to work out the answer to the mystery.

A man was staying in a motel. He went outside to his car and hooted on the horn. He then returned to his room. Why did he hoot on the car horn?

Group A: Turn to page 128 and answer the questions the students in Group B ask you.

10c | Strictly confidential PRIVATE

SPEAKING

1 Work in pairs. Which of the following pieces of information about you are the most confidential?

- your age
- the way that you vote
- your emails and where you surf on the internet
- your financial situation
- your employment record
- your school record

2 Which pieces of information in exercise 1 do you think the following people have the right to know? Explain your reasons.

- parents about their children
- husbands or wives about their partners
- employers about their staff
- schools or universities about their students
- governments about the people

LISTENING

1 🔘 2.25 Listen to the conversation between Camilla, Dave and Peter. Answer the questions.

1 What are they thinking of doing?
2 Who is for and who is against the idea?

2 🔘 2.25 Listen to the conversation again. Put the points in the correct order.

The new system

☐ will stop people wasting time.
☐ will show the staff that it is important to cut costs.
☐ will stop people from visiting gambling websites.
☐ will help to avoid problems with computer viruses.
☐ will make people feel unhappy.
☐ will cost money in the short term.

3 Do you think it is a good idea for companies (or schools) to introduce systems like this?

FUNCTIONAL LANGUAGE: advantages & disadvantages

1 Choose the correct words and phrases to complete the sentences.

1 We should think a little more about the *drawbacks / pros and cons*.
2 The *benefits / troubles* of this are pretty obvious.
3 There may be one or two hidden *drawbacks / problem*.
4 The good *disadvantage / thing* about this system is that it stops time-wasting.
5 The *advantages / trouble* is that our computer system is open to viruses.
6 You were worried about some of the *disadvantages / thing* of doing this.
7 I can't see any *gained / point* in waiting.
8 The other *benefits / problem* with this is the whole question of confidentiality.
9 I think there's a lot to be *benefit / gained*.

2 Look at tapescript 2.25 on pages 150–151 to check your answers.

3 Complete the conversation with the words in italics from exercise 1. Sometimes more than one answer is possible.

A: We've designed a new system that scans customers' emails to look for particular words.
B: What's the (1) _____ in that?
A: Well, the great (2) _____ of it is that we can send advertisements that match the things that people talk about.
B: But isn't there a (3) _____ with people who don't want to receive advertisements?
A: Maybe, but there are so many other (4) _____ – special offers, low prices and so on – that they'll want to use our service.
B: And it's a good (5) _____ for the advertisers, of course.
A: Yes, there's a lot to be (6) _____ for them. One of the (7) _____ in the past was that they didn't know who to send the advertisements to.

SPEAKING

Roleplay

1 Read the newspaper article about installing CCTV in schools.

Have your say:

Spying on our kids?

As we know, the behaviour of school children is getting worse across the UK. Vandalism, violence and bullying are all on the increase in our schools. More and more schools are trying to help solve this problem by installing

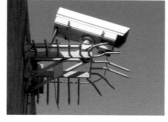

CCTV cameras in our schools so that the small minority who cause trouble can be caught.

In Crookton, our Mayor is thinking about spending some of his budget on such cameras. The cameras will be in classrooms, corridors, toilets and playgrounds.

A public debate on this issue will take place in the town hall this Friday. If you want to have your say, come along.

2 Work in four groups, A–D. You are going to prepare a list of five reasons for or against the introduction of CCTV cameras.

Group A: You represent the teachers in your town's schools. You are against the introduction of CCTV.

Group B: You represent the parents of school children in your town. You support the introduction of CCTV.

Group C: You represent school children in your town. You are against the introduction of CCTV.

Group D: You represent the local government in your town. You support the introduction of CCTV.

In your groups, prepare your reasons for or against the introduction of CCTV.

3 Now choose a representative from each group. Present your arguments for or against the introduction of CCTV.

VOCABULARY: idioms

1 Complete the idiomatic expressions 1–6 with a word from the box.

bright	cracking	feet	high	point	safe

1 Do you like to get up _____ and early or do you prefer to stay in bed as long as possible?
2 Do you know anyone who goes on and on and never gets to the _____ when they are speaking?
3 In general, do you live dangerously or play it _____?
4 What was the _____ point of your day yesterday and what was the worst moment?
5 When there is something you have to do, do you prefer to get _____ immediately or do you prefer to wait a bit?
6 When was the last time you didn't want to do something and you dragged your _____?

2 Find and underline these idioms in tapescript 2.25 on pages 150–151.

3 Work in pairs. Ask and answer the questions in exercise 1. Do you know any more English idioms? What are they?

GRAMMAR

Modals of speculation (present & past time)

We can use modal verbs to make guesses about the present, the past and the future.

The choice of modal verb shows how sure we are about our guess.

sure   less sure

◄──────────────────────────────►

must   *might (not)*   *may (not)*

sure   less sure

◄──────────────────────────────►

could   *can't*   *sure*

We use the modal verb + infinitive to make guesses about the present or the future.

> You **must be** very tired.
> I **might need** your help later.
> He **can't be** serious.

We use the modal verb + *be* + *-ing* form to make guesses about actions in progress now.

> She **must be having** problems at work.
> I'm not sure where he is. He **could be having** a bath.
> She **might be working** for the CIA.

We use the modal verb + *have* + past participle to make guesses about the past.

> They **must have arrived** by now.
> He **might not have known** her true identity.
> It **can't have been** a surprise.

FUNCTIONAL LANGUAGE

Advantages and disadvantages

The pros and cons of + noun/-*ing* form
The good/bad thing about + noun/-*ing* form *is …*

The advantage of + noun/-*ing* form
The benefit/benefits of + noun/-*ing* form
There's a lot to be gained from + -*ing* form

The disadvantage of + noun/-*ing* form
The drawback of + noun/-*ing* form
The trouble with + noun/-*ing* form
The problem with + noun/-*ing* form
There's no point in/There isn't any point in + -*ing* form
There's nothing to be gained from + -*ing* form

WORD LIST
Illusions

act *v* ***	/ækt/
audience *n C* **	/ˈɔːdɪəns/
fake *adj/n C*	/feɪk/
magician *n C*	/maˈdʒɪʃn/
perform *v* ***	/pəˈfɔːm/
pretend *v* *	/prɪˈtend/
public *n* ***	/ˈpʌblɪk/
reveal *v* ***	/rɪˈviːl/
stage *n C* ***	/steɪdʒ/
trick *n C* **	/trɪk/
vanish *v* *	/ˈvænɪʃ/

Word families

certain *adj* ***	/ˈsɜːtn/
certainly *adv* ***	/ˈsɜːtnli/
certainty *n C*	/ˈsɜːtnti/
definite *adj* **	/ˈdef(ə)nət/
definitely *adv* **	/ˈdef(ə)nətli/
impossibility *n C*	/ɪmˌpɒsəˈbɪləti/
impossible *adj* ***	/ɪmˈpɒsəbl/
improbability *n C*	/ɪmˌprɒbəˈbɪləti/
improbable *adj*	/ɪmˈprɒbəbl/
likelihood *n U*	/ˈlaɪklɪhʊd/
likely *adj* ***	/ˈlaɪkli/
possibility *n C* ***	/ˌpɒsəˈbɪləti/
possible *adj* ***	/ˈpɒsəbl/
possibly *adv* ***	/ˈpɒsəbli/
probability *n C*	/ˌprɒbəˈbɪləti/
probable *adj*	/ˈprɒbəbl/
probably *adv* ***	/ˈprɒbəbli/
uncertain *adj*	/ʌnˈsɜːtn/
uncertainty *n C*	/ʌnˈsɜːtnti/
unlikely *adj* **	/ʌnˈlaɪkli/

Verbs followed by infinitive

begin ***	/bɪˈgɪn/
claim ***	/kleɪm/
deserve **	/dɪˈzɜːv/
manage ***	/ˈmænɪdʒ/
pretend *	/prɪˈtend/
refuse ***	/rɪˈfjuːz/
seem ***	/siːm/
try ***	/traɪ/

Idioms

bright and early	/ˌbraɪt ən ˈɜːli/
drag your feet	/ˌdræg jə ˈfiːt/
get cracking	/ˌget ˈkrækɪŋ/
get to the point	/ˌget tə ðə ˈpɔɪnt/
high point	/ˈhaɪ ˌpɔɪnt/
play it safe	/ˌpleɪ ɪt ˈseɪf/

Other words & phrases

accuse *v* **	/əˈkjuːz/
admit *v* ***	/ædˈmɪt/
alien *n C*	/ˈeɪliən/
ape *n C*	/eɪp/
apologetic *adj*	/əˌpɒləˈdʒetɪk/
archaeological *adj*	/ˌɑːkiəˈlɒdʒɪkl/
army *n C* ***	/ˈɑːmi/
biological *adj*	/ˌbaɪəˈlɒdʒɪkl/
bullying *n U*	/ˈbʊliɪŋ/
bury *v* *	/ˈberi/
calm down *v*	/ˌkɑːm ˈdaʊn/
casino *n C*	/kəˈsiːnəʊ/
CCTV *n C*	/ˌsiːsiːtiːˈviː/
compartment *n C*	/kəmˈpɑːtmənt/
confidentiality *n U*	/ˌkɒnfɪdenʃˈræləti/
crazy *adj* **	/ˈkreɪzi/
dating agency *n C*	/ˈdeɪtɪŋ ˌeɪdʒənsi/
deaf *adj* **	/def/
equipment *n U* ***	/ɪˈkwɪpmənt/
float *v* *	/fləʊt/
furious *adj*	/ˈfjʊəriəs/
grave *n C* *	/greɪv/
guardian *n C*	/ˈgɑːdiən/
gun *n C* ***	/gʌn/
hack into *v*	/ˈhæk ˌɪntuː/
hang *v* ***	/hæŋ/
heel *n C*	/hiːl/
hoot *v*	/huːt/
imposter *n C*	/ɪmˈpɒstə/
in the long/short term	/ɪn ðə ˈlɒŋ/ˈʃɔːt tɜːm/
knight *n C*	/naɪt/

minority *n C* **	/maɪˈnɒrəti/
moral *adj* *	/ˈmɒrəl/
motel *n C*	/məʊˈtel/
murder *n C/v* **	/ˈmɜːdə/
murderer *n C*	/ˈmɜːdərə/
mysterious *adj*	/mɪˈstɪəriəs/
obvious *adj* ***	/ˈɒbviəs/
pharmaceutical *adj*	/ˌfɑːməˈsjuːtɪkl/
phone-in *n C*	/ˈfəʊnɪn/
productivity *n U*	/ˌprɒdʌkˈtɪvəti/
rabbit *n C*	/ˈræbɪt/
ruin *v*	/ˈruːɪn/
satellite *n C* *	/ˈsætəˌlaɪt/
scan *v*	/skæn/
scandal *n C/U*	/ˈskændl/
scare *v*	/skeə/
secrecy *n U*	/ˈsiːkrəsi/
secret agent *n C*	/ˌsiːkrət ˈeɪdʒənt/
software *n U* ***	/ˈsɒftweə/
spoil *v* *	/spɔɪl/
spy on *v*	/ˈspaɪ ˌɒn/
suspect *v* **	/səˈspekt/
tactic *n C*	/ˈtæktɪk/
technology *n C/U* ***	/tekˈnɒlədʒi/
terrorist *n C* *	/ˈterərɪst/
traitor *n C*	/ˈtreɪtə/
understandably *adv*	/ˌʌndəˈstændəbli/
upset *v* *	/ʌpˈset/
vandalism *n U*	/ˈvændəˌlɪz(ə)m/
weapon *n C* ***	/ˈwepən/
worthless *adj*	/ˈwɔːθləs/

11A | Olympic dreams

SPEAKING & VOCABULARY: sport

1 Work in pairs. Match at least one sport to each verb.

| catch | hit | jump | kick |
| pass | run | serve | throw |

| athletics | baseball | boxing | football |
| gymnastics | rugby | volleyball | waterpolo |

2 Can you think of one more sport for each verb?

3 🔘 2.26 Listen to someone describing how to play a sport. Which sport is the person talking about?

4 Now choose a different sport and describe it using the verbs in exercise 1.

5 Work in groups. Look at the sports in exercise 1 and discuss the questions.

- Which two sports are the most popular in your country?
- Which two sports is your country best at?
- Which two are the most enjoyable to do?
- Which two are the most interesting to watch?

READING

1 Read the article about a world champion sportswoman and answer the questions.

1 What sport does she compete in?
2 Is she famous in her home country?

2 Read the article again. Which topic 1–6 is not mentioned in the article?

1 Louise's sporting successes
2 why Louise chose paragliding
3 why it is important to be accepted as an Olympic sport
4 the process for acceptance as an Olympic sport
5 sports which have recently become Olympic sports
6 Louise's paragliding ambitions

Louise's Olympic dream

Louise Crandal has been named European Champion twice and has won the Women's World Cup on two successive
5 occasions. Louise's sport is one of a small number of sports where men and women sometimes compete together. In 1998, she was awarded her
10 first international championship gold medal in Argentina, beating all the men to do so. But despite her huge success, hardly anyone has heard of her.

15 ■ The reason lies with her chosen sport: paragliding. If she were a swimmer or a gymnast, Louise would be a household name. However, she fell in love with paragliding and not athletics. She first discovered the sport in 1992 when she was working in Switzerland as a waitress. Three years later, she entered her first competition.

20 ■ Paragliding first became popular in the 1970s and it is estimated that there are already 400,000 paragliders in Europe alone. The first world championships were held in 1979 and paragliding schools can now be found around the world. Paragliders say that they do their sport simply for the love of flying, but the World Paragliding Association is busy trying to
25 get the sport accepted as an Olympic sport. This will immediately make paragliding even more popular. It will help athletes to find sponsors and it will attract more people to the air.

■ To be accepted as an Olympic event, a sport must be played in at least 75 countries on at least four continents (for women's sports 45 countries
30 on three continents). The new sports that have been introduced in recent Olympic Games reflect changing fashions around the world. Snowboarding was introduced in Nagano in 1998, and the first Olympic Taekwondo

3 Complete the sentences with words from the article.

1 Can you name two athletes who are h_____ names in your country?
2 In which sport would you like to c_____ in the Olympic Games?
3 What was the last sporting e_____ that you went to?
4 Which companies are the best-known s_____ of sport in your country?

4 Work in pairs. Ask and answer the questions in exercise 3.

competitions were held in Sydney in 2000. Air sports such as paragliding, hang-gliding and skydiving are becoming increasingly
35 popular. Official competitions for paragliding are held in more and more countries each year, and there is reason to hope that paragliding will be added to the Olympic list before long.

◼ When that happens, Louise will finally become a household name – at least in her native Denmark. But in the meantime, what
40 will she be doing when the Olympics are being shown on TV? The one thing she enjoys most, of course: flying.

GRAMMAR: passive

1 Complete the table with examples from the article.

active	passive
present simple They **hold** official competitions.	(1) Official competitions ____ _____.
present continuous They **are showing** the Olympics on TV.	(2) The Olympics _____ _____ __.
past simple They **introduced** snowboarding.	(3) Snowboarding _____ _____.
present perfect They **have named** Louise European champion.	(4) Louise _____ _____.
future simple They **will add** paragliding to the Olympic list.	(5) Paragliding _____ _____.
modal verbs People **must play** a sport.	(6) A sport _____ _____.

2 Choose the correct form to complete the sentences.

1 Where *did the first modern Olympics hold / were the first modern Olympics held* in 1896?
2 How many times *have the Olympics cancelled / have the Olympics been cancelled* because of war?
3 Approximately how many gold medals *are awarded / award* at the Olympics?
4 Which country *has won / has been won* the most gold medals since the Olympics started?
5 How many different sports *can watch / can be watched* at the Olympics?
6 When *did the Olympics see / were the Olympics seen* on TV for the first time?
7 How many people *watch / are watched* the Olympics on TV?
8 Which sport *introduced / was introduced* as an Olympic event in 1996?
9 When *did the Olympic flag use / was the Olympic flag used* for the first time?

3 Match the answers in the box to the questions in exercise 2. Check your answers on page 129. Now turn the answers into full sentences.

Athens		beach volleyball	the United States
3	28	300	1920	1960	4 billion

1 The first modern Olympics were held in Athens.

4 Work in pairs. Write three similar quiz questions about sports in your country. Use passives where possible. Then test your classmates.

Use the passive
• to talk about an action when the agent (the person or thing that does the action) is unknown or unimportant.
• to emphasize what happened rather than who did it.

If we want to name the agent, we use *by*.
  The modern Olympics were started **by** *Pierre de Frédy.*
  (We only name the agent when the information is important or unusual.)

Make the passive with the appropriate tense of the verb *to be* + past participle.
  How **are** *Olympic sports* **chosen**?
  The 2008 games **are being held** *in China.*
  Tickets **must be bought** *a long time in advance.*

❯ SEE LANGUAGE REFERENCE PAGE 114

VOCABULARY: nouns & adjectives (describing people)

1 Match the adjectives in the box to the sentences.

> agile ambitious determined enthusiastic
> intelligent powerful ruthless talented

1 He will not let anything stop him from doing what he has decided to do.
2 He's always really interested in and excited by his sport.
3 I've never known anyone who wants so much to be successful.
4 She can really move very quickly and very easily.
5 She has so much natural ability.
6 She is very, very strong.
7 She thinks clearly and quickly.
8 The only thing that is important to him is success. He doesn't mind if other people suffer in the process.

2 Make nouns from the adjectives in exercise 1. Use a dictionary to help you.

agile   agility

3 Work with a partner. Discuss these questions.

- Think of a well-known sports personality. Which of the words in exercises 1 and 2 can you use to describe this person?
- What special qualities do you think children need to become very successful at sport?

READING & LISTENING

1 Read the article below about a child sports star. Choose the best summary 1–3 of the article.

1 An Olympic gymnast wants her parents to get divorced.
2 An Olympic gymnast wants her parents to give her more money.
3 An Olympic gymnast wants to be able to control her own life.

2 Work in pairs. Discuss these questions.

- What sacrifices do you think Dominique has had to make to become an Olympic star?
- Do you think that winning an Olympic medal is worth all these sacrifices?

3 🔘 **2.27** Listen to a psychologist talking about child sports stars and answer these questions.

1 Which two sports do they talk about?
2 Does the psychologist think the child star phenomenon is a positive one? Why or why not?

4 🔘 **2.27** Listen to the interview again and put the points below in the order they are mentioned.

☐ Child sports stars can have health problems when they get older.
☐ Child sports stars do not have a normal childhood.
☐ It's important for tennis players to be successful before they are sixteen.
☐ Sometimes, it is the parents of the sports star who get the money.
☐ Sports stars are getting younger and younger.
☐ The first child sports stars appeared in the 1970s.

Olympic gymnast calls for a divorce

A teenage gymnast who won an Olympic gold medal for the USA wants a 'divorce' from her parents.

Dominique Moceanu, seventeen, wants to be legally declared an adult to stop her parents having any control over her or her money. 'I kill myself training and going to school,' said Moceanu. 'They haven't been working since 1996. Where does their income come from? Me.'

She added that the problems were more than just about money. 'I never had a childhood,' she said. 'I always had to be in the gym. I used to think, 'Don't you guys know anything besides gymnastics? Can't you be my mom and dad instead of me being your business?'

GRAMMAR: verbs with two objects

Some verbs can have two objects: an indirect object and a direct object.

	indirect object	direct object
His parents bought	him	a tennis racket.
The judges gave	Nadia	ten points.

You can also put the direct object immediately after the verb. You need a preposition (*to* or *for*) before the indirect object.

*His parents bought a tennis racket **for** him.*
*The judges gave ten points **to** Nadia.*

Note that in passive sentences both the direct and indirect objects can become the subject of the sentence.

active:
Her dad taught her the basics of the game at a very young age.
passive 1: indirect object as subject
She was taught the basics of the game at a very young age.
passive 2: direct object as subject
The basics of the game were taught to her at a very young age.

> ● SEE LANGUAGE REFERENCE PAGE 114

1 Rewrite the sentences by putting the indirect object before the direct object.

1 They gave their daughter some skis for her second birthday.

1 They gave some skis to their daughter for her second birthday.
2 Every day, they showed films about skiing to her.
3 Before bed, they read stories about the mountains to her.
4 They also bought a house in the mountains for her.
5 They found the best ski instructor in the world for her.
6 They promised all sorts of rewards to her.

2 Rearrange the words to make sentences.

1 He was given a lot of support.

1 a given he lot of support was .
2 game he of taught the the was rules .
3 father's he his medals shown was .
4 bought equipment expensive for him most the was .
5 drugs given he special was .
6 a judges lot money of offered the to was .

3 Work in pairs. Answer the questions for you. Give details about what and who.

When was the last time you …
● bought something for somebody?
● lent something to somebody?
● made something for somebody?
● were given a present?
● were shown some photographs?

I bought an MP3 player for my boyfriend.

SPEAKING

1 Work in groups. Discuss these questions.

● Why do so many countries want to host the Olympic Games?
● Has your country ever hosted the Olympic Games?
● If yes, when? Which city was the host?

2 Work in groups. Choose a city in your country which you think could host the Olympic Games. Then make a list of five reasons why it would be an ideal location.

3 Explain to the class which city you think it should be and why.

> *Useful language*
>
> *We believe … is ideally suited because of its …*
> *It would make the ideal host thanks to its …*
> *In addition, it has …*
> *What's more, it can offer …*
> *In conclusion, we are confident that …*

11B | The sporting year

READING

1 Read the guidebook extracts 1–3 and match them to photos A–C.

1 This week-long event is one of the highlights of the racing calendar. People bet serious amounts of money, but the action on the track is often secondary to the fashions on show. Remember that you cannot wear casual clothes in some parts of the course. ✳

2 The annual race between Oxford and Cambridge Universities began in 1829. It is now one of the highlights of London's year. Huge crowds wait outside pubs and on bridges along the river for the two teams to appear. ✳

3 It is nearly 30 years since there was a British finalist in the Women's Singles and even longer for the men, but this is one of Britain's most popular sporting events. Don't forget to eat the traditional strawberries and cream while you are waiting to get in. ✳

2 Read the emails a–c and match them to the events 1–3 in exercise 1.

a | the tickets

We got them at last – the tickets I mean! And you'll never believe it, but we've got tickets for the Centre Court, so we should see the men's semi-finals. They cost a small fortune, but it's worth it! We thought we were going to have to wait outside all night to get them, but in the end Jen found this Internet agency that specialises in getting tickets for sporting events. And they had the tickets delivered to us by special courier this morning!

b | birthday!

I'm so excited!
Have you heard about Beth's birthday plans? She wants to go to a day at the races! I've never been before, but I think it's a great idea. I love the whole idea of dressing up and drinking champagne in the Royal Enclosure and all that! So we've all got to get our outfits ready for the big day. We're all having hats made especially for us. Beth's got a friend from Art College who makes hats and she's going to do them for us. Liz has said she's going to have her hair dyed black for the occasion! I don't know why – she's only got about three grey hairs. Do you fancy joining in? It'll be a laugh. Let me know if you're interested and I'll get hold of a ticket for you too.

c | meet up

Hi there! Thanks for the message. I tried getting back to you but your mobile was out of order. Why don't you have it checked out? That's the second time it's happened in the last week. But to answer your question, yes, we had a great time. I can't believe I've lived here so long and never been to see it before! You were right, it was totally impossible to get to the finish line. But we did get a place in that pub you recommended. What a great spot! But there were so many people! Massive crowds. I had no idea it was so popular. It's a shame you couldn't come. Maybe we can go together next year?

3 Read the sentences a–g and decide which event 1–3 they are describing.

a For some people, it is more of a social occasion than a sporting event.
b It is very difficult to get tickets.
c It is very rare for the British to win.
d It only happens on one day every year.
e It's not a good idea to wear jeans and trainers.
f It's very difficult to see the end of the event.
g You don't have to pay to watch.

4 Which event in exercise 1 would you most like to attend? What are the most important sports events in your country? Have you ever been to any of them?

GRAMMAR: causative

Use *have* something *done* to talk about an action that you ask someone else to do for you.
> **We're having hats made.**
> (= We asked or paid someone to make hats for us.)

Note that it is not necessary to say who does the action, as it is usually understood. If you want to say who does the action, use *by* + the person.
> *They had the tickets delivered **by special courier.***

form	object	past participle
has/have is/are having had is/are going to have	hats, them, etc.	made, delivered, etc.

⊙ SEE LANGUAGE REFERENCE PAGE 114

1 Find and correct the mistake in five of these sentences.

1 We had pizzas send to our room.
2 He's having repaired his bike.
3 He has his shorts ironing for him.
4 She's going to have her hair cut very short.
5 They were their house painted last week.
6 She's having her hair dyed.
7 You should have your eyes testing.
8 Why don't you have your shopping delivered?

2 Rewrite the sentences using the words given and the causative.

1 The newsagent delivers the sports press to his house every morning.
He has the _____ every morning.
2 An assistant shaves his head before every match.
He has his _____ before every match.
3 His sponsors make special boots for him.
He has his _____ by his sponsors.
4 A top fashion designer designs his clothes.
He has his _____.
5 His accountant looks after his money.
He has _____.

3 Work in pairs. All the sentences in exercise 2 are about one of the people in the box. Who?

a singer   an actor   a football player
a tennis coach   a teacher   a foreign student

4 Choose another person from the box in exercise 3. Write three sentences about him/her using *the causative*. Ask the class to guess who you are talking about.

She has the board cleaned by a student.

SPEAKING & VOCABULARY: services

1 Complete these questions using the past participles of the verbs in the box.

bring   test   cook   cut   deliver
develop   service   serve   iron

1 Where do you usually …
have your photos _____?
have your hair _____?
have your car _____?

2 How often do you …
have your eyes _____?
have your meals _____ for you?
have your clothes _____ for you?

3 Would you like to …
have champagne _____ to your bedroom?
have breakfast _____ in bed?
have flowers _____ to your home every day?

2 Work in pairs. Ask and answer the questions in exercise 1.

PRONUNCIATION: /ɪə/ & /eə/

1 ⊙ 2.28 Listen to the pronunciation of these words. Can you think of any other words that contain these sounds?

ear /ɪə/   air /eə/

2 Underline all the words in this text that contain /ɪə/. Circle all the words that contain /eə/.

If you have a moment to spare on Christmas morning, go down to the beach near Brighton town centre where you can see another British sporting tradition. Every year, a group of about 50 people go for a swim in the sea. With a water temperature that is rarely more than seven degrees and an air temperature that is close to zero, most people keep their swim very short. More experienced swimmers stay in the water for nearly twenty minutes. The idea began in 1860 and there are similar events in other parts of the country.

3 ⊙ 2.29 Listen to check your answers in exercise 2.

11c | Sport relief

SPEAKING

1 Work in small groups. Look at the ideas for ways to raise money for charity and answer the questions.

1 A tennis match between the Wimbledon champion and the president of your country. How much would you pay for a ticket to watch the match?
2 A friend of yours is going to run a marathon and wants people to sponsor her/him. How much money would you give him/her?
3 A lottery. The prize is an evening out with the sports personality of your choice. How much would you spend on tickets in this lottery?

2 Work in groups of three students, A–C. You have three minutes to read some information about a charity.

Then close your books and tell the other people in your group as much as you can remember about your charity.

A: Turn to page 129.
B: Turn to page 131.
C: Turn to page 132.

3 Now imagine that your group works for the national lottery. You have £100,000 that you can give to the sports charities in exercise 2. You can either give all of the money to one charity or divide it between several charities.

Decide as a group what you will do with the money.

4 Tell the rest of the class your decision and explain your reasons.

LISTENING

1 🔘 2.30–2.34 Listen to five short conversations and say if the sentences are true (T) or false (F).

1 Dave is going to cycle from London to Brighton to raise money for charity.
2 He wants his colleagues to cycle with him.
3 Everybody in the office agrees to give some money.

2 🔘 2.30–2.34 Listen to the conversations again and complete the sentences with Camilla (C), Avril (A), Derek (D), Linda (L) or Clive (CL).

1 _____ doesn't have much money at the moment.
2 _____ doesn't think that Dave will complete the cycle ride.
3 _____ gives the least amount of money.
4 _____ gives £20.
5 _____ has received some good news.
6 _____ is extremely busy.
7 _____ is not happy about doing somebody else's work.
8 _____ wants a cup of tea.

VOCABULARY: *make* & *do*

1 Find these words and phrases in tapescripts 2.30–2.34 on pages 152–153. Then mark them *make* (M) or *do* (D).

a cup of tea *M*	some work *D*	a donation
the shopping	the accounts	a mess
a mistake	someone a favour	sport

112

2 Complete the questions with the correct verb form of *make* or *do*.

1 Who _____ the most mess in your home?
2 Have you ever _____ a donation to charity?
3 How often do you _____ sport?
4 Who usually _____ the accounts in your home?
5 Who was the last person who ____ you a favour?
6 What is the biggest mistake you have ever _____?
7 Who usually ____ the shopping in your home?

3 Work in pairs. Ask and answer the questions in exercise 2.

FUNCTIONAL LANGUAGE: question tags (checking)

> Use a question tag after a sentence to check information that you think is true.
>   *That was a great film, **wasn't it**?*
>
> Use a negative tag after a positive main verb.
>   *It's time to go, **isn't it**?*
> Use a positive tag after a negative main verb.
>   *You can't speak Japanese, **can you**?*
>
> Make question tags with an auxiliary verb and a pronoun. The voice falls on the tag.
>
> *It's easy, **isn't it**?*
> *You're not busy, **are you**?*
> *She lives near here, **doesn't she**?*
> *We didn't have any homework, **did we**?*
>
> ❯ SEE LANGUAGE REFERENCE PAGE 115

1 Complete the phrases in column A with a question tag from column B.

A		B	
1	You aren't working,	a	aren't you?
2	You can drive,	b	are you?
3	You don't have children,	c	weren't you?
4	You didn't like it,	d	do you?
5	You play tennis,	e	haven't you?
6	You're older than me,	f	did you?
7	You've been to London,	g	don't you?
8	You were a bit tired,	h	can't you?

2 Complete the phrases with an appropriate question tag. Then check your answers in tapescripts 2.30–2.33 on page 152.

1 We can use first names, _____?
2 It's about the photocopying machine, _____?
3 You're not taking any time off work, _____?
4 You said something about that last week, _____?
5 It was just £2, _____?
6 You've taken the job, _____?
7 She hasn't given much, _____?
8 You'll sponsor me for the cycle ride, _____?

3 Work in pairs. Write six things about your partner that you think are true.

You've got two brothers. You don't like football.

4 Now check the information with your partner. Use question tags.

A: You've got two brothers, haven't you?
B: Yes, I have.

DID YOU KNOW?

1 Work in pairs. Read the information about the British royal family and discuss these questions.

The British royal family has no real political power. Much of their time is devoted to sport and charity. They hold positions in various sports organizations and they are often asked to present the medals at important events. They also take part in various sports. Horse-riding and polo are traditionally very popular with the royals. Members of the family are also very involved in work for charity. They work as unpaid patrons of many charitable organizations and help raise money.

• What else do you know about the royal family?
• Is the head of state in your country involved with any sports or charities?

GRAMMAR

Passive

We use the passive voice:

- to talk about an action when the agent (the person or thing that does the action) is unknown or unimportant.
  *The captain **was shown** the red card in the second minute of the game.*

- to emphasize what happened rather than who did it.
  *The first World Cup **was held** in Uruguay in 1930.*

If we want to name the agent, we use *by*. We name the agent when it is important or unusual, or because we want to make this information more noticeable.
  *The gold medal **was won** by Michael Johnson.*

	active	passive
present simple	They **play** tennis indoors.	Tennis **is played** indoors.
present continuous	They **are holding** the next games in Russia.	The next games **are being held** in Russia.
past simple	They **changed** the rules.	The rules **were changed**.
past continuous	Officials **were showing** them around the city.	They **were being shown** around the city.
present perfect	They**'ve done** it.	It's **been done**.
future 1 (future plans)	They**'re going to cancel** the games.	The games **are going to be cancelled**.
future 2 (*will*)	We**'ll finish** it soon.	It**'ll be finished** soon.
modal verbs	You **must write** it down.	It **must be written** down.
infinitive	I want you **to help** me.	I want **to be helped**.

Verbs with two objects

Some verbs can have two objects: an indirect object and a direct object.

	indirect object	direct object
She sent	her father	a letter.

	indirect object	direct object
She made	me	a special cake.

With these verbs, we can also put the direct object immediately after the verb. When we do this, we need to use *to* or *for* before the indirect object.
  *She sent a letter **to** her father.*
  *She made a special cake **for** me.*

Other verbs that can have two objects (and are used with *to*) include: *bring, give, offer, pay, promise, read, send, show, teach, tell, write.*

Other verbs that can have two objects (and are used with *for*) include: *buy, find, get, keep, make, write.*

When we use these verbs in the passive voice, both the direct and indirect objects can become the subject of the sentence.

active: *They gave him a lot of support.*
passive 1: ***He** was given a lot of support.*
passive 2: ***A lot of support** was given to him.*

Causative

We use the causative to talk about an action that you ask someone else to do for you.

  *She **has her hair** cut every Friday.*
  (= She pays someone to cut her hair.)

  *We **had champagne brought** to our room.*
  (= We asked room service to bring champagne to our room.)

We do not usually need to say who does the action, because this is usually understood from the context. We use *by* if we want to say who does the action.

  *He has his suits made **by** the most expensive tailor in town.*

subject	verb	object	past participle
He/She/ They, etc.	has/have is/are having had is/are going to have	the car/ the TV/ it	repaired/ mended/ fixed

FUNCTIONAL LANGUAGE
Questions tags (checking)

We can use tags after a sentence to check information that we think is true.

> Wimbledon is in London, **isn't it**?
> You went there last year, **didn't you**?

We use a negative tag after a positive main verb, and we use a positive tag after a negative main verb.

> You've already given some money, **haven't you**?
> You didn't call me this morning, **did you**?

We use an auxiliary verb in the tag. The auxiliary verb corresponds to the main verb in the opening part of the sentence. We use *do/don't/does/doesn't* if the main verb is in the present simple. We use *did/didn't* if the main verb is in the past simple.

> I can pay by credit card, **can't I**?
> She isn't waiting for us, **is she**?
> He works with you, **doesn't he**?
> They didn't know, **did they**?

The voice (intonation) falls on the tag to show that we are checking information.

WORD LIST
Sport

athletics *n U*	/æθˈletɪks/
baseball *n U*	/ˈbeɪsbɔːl/
beat *v* ***	/biːt/
boxing *n U*	/ˈbɒksɪŋ/
catch *v* ***	/kætʃ/
champion *n C* *	/ˈtʃæmpɪən/
championship *n C* *	/ˈtʃæmpɪənʃɪp/
coach *n C/v* *	/kəʊtʃ/
dive *v*	/daɪv/
field *n C* ***	/fiːld/
finalist *n C*	/ˈfaɪnəlɪst/
football *n U* **	/ˈfʊtbɔːl/
gym *n C*	/dʒɪm/
gymnast *n C*	/ˈdʒɪmnæst/
gymnastics *n U*	/dʒɪmˈnæstɪks/

hang-gliding *n U*	/ˈhæŋˌɡlaɪdɪŋ/
hit *v* ***	/hɪt/
jump *v* ***	/dʒʌmp/
kick *v* ***	/kɪk/
marathon *n C*	/ˈmærəθən/
medal *n C*	/ˈmedl/
paraglider *n C*	/ˈpærəˌɡlaɪdə/
paragliding *n U*	/ˈpærəˌɡlaɪdɪŋ/
pass *v* ***	/pɑːs/
penalty *n C* *	/ˈpenəlti/
polo *n U*	/ˈpəʊləʊ/
player *n C* ***	/ˈpleɪə/
race *n C/v* ***	/reɪs/
racket *n C*	/ˈrækɪt/
rugby *n U*	/ˈrʌɡbi/
run *v* ***	/rʌn/
semi-final *n C*	/ˌsemiˈfaɪnl/
serve *v* ***	/sɜːv/
skydiving *n U*	/ˈskaɪˌdaɪvɪŋ/
snowboarding *n U*	/ˈsnəʊˌbɔːdɪŋ/
throw *v* ***	/θrəʊ/
water polo *n U*	/ˈwɔːtə ˌpəʊləʊ/

Nouns and adjectives

agile *adj*	/ˈædʒaɪl/
agility *n U*	/əˈdʒɪləti/
ambitious *adj*	/æmˈbɪʃəs/
ambition *n C* *	/æmˈbɪʃn/
determined *adj* *	/dɪˈtɜːmɪnd/
determination *n U* *	/dɪˌtɜːmɪˈneɪʃn/
enthusiastic *adj* *	/ɪnˌθjuːzɪˈæstɪk/
enthusiasm *n U* *	/ɪnˈθjuːzɪˌæzəm/
intelligent *adj* **	/ɪnˈtelɪdʒ(ə)nt/
intelligence *n U* **	/ɪnˈtelɪdʒ(ə)ns/
power *n U* ***	/ˈpaʊə/
powerful *adj* ***	/ˈpaʊəfl/
ruthless *adj*	/ˈruːθləs/
ruthlessness *n U*	/ˈruːθləsnəs/
talent *n C*	/ˈtælənt/
talented *adj*	/ˈtæləntɪd/

Make & do

make	a cup of tea
	a donation
	a mess
	a mistake
do	some work
	the shopping
	the accounts
	someone a favour
	some sport

Other words & phrases

acceptance *n U*	/əkˈseptəns/
achievement *n C* **	/əˈtʃiːvment/
anorexia *n U*	/ˌænəˈreksɪə/
award *v/n C* **	/əˈwɔːd/
bet *v/n C* *	/bet/
calendar *n C*	/ˈkæləndə/
cancel *v*	/ˈkænsl/
casual *adj*	/ˈkæʒuəl/
charitable *adj*	/ˈtʃærɪtəbl/
check out *v*	/ˌtʃek ˈaʊt/
childhood *n C*	/ˈtʃaɪldhʊd/
contribution *n C* ***	/ˌkɒntrɪˈbjuːʃn/
courier *n C*	/ˈkʊrɪə/
cycle *n C* **	/ˈsaɪkl/
declare *v* **	/dɪˈkleə/
design *v* ***	/dɪˈzaɪn/
devote *v*	/dɪˈvəʊt/
disability *n C*	/ˌdɪsəˈbɪləti/
donation *n C*	/dəʊˈneɪʃn/
downhill *adv*	/daʊnˈhɪl/
dress up *v*	/ˌdres ˈʌp/
dye *v*	/daɪ/
estimate *v* **	/ˈestɪmeɪt/
fed up *adj*	/ˌfed ˈʌp/
fill in *v*	/ˌfɪl ˈɪn/
foundation *n C* **	/faʊnˈdeɪʃn/
gang *n C*	/ɡæŋ/
glory *n U*	/ˈɡlɔːri/
host *v*	/həʊst/
in the meantime	/ɪn ðə ˈmiːn taɪm/
increasingly *adv* **	/ɪnˈkriːsɪŋli/
iron *v*	/ˈaɪən/
majesty *n U*	/ˈmædʒəsti/
massive *adj* *	/ˈmæsɪv/
native *adj* *	/ˈneɪtɪv/
official *adj* ***	/əˈfɪʃl/
outlook *n C*	/ˈaʊtlʊk/
participate *v*	/pɑːˈtɪsɪˌpeɪt/
patron *n C*	/ˈpeɪtrən/
phenomenon *n C*	/fəˈnɒmɪnən/
psychological *adj* *	/ˌsaɪkəˈlɒdʒɪkl/
psychologist *n C*	/saɪˈkɒlədʒɪst/
relief *n U* ***	/rɪˈliːf/
royal *adj* **	/ˈrɔɪəl/
sacrifice *n C*	/ˈsækrɪˌfaɪs/
shave *v*	/ʃeɪv/
strawberry *n C*	/ˈstrɔːbəri/
successive *adj*	/səkˈsesɪv/
take part *v*	/ˌteɪk ˈpɑːt/
tiny *adj* **	/ˈtaɪni/
train *v* ***	/treɪn/
trainers *n pl*	/ˈtreɪnəz/
unpaid *adj*	

12A | Money matters

SPEAKING

1 Work in pairs. Look at the photo below and put these things in order of importance (1 = most important → 7 = least important) for the person.

- ☐ a roof over your head
- ☐ something to eat
- ☐ money in your pocket
- ☐ a steady job
- ☐ friends and family
- ☐ someone to share your life with
- ☐ hope for the future

2 Which of the things in exercise 1 are most important to you?

3 Discuss these questions.

- Are there many beggars and homeless people in your town?
- Do you ever give them any money? Why or why not?
- Who do you think should be responsible for helping them?

READING

1 Read the first part of a magazine article story about how Sheila and Akan met. How do you think the story ends? Discuss your ideas with a partner.

2 Turn to page 134 and read the second part to see if you were right.

'I never thought it would happen to me'

Every day on her way to work, Sheila Fletcher, a senior nurse from north London, passed a group of homeless men outside the Underground. She never paid any attention until, one day, she noticed a man who seemed different from the others. 'I don't know why,' said Sheila, 38, 'but I gave him £5. When I gave him the money, he looked so vulnerable, like a little boy.'

Sheila thought about him all day at work and realized that she wanted to see him again. That afternoon, he was there again and he smiled when he saw her. She didn't give him any money, but they talked for a few minutes without saying much. For the next three days, they chatted morning and afternoon and Sheila learnt more about him.

He told Sheila that his name was Akan and he came from Cyprus. He had lost his job in a shoe factory and he had lost his home at that time. He said that his friends didn't want to know him any more and he had been on the streets for eight weeks. He wanted to return to Cyprus, but he thought that he would never have the money.

On the fifth afternoon, Sheila stopped, as usual. 'It was cold and wet,' she says. 'I couldn't leave him in the street. I knew it was crazy to invite a beggar to my home, but I wasn't worried.' At home, they chatted for hours about their families, their lives and their interests. Much later, feeling tired, Sheila told Akan that he could sleep on the sofa, and, before going to her room, she kissed him goodnight.

Suddenly, Akan looked agitated. 'Wait,' he said. 'I have to tell you something. I know it will shock you, but I have to tell you.' With tears rolling down his cheeks, Akan told Sheila that he was a heroin addict. Sheila was angry with herself, thinking she had been stupid to fall in love with an addict. After staying awake all night, she knew that although she loved him, she couldn't let him stay with her.

The next day, Sheila took Akan to a travel agent's and bought him a ticket to Cyprus. She didn't know if she felt happy or sad that he was returning home.

3 Read the two parts of the magazine article again. Correct the statements about Sheila and Akan.

1 Akan was from London.
2 He had been homeless for years.
3 Sheila gave him money every time she saw him.
4 Akan still has a lot of good friends.
5 Sheila was sad when she found out that Akan was a heroin addict.
6 Sheila thought it was stupid to fall in love with a homeless beggar.
7 Akan waited for a week before phoning Sheila.
8 When she arrived in Cyprus, Akan told her he was going to give up heroin.

4 Work in pairs. Discuss these questions.

● Do you think that Sheila and Akan's relationship will last?
● What kind of problems do you think they will face in the future?

GRAMMAR: reported speech & thought

When we report someone's words or thoughts, the verb forms usually move into the past.

direct speech	reported speech
'My name **is** Akan.'	He said his name **was** Akan.
'I **lost** my job in a shoe factory.'	He said he **had lost** his job in a shoe factory.
'I **will never have** the money.'	He thought he **would never have** the money.
'I **can't** let him stay with me.'	She knew that she **couldn't** let him stay with her.

We also make changes to pronouns and time expressions.
'I lost **my** home **then**,' said Akan.
He said **he** had lost **his** home **at that time**.

say and *tell*
● Use *tell* + the person you're talking to + reported speech
Akan **told Sheila** that he was a heroin addict.
Not ~~Akan said Sheila that he was a heroin addict.~~
● Use *say* + reported speech (do not refer to the person you're talking to).
He **said** that his friends didn't want to know him.
Not ~~He said her that his friends didn't want to know him.~~

❯ SEE LANGUAGE REFERENCE PAGE 124

1 Underline the examples of reported speech and thought in the magazine article.

2 Rewrite the sentences in direct speech or thought. Use these words to help you.

I me my you your tomorrow ago today

1 'I really miss my family.'

1 He said he really missed his family.
2 She told him she was a nurse.
3 He said he had arrived in London four years before.
4 She told him she couldn't stop thinking about him and his sad story.
5 He said he didn't understand why she wanted to help him.
6 She thought she would book him a flight home the next day.
7 He said his family would be delighted to welcome her to Cyprus.
8 She decided that she was going to fly to Cyprus that day.

3 Report the speech and thought below. Use *told, said, thought* or *decided*. Pay attention to the underlined phrases.

1 She said she really had to get her work done that night.

1 'I'm sorry Sam, I really have to get my work done <u>tonight</u>.'
2 'I can't go out <u>tonight</u>, Bill, I've got some work to do.'
3 'David, I've just typed and printed the report for you.'
4 'I'll never understand why John did that.'
5 'I'm going to tell him what happened first thing <u>tomorrow</u>.'
6 'Jane, I'm really sorry I didn't phone you <u>last night</u>.'

4 Work in pairs. Imagine a situation for each of the sentences in exercise 3. Who is speaking to whom?

5 What was the longest conversation you've had in the last day? Who were you talking to? What did you talk about? Report the conversation to your partner.

I had a conversation with my girlfriend yesterday evening. She said she needed a holiday. I told her I wanted to take some time off, too. We decided to book a week in France.

READING & SPEAKING

1 Look at the survey. What is it investigating?

1 people's spending habits
2 how much money people earn
3 people's attitudes to money

2 Answer questions 1–6 in the survey. Then work in pairs and compare your answers.

3 With your partner, complete question 7. Compare your sentence with the rest of the class and choose the best one.

The Money Survey

Complete the survey and you could win one of our fabulous prizes.

1 Is money important to you?

a) Yes, but other things are as important.
b) Yes, of course. You can't do anything without money.
c) No, not really, so long as I've got enough to survive.

2 Do you worry about money?

a) Yes, all the time.
b) Only at the end of the month.
c) No, not on the whole.

3 What do you do with your money?

a) donate it   c) enjoy it   e) invest it
b) lend it   d) save it   f) spend it

4 What is your main source of income?

a) your job   b) your family
c) the government   d) other (please specify)

5 Who or what influences the way you spend your money?

a) your friends
b) your family
c) your bank
d) information on TV or in the papers?

6 Which of these prizes would you most like to win?

a) a holiday for two
b) a Smart™ car
c) £5,000
d) £1,000 a year for the next ten years

7 In no more than fifteen words, describe your attitude to money*:

_____

_____

* **The best answers here may be used as a slogan in an advertising campaign for Western Commercial Bank.**

If you want to take part in our prize competition, fill in the information below and send it to us by 30 June.

Name:

_____

Address:

_____

_____

Age: under 18 ☐   18–25 ☐   25–35 ☐   over 35 ☐

LISTENING

1 ● 2.35 Listen to a woman from Western Commercial Bank talking about the results of the survey. Tick the most popular answers for each question on the survey in the Reading section.

2 ● 2.35 Listen again and say if the sentences are true (T) or false (F).

1 The people who answered the questions were under eighteen.
2 The survey took place in a café.
3 The woman was surprised by the answers to the second question.
4 A lot of young people give money to charity.
5 Very few young people invest their money.
6 About half of the people in the survey have a job.
7 Most of them share a flat with friends.
8 Newspapers and the TV influence most people's money decisions.

GRAMMAR: reported questions

To report a *wh-* question
- move the verb tenses into the past.
- drop the question mark.
- change the word order.
  '*What are you saving your money for?*'
  He asked me what I was saving my money for.

Note that in *yes/no* questions you also use *if* or *whether* to introduce the question.
  '*Do you have a savings account?*'
  She wanted to know **if/whether** *I had a savings account.*

Note that you do not need an auxiliary verb (*do/does/did*) to report questions in the present simple or the past simple.
  He asked me whether I saved money regularly.
  Not *He asked me whether I did save money regularly.*

● SEE LANGUAGE REFERENCE PAGE 124

1 Find five examples of reported questions in tapescript 2.35 on page 153.

2 Put the reported questions into direct speech.

1 'Have you got a job?'

1 They asked me if I had a job.
2 They wanted to know whether I lived at home.
3 They asked me what I had studied at university.
4 They wanted to know what I was going to do in the holidays.
5 They asked me who my greatest hero was.
6 They asked me if I could speak any other languages.

3 Work in pairs. Choose and discuss eight of the questions.

- Would you like to be a millionaire?
- Do you think money can buy happiness?
- What is your greatest ambition?
- Who do you admire most?
- What makes you feel happy?
- How many bank accounts do you have?
- Are you often in debt?
- Have you ever paid a bill late?
- When did you last read a financial newspaper?
- Do you prefer giving or receiving?
- Have you ever dreamed about money?
- How often do you go on holiday?
- Is it easy for you to save money?

4 Work with a different partner. Tell your new partner about the questions you asked and the answers you received in exercise 3. Use *I asked her/him …*

SPEAKING & VOCABULARY: verb collocations (money)

1 Complete the questions with a verb from the box.

get into	withdraw	write	take out
open	pay	make	buy

1 When was the last time you _____ a bill in cash?
2 How old were you when you _____ your first bank account?
3 Do you prefer to _____ cash from the bank or from a cash machine?
4 How many cheques have you _____ in the last three months?
5 Is it easy for young people to _____ a mortgage these days?
6 Have you considered _____ stocks and shares?
7 What's the quickest way to _____ a million?
8 Do you agree that it's far too easy to _____ debt these days?

2 Work in pairs. Ask and answer the questions in exercise 1.

12B | Sue!

READING

1 Work in pairs. Look at the cartoons A–E. Something is going wrong in each one. What is it?

2 Read the newspaper articles 1–5 below. Match them to the cartoons in exercise 1.

3 Read article 1 again and find words that match these definitions.

1 a person who takes another person to court
2 a financial agreement
3 asking a law court to change its decision
4 taking a person to court to get money from them because they have done something bad to you
5 money that is paid because you have done something bad to another person
6 extreme unhappiness

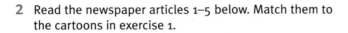

1 A grandmother from Kansas City is suing a Florida theme park because she says that one of the attractions is too frightening. The plaintiff, Mrs Darlene Joel, refused the offer of a small out of court settlement. She has asked for $15,000 in damages for the emotional distress she suffered. However, the court is expected to turn down Mrs Joel's claim in the judgment later today. Her lawyers are already planning an appeal.

2 In March 2003, Mr Merv Grazinski of Oklahoma City bought a new 10-metre Winnebago motor home. On his first trip, he set the cruise control at 70 mph and went into the back of the vehicle to make himself a cup of coffee. Within minutes, the motor home had crashed. Mr Grazinski was not hurt but he wanted his money back. In court, he insisted that he was not responsible. He pointed out that the instruction manual did not tell him to stay in the driver's seat when he was using cruise control. The manufacturers denied responsibility and asked the judge to throw out the claim.

3 At an Elton John concert in a San Diego stadium, Robert Glaser needed to go to the men's room. However, when he got to the toilet, he was surprised to find a woman using it. When he asked a stadium official to show him to another men's room, he was informed that all the toilets in the stadium were unisex. Too embarrassed to share a toilet with a woman, Glaser had to wait until the end of the concert, four hours later. He complained that he had suffered emotional distress and sued the stadium for $5.4 million.

4 CHERYL VANDEVENDER, a shop worker in West Virginia, seriously injured her back at work after opening a jar of pickles. Her doctor told her to take some time off work. Her manager warned her that she would lose her job if she did not return to work within twelve months. Nearly a year later, she returned to the shop and her manager told her to fill up a fridge. After only twenty minutes, her back was injured again. This time, Ms Vandevender decided to sue the company, Sheetz Inc.

5 Veronica Martin and her husband were eating hamburgers from a fast food chain when a hot pickle fell out of the burger and burnt Victoria's chin. Her lawyers have asked a court in Knoxville, Texas, to award $110,000 in damages for medical bills, loss of earnings and emotional distress. Her husband, Darrin, has claimed that he lost the 'services and companionship' of his wife and is also suing for $15,000. A company spokesman said that all its products were safe.

4 Now read articles 2–5 again. What do you think the judge decided in each case?

5 Match the articles 2–5 to the judges' decisions a–d.

a In order to avoid legal costs, the company reached a secret settlement with the couple, but refused to discuss details or to accept any responsibility.

b The judge, however, agreed with the plaintiff and order the company to pay $1.75 million in damages and replace the vehicle.

c But the real emotional distress came later when the judge said the claim was not serious, and the Supreme Court refused to hear an appeal.

d The court decided that the company had acted in an illegal and unfair way towards its employee and ordered it to pay over $2 million in damages.

6 Work in pairs. Discuss these questions.

- Do you think that Mrs Joel (article 1) was right to sue the theme park? Why or why not?
- For what reasons do people sue in your country?
- Can you think of any recent examples?

7 All five of the stories you read in exercise 2 were reported in newspapers in the United States. Later it was discovered that one of the stories was untrue. Which one, do you think? Explain your reasons.

GRAMMAR: *tell* & *ask* with infinitive

You can use *tell/ask* + object + *(not) to* + infinitive to report instructions, orders or requests.

direct speech	reported speech
'Can you show me the men's room?'	He **asked an official to show** him the men's room.
'Don't go back for three weeks.'	Her doctor **told her not to go back** for three weeks.

> SEE LANGUAGE REFERENCE PAGE 124

1 Put the sentences into reported speech.

1 'Can you describe the attraction?' the judge asked her.
2 The instruction manual told drivers: 'Use cruise control for long-distance trips on the freeway.'
3 'Stop wasting the court's time!' the judge told him.
4 'Don't interrupt me when I'm speaking,' she told her son.
5 'Could you give me the name of a good lawyer?' she asked her friend.
6 'Can you call an ambulance?' she asked her husband.

2 Write five sentences about things that your teacher has recently told or asked you to do.

She asked me to do some grammar exercises. He told me to listen to the news on BBC radio.

VOCABULARY: reporting verbs

1 Match the highlighted verbs in the newspaper articles to the definitions 1–6.

1 gave someone some information
2 continued saying that something was true
3 said that something was not true
4 said that something was true, although you knew that other people may not agree
5 said you were not happy about something
6 told someone that something bad may happen

2 Match the sentences to the reporting verbs in exercise 1.

1 'It's not true that the attractions in our theme park are dangerous.'
2 'Danger! This attraction is not suitable for people with a heart condition.'
3 'Please, Gran. I really, really, really want to try it.'
4 'The park will close in forty-five minutes.'
5 'This is the best theme park in the world.'
6 'We had to wait far too long for some of the attractions.'

SPEAKING

1 Work in groups. Read the information below and decide how much money the woman should receive.

A woman went to a fast-food restaurant and bought a cup of coffee. She placed the cup between her knees and as she was taking the lid off the cup of coffee to add cream and sugar, she spilled the coffee, which burned her legs. She decided to sue the company that owned the restaurant and she found a lawyer who agreed to help her.

2 Compare your ideas with other groups and explain your reasons.

Now turn to page 126.

121

12c | Gifts of gold

SPEAKING

1 Work in pairs. Discuss these questions.

1 Do you know anyone who:
- has got engaged?
- has graduated from university?
- has had their golden (50th) wedding anniversary?
- has moved to a new home?
- has retired?
- has been promoted to a top job?
- has worked for the same company for 25 years?

2 Did these people do anything to celebrate these occasions?

3 What would you do to celebrate these occasions?

2 Choose three occasions from the list in exercise 1 that you think are the most important in a person's life.

Now choose an appropriate present for each of these occasions. Explain your reasons.

PRONUNCIATION: intonation (social expressions)

1 🔘 2.36 Listen to the recording. Who sounds more friendly, the man or the woman?

2 Practise saying the words and phrases in a friendly way.

1	Thank you very much.	5	Take care.
2	Sorry.	6	Have a nice day.
3	See you soon.	7	Excuse me.
4	Well done!	8	Pardon?

FUNCTIONAL LANGUAGE: social expressions

1 Match the comments 1–8 to the best response a–h.

1 Bad news, I'm afraid. I didn't get the job.
2 Excuse me, would you mind taking a photo of us?
3 Good luck for the big day tomorrow.
4 Guess what! We've decided to get married.
5 I'm afraid I can't come out for dinner this evening.
6 Thank you so much. It was really kind of you.
7 We'll really miss you.
8 Well, I must be going. The plane leaves in half an hour.

a Excellent news! Congratulations!
b Not at all. My pleasure.
c Of course. Are you ready? Say 'cheese'.
d Oh well, never mind. Another day, maybe?
e Oh, what a shame. That's really bad luck.
f OK. Have a safe journey and all the best.
g The same to you. I'll keep my fingers crossed.
h We'll miss you, too. Keep in touch, OK?

2 🔘 2.37 Listen to the recording to check your answers.

3 Choose an appropriate response from exercise 1 for each of these situations.

1 A friend tells you that she has broken her leg, and so she can't come to your party at the weekend.
2 A friend tells you that she has just got engaged to her boyfriend and is going to live at the other end of the country after the wedding.
3 A friend tells you that she has got a very important interview for a new job tomorrow.
4 A friend thanks you for lending her your car last week.
5 An American friend tells you that her mother is ill and that she must return to New York tomorrow.

LISTENING

1 Look at the picture. Why do you think Derek and his colleagues are smiling? Give a reason for each of the people.

2 🔊 2.38–2.40 Listen to three conversations to find out if you were correct.

3 🔊 2.38–2.40 Listen to the conversations again. Match the sentences 1–6 with the phrases a–f.

1 'I'm going to be a little late,'
2 'I can't remember when I joined the company,'
3 'I feel I need a change,'
4 'Please don't tell anyone,'
5 'I'm more than happy to take early retirement,'
6 'Do you want to come with me?'

a Derek said to Dave.
b Camilla said to Derek.
c Derek said to Camilla.
d Derek said to Camilla.
e Derek asked to Avril.
f Clive said to Derek.

4 Work in pairs. Prepare and practise the conversation.

A: You work in the office, but you were ill yesterday and you do not know the news. You ask a friend to tell you what happened.

B: You work in the office. Your friend was ill yesterday and does not know what happened. Tell him/her the news.

DID YOU KNOW?

1 Work in pairs. Read the information about the US Congressional Gold Medal and discuss these questions.

> THE US CONGRESSIONAL GOLD MEDAL is an award that is given to individuals and institutions to honour special achievements. The first person to receive the medal was George Washington and other winners include Nelson Mandela and Mother Teresa of Calcutta. The medal is also awarded for achievements in the arts (Walt Disney, Frank Sinatra, John Wayne), sport (the runner, Jesse Owens and the boxer, Joe Louis) and the sciences (Thomas Edison).

- Who would you give a Congressional Gold Medal to? Give your reasons.
- Does your country give medals for special achievements?
- Who has won medals and what were their achievements?

GRAMMAR

Reported speech & thought

We use reported speech to report someone's words or thoughts.

Direct form: *'I'm very tired,' she said.*
Reported form: *She said she was very tired.*
Direct form: *'It's boring,' he thought.*
Reported form: *He thought it was boring.*

We usually change the verb forms into the past in reported speech and thought. However, this is not always necessary.

direct form	reported form
'I work ...'	*She said she worked ...*
'I'm working ...'	*She said she was working ...*
'I've worked ...'	*She said she had worked ...*
'I worked ...'	*She said she had worked ...*
'I was working ...'	*She said she had been working ...*
'I'll work ...'	*She said she would work ...*
'I'm going to work ...'	*She said she was going to work ...*
'I must work ...'	*She said she had to work ...*
'I can work ...'	*She said she could work ...*

When we are reporting, we often need to change pronouns and time expressions.

Direct form: *'I'm going to see my doctor tomorrow.'*
Reported form: *She said she was going to see her doctor the following day.*

Because the time of the reporting may be different from the time of the direct speech or thought, we may need to change the expression to make the meaning clear.

Direct form: *'I'll do it now.'*
Reported form: *She said she'd do it immediately.*

Other time expressions that may change include the following: *now (immediately), today (that day), yesterday (the day before), tomorrow (the following day), this (that), last (the ... before), next (the following ...).*

Two very common verbs for reported speech are *say* and *tell. Say* is followed immediately by the reported speech. We do not refer to the person we were talking to. *Tell* is followed by an object (the person we were speaking to), and then the reported speech.

> *He said (that) he loved her.*
> Not ~~He said her that he loved her~~.
> *He told her (that) he loved her.*
> Not ~~He told that he loved her~~.

Reported questions

When we report questions, we
- also move the verb form into the past.
- drop the question mark.
- change the word order.

Direct form: *'What's the time?'*
Reported form: *She asked what the time was.*

In the reported form, we put the subject before the verb, so we do not need to use the auxiliaries *do/does/did* in the present and past tenses.

Direct form: *'Where do you live?'*
Reported form: *She asked me where I lived.*
Not *'~~She asked me where I did live~~.'*

With *yes/no* questions, we use *if* or *whether* to introduce the question.

Direct form: *'Do you read the financial newspapers?'*
Reported form: *He asked me if/whether I read the financial newspapers.*

Tell & *ask* with infinitive

To report instructions, orders or requests, we can use *tell/ask* + object + *(not) to* + infinitive.

Direct form: *'Can you hurry up?'*
Reported form: *She told/asked me to hurry up.*

Direct form: *'Don't be late'.*
Reported form: *I told/asked them not to be late.*

FUNCTIONAL LANGUAGE
Social expressions

All the best.
Another day/time, maybe.
Bad news, I'm afraid.
Congratulations!
Excellent news!
Good luck for …
Guess what?
Have a safe journey.
I must be going.
I'll keep my fingers crossed.
Keep in touch.
My pleasure.
Never mind.
Not at all.
Say 'cheese'.
The same to you.
What a shame.

WORD LIST
Money

bank account *n C*	/ˈbæŋk əˌkaʊnt/
cash machine *n C*	/ˈkæʃ məˌʃiːn/
dependent *adj* **	/dɪˈpendənt/
earnings *n pl*	/ˈɜːnɪŋz/
financial *adj* ***	/faɪˈnænʃl/
financially *adv*	/faɪˈnænʃəli/
get into debt	/ˌget ɪntə ˈdet/
invest *v* *	/ɪnˈvest/
investment *n C* ***	/ɪnˈvestmənt/
make money	/ˌmeɪk ˈmʌni/
open an account	/ˌəʊpən ən əˈkaʊnt/
pay a bill	/ˌpeɪ ə ˈbɪl/
save *v* ***	/seɪv/
savings account *n C*	/ˈseɪvɪnz əˈkaʊnt/
share *n C*	/ʃeə/
stock *n C*	/stɒk/
take out a mortgage	/ˌteɪk aʊt ə ˈmɔːgɪdʒ/
withdraw *v* *	/wɪðˈdrɔː/
write a cheque	/ˌraɪt ə ˈtʃek/

Reporting verbs

claim ***	/kleɪm/
complain ***	/kəmˈpleɪn/
deny ***	/dɪˈnaɪ/
inform ***	/ɪnˈfɔːm/
insist **	/ɪnˈsɪst/
warn ***	/wɔːn/

Other words & phrases

agitated *adj*	/ˈædʒɪˌteɪtɪd/
appeal *n C* *	/əˈpiːl/
as a matter of fact	/æz ə ˌmætər əv ˈfækt/
astonishing *adj*	/əˈstɒnɪʃɪŋ/
attract *v* **	/əˈtrækt/
beggar *n C*	/ˈbegə/
campaign *n C* *	/kæmˈpeɪn/
cheek *n C* **	/tʃiːk/
chin *n C* **	/tʃɪn/
close down *v*	/ˌkləʊz ˈdaʊn/
companionship *n U*	/kəmˈpænjənʃɪp/
cruise *v*	/kruːz/
damages *n pl*	/ˈdæmɪdʒəz/
distress *n U*	/dɪstres/
duty *n C* ***	/ˈdjuːti/
edition *n C*	/ɪˈdɪʃn/
emphasis *n C* **	/ˈemfəsɪs/
freeway *n C*	/ˈfriːweɪ/
gentle *adj* *	/ˈdʒentl/
help out *v*	/ˌhelp ˈaʊt/
heroin *n U*	/ˈherəʊɪn/
homeless *adj*	/ˈhəʊmləs/
honour *v*	/ˈɒnə/
investigate *v* **	/ɪnˈvestɪˌgeɪt/
kick out *v*	/ˌkɪk ˈaʊt/
limited *adj* **	/ˈlɪmɪtɪd/
lounge *n C*	/laʊndʒ/
manual *n C*	/ˈmænjʊəl/
manufacturer *n C*	/ˌmænjʊˈfæktʃərə/
men's room *n C*	/ˈmenz ˌruːm/
motor home *n C*	/ˈməʊtə ˌhəʊm/
multiplex *n C/adj*	/ˈmʌltɪˌpleks/
outline *v*	/ˈaʊtlaɪn/
painter *n C*	/ˈpeɪntə/
pickle *n C*	/ˈpɪkl/
plaintiff *n C*	/ˈpleɪntɪf/
predictable *adj*	/prɪˈdɪktəbl/
reflect *v* ***	/rɪˈflekt/
report *n C* ***	/rɪˈpɔːt/
responsibility *n C* ***	/rɪˌspɒnsəˈbɪləti/
settlement *n C*	/ˈsetlmənt/
steady *adj* *	/ˈstedi/
student union *n C*	/ˌstjuːdnt ˈjuːnjən/

sue *v*	/suː/
suitable *adj* ***	/ˈsuːtəbl/
supreme *adj*	/suːˈpriːm/
survey *n C/v* **	/ˈsɜːveɪ (n); səˈveɪ (v)/
target *n C* ***	/ˈtɑːgɪt/
tear *n C* **	/teə/
theme park *n C*	/ˈθiːm ˌpɑːk/
throw out *v*	/ˌθrəʊ ˈaʊt/
unfair *adj* *	/ʌnˈfeə/
unisex *adj*	/ˈjuːnɪseks/
vehicle *n C* ***	/ˈviːɪkl/
with immediate effect	/wɪð ɪˌmiːdɪət ɪˈfekt/

Abbreviations for word list

n	noun
v	verb
adj	adjective
adv	adverb
prep	preposition
sb	somebody
sth	something
C	countable
U	uncountable
pl	plural
s	singular

*** the most common and basic words
** very common words
* fairly common words

Communication activities

1A Grammar exercise 3 page 7
Student A

1A Speaking exercise 1 page 7

I come from …   I have …   I'm feeling …
I live in …   I really like …   I always …
I work for …   I am looking for …

1B Speaking exercise 1 page 11

Grammar exercise 2

1 (a) About 5 million. (b) About 25 million.
   (c) About 50 million.
2 (a) Queen Elizabeth II was born.
   (b) The Normans invaded England.
   (c) England won the World Cup.
3 (a) Never, at least not in theory.
   (b) On the Queen's birthday.
   (c) When you are at a demonstration.
4 (a) The Campaign for the Real Europe.
   (b) The Commission for Racial Equality.
   (c) The Committee for the Revolution in England.
5 (a) 100. (b) 911. (c) 999.
6 (a) Most immigrants from India and Pakistan.
   (b) Some people in Cornwall.
   (c) Some people in London.

Grammar exercise 3

1 (a) Queen Elizabeth II. (b) Diana Spencer.
   (c) Margaret Thatcher.
2 (a) The Conservatives. (b) The Labour Party.
   (c) The Liberal Democrats.
3 (a) It is a famous nightclub.
   (b) It is the headquarters of the Secret Service.
   (c) The prime minister lives there.
4 (a) People eat chocolate eggs.
   (b) People have a day off work.
   (c) People watch firework displays.
5 (a) 1918 (b) 1938 (c) 1968
6 (a) Henry I (b) Henry V (c) Henry VIII

2A Vocabulary exercise 5 page 19
Student A

1 Complete the questions below using some of the phrasal verbs from page 19.

1 When was the last time you had to solve a difficult problem? What was it? How did you _____ it _____?
2 When was the last time you _____ someone _____ at an airport? Who was it? Where were they going?
3 Have you ever _____ any money in the street? What did you do with it?

2 Discuss the questions with your partner.

12B Speaking exercise 2 page 121

This was not the first time that the company had received complaints about their hot coffee. Company documents showed that they had received at least 700 complaints in the previous ten years. In some of these cases, the company had made a settlement with the plaintiff before the case went to court. In one case (of a woman who suffered similar burns), the company paid $230,000.

How much money should the woman receive? Does this information change your opinion?

Compare your ideas with the ideas of other groups and explain your reasons.

Now turn to page 129.

3C Vocabulary exercise 4 page 33
Student A

You've only just met. You haven't been to your friend's house before. Your friend is still in the kitchen preparing the food when you arrive. You really enjoy the evening. Your new friend is a great cook and a really interesting person. You'd like to get to know him/her better.

Think of four requests using the verbs in the box.

| close | give | have | leave | open | call |
| pass | put | smoke | take | use | do |

If you refuse a request, give a reason.

4B Speaking exercise 1 page 39

Student A

Ask questions to find out the missing information in the text.

Who is the second president?

There are a number of strange coincidences that link American presidents _____ and Kennedy. Both of them have seven _____ in their _____ and Lincoln had a secretary called _____ , while Kennedy's secretary was called Lincoln. Lincoln was _____ in 1860 and Kennedy one hundred years later in 1960, and the next president, in both cases, was called Johnson. Both men were _____ on a Friday, and both times, the men were with their wives. John Wilkes Booth shot Lincoln in a _____ and then ran to a warehouse; Lee Harvey Oswald shot Kennedy from a warehouse and then ran to a _____. Both killers have fifteen letters in their names.

5B Speaking exercise 1 page 51

Student A

> **The boss**
> A party is good for the staff because it is an opportunity for people to get to know each other better. For this reason, you don't mind paying as long as it isn't too expensive. You think that it is important that the staff decide what kind of party they want, but the final decision is yours.

6A Speaking exercise 2 page 59

Group A

- *interested in water sports*
- *would like a babysitter a few evenings a week*
- *the younger children love anything to do with animals*

6A Reading exercise 2 page 56

What kind of holiday person are you?

Mostly As
You are obviously hyper-organized and you like to make sure that you have everything under control months ahead of time. But have you ever thought that maybe you're a bit too organized? Sometimes it can be fun to make decisions at the last minute.

Mostly Bs
You know that planning ahead makes sense, and you like to make sure that the big decisions have been taken in plenty of time. But you still leave some space for flexibility and you are quite happy to change your plans if something better comes along.

Mostly Cs
You love to leave everything till the last minute. You think that way you can make the best of every opportunity that comes your way. But you may be missing out by letting fate and last minute bargains make your decisions for you. Why not try making your own decision for a change. You may like it!

6A Speaking exercise 1 page 57

Student A

> You're on holiday with a friend, but he/she isn't feeling well and has decided to stay in bed this morning. You'd like to wander around and explore the resort. You also want to do a bit of shopping. It would certainly be more fun with some other people. If your friend isn't feeling better later, you think you'll find out if it's possible to do some water-skiing.

7A Speaking exercise 2 page 69

> **Life changes**
>
> **You have recently:**
> - started work as an early morning newsreader.
> - gone back to college to train to be a nurse.
> - become a ski instructor.
> - opened a beach bar on a tropical island.
> - married a millionaire.
> - signed up at circus school to train to be a clown.
> - been chosen to star in a Hollywood movie alongside a very famous actor/actress.
> - had five children (quintuplets).

7B Reading exercise 4   page 71

Student A

1 Where does Maria live? How long has she lived there?
2 What preparations has she made for her party?
3 How many husbands has she had? Can you remember their names?
4 How many grandchildren and great-grandchildren has she got?

7B Speaking exercise 1   page 71

Group A

1 How has your town changed in your lifetime? Is it a lot bigger?
2 Have a lot of immigrants moved into your town? If yes, from where?
3 Have a lot of new houses been built? If yes, where and what kind of houses?
4 What other new buildings are there?
5 Have the shops and shopping areas changed?
6 Can you think of any other changes?

7C Roleplay exercise 5   page 73

Student A

You have won a holiday for two in Venice. You don't know whether to take your mother or your boyfriend/girlfriend with you. Tell your friend the following facts one by one:

- You have won a holiday for two in Venice.
- You're thinking about taking your mother with you to celebrate her 60th birthday.
- She's been having a hard time recently and she needs a break.
- You know your girlfriend/boyfriend will be jealous.
- It's your second anniversary at the same time, so it would also be nice to use the holiday to celebrate that.

10B Speaking exercise 2   page 101

Group A

The man was staying in a motel with his wife, who was deaf. He went outside to get something from his car, but then forgot which room was his. He hooted loudly on his horn. The other guests opened their doors or looked out of their windows to find out what was happening. However, his wife was deaf so she didn't hear him. She didn't look out of the window or open the door, so he knew which room was his. He was then able to return to his room.

8A Speaking exercise 2   page 79

Student A

New road endangers wildlife says report
A report published today says that the new Arne Valley road will endanger local wildlife. According to the report, the new bridge over the River Arne will destroy an area of outstanding natural beauty. The Arne Valley is home to the Arne orchid and three species of very rare butterflies. The report says that these vulnerable species may disappear completely as a result of the building of the new road. The spokeswoman for the Ministry of Transport was unavailable for comment.

6A Speaking exercise 2   page 59

Group B

- *want somewhere warm and sunny*
- *don't want to be based in a town*
- *love camping*

8A Speaking exercise 1   page 77

Group A

1 A factory is going to close in the north of your country and 800 people are going to lose their jobs.
2 A man has killed a policeman. He says he got the idea after watching a recent violent Hollywood thriller.
3 The fifteen-year-old daughter of an important politician in the government is going to have a baby with her seventeen-year-old boyfriend.
4 The most famous footballer in your country has announced that he is going to retire next year.
5 The police have arrested a well-known pop star after finding drugs and a gun at his house.

11C Speaking exercise 2 page 112

Student A

The **British Wheelchair Sports Foundation** can play an important part in the lives of people with disabilities. For some people, it can help them to build confidence and a positive outlook on life. For others, it can help them to stay healthy and to explore new talents. For everyone, sport can provide a sense of achievement. The British Wheelchair Sports Foundation organizes sports camps and sports events for both adults and children of all ability levels.

1B Speaking exercise 2 page 11

Student B

1 Margaret Thatcher was the first woman prime minister. Diana Spencer was the Princess of Wales, who died in a car crash in Paris in 1997.
2 The three main political parties in England are the Conservatives (blue), the Labour Party (red) and the Liberal Democrats (orange).
3 The photo shows No. 10 Downing Street, the official home of the prime minister.
4 Every year, on 5 November, people celebrate Guy Fawkes' Night with large fires and fireworks. It is not a national holiday. Chocolate eggs are a tradition at Easter.
5 Women who were aged 30 or over were first allowed to vote in 1918. Ten years later, in 1928, women had the same rights as men and could vote when they were 21. Eighteen became the voting age for men and women in 1969.
6 King Henry VIII, who was king from 1509–1547, married six times.

6A Speaking exercise 1 page 57

Student B

You're staying in the hotel on business. You have a conference tomorrow but today is free. You know the resort well. When you have free time, you often hire a speedboat, but it isn't much fun on your own. You also like windsurfing. But, first of all, you need to go to the shops to buy a new battery for your laptop computer.

11A Grammar exercise 3 page 107

1 Athens   2 3   3 300   4 The United States   5 28
6 1960   7 4 billion   8 beach volleyball   9 1920

2A Vocabulary exercise 5 page 19

Student B

1 Complete the questions below using some of the phrasal verbs from page 19.

1 What's the best way to help someone _____ a disappointment?
2 Do you ever _____ hitch hikers _____ in your car? Why or why not?
3 When was the last time someone _____ you _____ outside your house? Why were you in their car?

2 Discuss the questions with your partner.

8C Speaking exercise 2 page 82

Student A

Clyde: This is a stickup. You're gonna give me all your money, and you'll be OK.
Clerk: _____
Clyde: You heard me. The money. I don't wanna have to use this.
Clerk: _____
Clyde: I am in a bank, right?
Clerk: _____

12B Speaking exercise 2 page 121

The restaurant's coffee was served at 82.2℃, which is more than 10% hotter than some other restaurants. According to one of the company's executives, the company knew that the coffee sometimes caused serious burns. However, the company had decided not to warn customers about the danger and did not plan to change the way it served coffee.

A few days before the case began in court, the judge asked the company and the woman's lawyer to come to a meeting. At the meeting, the judge said that he thought the restaurant should pay $225,000. However, the company continued to deny responsibility, arguing that the woman should not have put the coffee between her legs and claimed that her injuries were more serious because she was old.

How much money should the woman receive? Does this information change your opinion?

Compare your ideas with the ideas of other groups and explain your reasons.

Now turn to page 131.

5B   Speaking exercise 1   page 51
Student C

> **The gossip**
>
> You think a party is a great idea. A disco would be nice and you have lots of friends who would like to come. You know some very good clubs in the centre of town and you think that everyone would like them. These clubs are often closed on Monday and Tuesday nights, so the company could rent one. It could be a fantastic night out.

1B   Speaking exercise 2   page 11
Student A

> 1 The population of Scotland is approximately 5 million. The total population of the United Kingdom is about 60 million.
> 2 In 1066, the Normans successfully invaded England. Their leader, William the Conqueror became king. It was the last successful invasion of England.
> 3 According to the law, the police cannot arrest anybody without a good reason.
> 4 The CRE is the Commission for Racial Equality, an organization that fights racism.
> 5 In the UK, you telephone 999 for police, fire or ambulance. You dial 100 for the operator. 911 is the number for the emergency services in the United States.
> 6 Cornish is spoken by some people in Cornwall, in the south-west of England.

7C   Roleplay exercise 6   page 73
Student A

You know the following things about your friend:

> • Your friend is a really good student.
> • Your friend is doing well on his/her course.
> • He/She always gets good marks.
> • Your friend works too hard, he/she needs to get out more.
> • He/She is pretty serious about his/her new boyfriend/girlfriend.

Listen to his/her dilemma and try to help.

10A   Speaking exercise 1   page 97
Group A

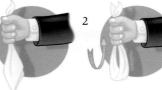 

1   2   3

The self-tying handkerchief

• To do this trick you need a handkerchief with a knot tied in one corner. Put the handkerchief in your right pocket.
• Tell your partner that you're going to tie a knot in a handkerchief using only one hand. Pull the handkerchief out of your pocket with your right hand, keeping the knot hidden in your hand (see picture 1).
• Pick up the opposite corner of the handkerchief with your left hand, and put it into your right hand (see picture 2).
• Pretend the trick is difficult. (You succeed on the third attempt!) Drop the end of the handkerchief without the knot out of your right hand with a snap. Pick up the other end with your left hand as before and repeat, again letting go of the end without the knot.
• On the third try, let go of the knotted end instead of the expected corner (see picture 3) and there you are: a one-handed knot!

4B   Speaking exercise 1   page 39
Student B

Ask questions to find out the missing information in the text.

Who is the second president?

There are a number of strange coincidences that link American presidents Lincoln and _____. Both of them have seven letters in their names and Lincoln had a secretary called Kennedy, while Kennedy's _____ was called Lincoln. Lincoln was elected in 1860 and Kennedy one hundred years later in 1960, and the next president, in both cases, was called _____. Both men were assassinated on a Friday, and both times, the men were with their _____. John Wilkes Booth shot Lincoln in a theatre and then ran to a _____; Lee Harvey Oswald shot Kennedy from a _____ and then ran to a theatre. Both killers have fifteen _____ in their _____.

8A   Speaking exercise 1   page 77
Group B

> 1 A photographer from your newspaper has taken nude photographs of a famous TV presenter in your country.
> 2 A top Hollywood film star has separated from his girlfriend after three years together.
> 3 Medical scientists have developed a powerful new drug for heart disease.
> 4 The government has announced that they are going to increase the tax on cigarettes by 6%.
> 5 Thieves have stolen a valuable painting from the home of a famous businessman in your country.

8A Speaking exercise 2 page 79
Student B

Local residents promise to fight new road
Arne Valley police have arrested a man who threw an egg at the Minister for Transport outside the Houses of Parliament today. The man was protesting against plans to build a new road in the Arne Valley. The man, from the village of Arneford, is from one of 24 families in the area who will lose their homes when the road is built. In a statement to the press, the man's solicitor said that this was only the beginning of the protests. 'The road will completely destroy the historic village of Arneford,' he said. 'All the local residents are against the project and have promised to fight the new road.'

3c Vocabulary exercise 4 page 33
Student B

You've only just met. Your friend hasn't been to your house before. Your friend arrives early. You're still in the kitchen preparing the food when he/she arrives. You don't really enjoy the evening. Your new friend is a bit boring. You haven't really got a lot in common.

Think of four requests using the verbs in the box.

close	give	have	leave	open	call
pass	put	smoke	take	use	do

If you refuse a request, give a reason.

7B Speaking exercise 1 page 71
Group B

1 How have people's lifestyles changed in your country during your lifetime?
2 Do people still do the same kind of jobs?
3 Have any new industries developed? Have any old industries disappeared?
4 Has family life changed?
5 Do people still do the same kinds of things in their free time? Do they spend their money on the same things? Are their hopes and dreams the same?
6 Can you think of any other changes?

9A Speaking exercise 1 page 89
Group A

You represent a youth association. You believe that it is very important to offer teenagers a variety of free time activities. You want to see the shopping area offering much more than just shops and cinemas. It's very important that the centre has good public transport because most teenagers do not have their own car.

12B Speaking exercise 2 page 121

The woman was 79 years old and the burns were extremely serious. She needed to spend seven days in hospital. Apparently, she only decided to sue the company when they refused to pay $800 for her medical bills.

How much money should the woman receive? Does this information change your opinion?

Compare your ideas with the ideas of other groups and explain your reasons.

Now turn to page 133.

7B Reading exercise 4 page 71
Student B

1 Where is Maria going to celebrate her birthday?
2 How old was she when she got married the first time?
3 How long was she married to her second husband?
4 How many children did she have? Are any of them still alive?

11c Speaking exercise 2 page 112
Student B

FARE is based in one of the poorest parts of Glasgow, where more than 50% of children are living in poverty. The area is controlled by gangs that come together to fight, often in a local sports ground, that is known as the 'killing fields'. Children grow up with fear and violence as part of their lives. FARE organizes a programme of sports (including football, basketball and tennis) that brings these children together, helps them to build new relationships and to break the cycle of violence in this part of the city.

10B Speaking exercise 1 page 101

Group B

The woman worked in a circus and she was the assistant in a knife-throwing trick. The new shoes that she bought had higher heels than her usual pair. When she went to work, she forgot to tell her colleague about her new shoes. She was now four centimetres taller. Unfortunately, the first knife killed her.

8C Speaking exercise 2 page 82

Student B

> Clyde: _____
> Clerk: I'm sorry, sir?
> Clyde: _____
> Clerk: But we don't have nuttin. We're right out.
> Clyde: _____?
> Clerk: No, sirree. We're closed. We've been closed down for weeks.

5B Speaking exercise 1 page 51

Student D

> The lazy worker
> You don't really want to go out with people from work on a Friday night or at the weekend – you've got better things to do. But if the company is going to pay for an expensive meal in a restaurant or a good party, you don't mind. In fact, you don't mind organizing everything – booking a place and making other arrangements. It would be a nice change from your usual boring job.

11C Speaking exercise 2 page 112

Student C

> **SportsAid** is a national organization that provides financial help to sportsmen and women between twelve and eighteen years old. These young sports people have already shown a special talent in their sport, but they come from families who do not have enough money to support their children's sporting ambitions. The money will help to pay for training, equipment and for travel to competitions. Without this help, these young people will turn their backs on sport. With help from SportsAid, they will have the chance to become international stars in their chosen sport.

7C Roleplay exercise 2 page 73

Student B

> You have been invited to meet your new partner's parents. This means going away for the weekend. You really want to go but you have an important exam next week and you should really spend the weekend studying for it. Tell your friend the following facts one by one:
>
> - You've been invited to your partner's parents' house for the weekend next weekend.
> - You've got a really important exam next week.
> - You haven't done enough studying for the exam – you know you won't pass if you don't study more.
> - It's really important to your partner that you go.
> - You really don't want to offend him/her or his/her parents.
> - It's a four-hour train journey to get there.

6A Speaking exercise 2 page 59

Group C

> – good beaches very important
> – like to visit markets and buy souvenirs
> – want lots of night life

9A Speaking exercise 1 page 89

Group B

You represent an old age pensioners' association. You want to see cheap and easy public transport to the shopping area. This would probably be easier if the shopping centre was near the centre of town. You also want to make sure the centre is easily accessible for wheelchair users. You would also like to see cultural activities that will appeal to older people.

12B Speaking exercise 2 page 121

After seven days of listening to the evidence, the jury decided that the restaurant was responsible. The jury decided that the company should pay $160,000 in compensatory damages and an additional $2.7 million in punitive damages. The trial judge later reduced the amount of punitive damages to $480,000.

Do you think the court's decision was fair?

10A Speaking exercise 1 page 97
Group B

The vanishing coin

- Show your partner a coin in your left hand, then rub it in your right elbow (see picture 1). Tell your partner that you are going to make the coin disappear!
- After a few moments drop the coin onto the table and say it usually works better with the right hand. Pick the coin up and pretend to put it into your right hand, but in fact leave it in your left hand.
- Then pretend to rub the coin into your left elbow with your right hand. At the same time, lift your left hand, which is still holding the coin, up behind your ear (see picture 2).
- Drop the coin into the back of your shirt collar, and then show that the coin has vanished, and both hands are absolutely empty!

9B Reading exercises 2 & 3 page 90

Match the descriptions with three of the stores on the Eezeemall homepage.

1 Posters, reviews, memorabilia and of course … hundreds upon hundreds of films. Take our word for it, there are enough DVDs, videos and screenplays to keep the keenest film buff happy for a long, long time! This month's special star is Clint Eastwood. Check out the special prices on all his films, take a look at some of the scenes that were not included in the movies (outcuts), and there's even a chance for a few lucky customers to win a trip to Almeria, the Spanish home of spaghetti Westerns.

2 The first stop for all children, no matter how old. Whether you're looking for that special first toy for a recent arrival or shopping around for an unusual gift for the person who's got everything – you've come to the right place. Not many other shops can offer the incredible range we offer. From bikes and trikes to a ride in a Formula One car. From educational toys to once in a lifetime experiences (check out this month's special offer – a champagne ride in a hot-air balloon), we've got exactly what you're looking for. There's almost too much choice!

3 Flowers, plants, herbs, spices and so much more! Take our advice. Don't waste precious time travelling out to your local garden centre, where there are too many people and too little choice to find exactly what you're looking for. Make all your gardening decisions in the comfort of your own home! And with the expert help of the country's best-known landscape gardeners. Email your queries to the experts, or take a look at a couple of their favourite designs.

7C Roleplay exercise 5 page 73
Student B

You know the following things about your friend:

- His/Her mother loves Italy.
- Your friend spends a lot of time with his/her mother and they are very close.
- Your friend's partner is very much in love with him/her but is sometimes quite jealous.
- Your friend and his/her partner don't spend much time together because they work different hours.

Listen to his/her dilemma and try to help.

12A Reading exercise 2 page 116

A week later, Sheila went with Akan to the airport. 'We kissed goodbye and I thought I would never see him again,' says Sheila. 'But I knew that he was sad to be leaving me, too. He promised that he would phone.'

5 Sheila went back to her work at the hospital and didn't hear from Akan for over two months. Then, one day, the phone rang. Akan explained that he missed Sheila and that he thought about her all the time. He said that he had given up heroin and that he had found a
10 job. He begged her to come and visit him.

Sheila asked her friends for advice and they all thought it was astonishing that she was even thinking of seeing him again. But Sheila couldn't imagine life without him and a few months later, she flew to Cyprus. Akan
15 met her at the airport, and she couldn't believe how much his appearance had changed. He looked tanned and healthy, and had put on weight, so different from the homeless man she had seen outside the Underground station. He told her that she had
20 inspired him to change his life, that he was a new man.

Sheila and Akan were married four weeks later. 'I never thought it would happen to me,' she says. 'But it goes to show that you find true love where you least expect it.'

9A Speaking exercise 1 page 89
Group C

You represent a local parents' association. You think that it is very important that the shopping area offers plenty of facilities for families with young children, including parks, playgrounds and indoor play areas. You would prefer to see the area outside the town, away from traffic and noise.

8A Speaking exercise 2 page 79
Student C

New road will cut journey times by 12 minutes
The government has announced plans for a new road in the west of the country. The new 14 mile road, which will cross the Arne Valley, will provide a new connection between the A40 and the M5. A spokeswoman for the Department of Transport said that the journey time between the Arne Valley and Birmingham will be reduced by about 12 minutes. The project will cost £67 million and work will start within two years. At a press conference earlier today, the spokeswoman said that the new road will reduce heavy traffic on the A40. 'This is good news for local businesses and local residents. The area has needed decent road connections for a long time,' she said.

6A Speaking exercise 1 page 57
Student C

You're on holiday on your own because you think it's a good way to make new friends. You want to go into town to find out about hiring a car. You have read that there is a very interesting old town about 40 kilometres from your resort, and you would like to visit it. With a car you could also visit the most beautiful beaches which are further along the coast.

1A Grammar exercise 3 page 7
Student B

9A Pronunciation exercise 4 page 86

5B Speaking exercise 1 page 51
Student B

The workaholic
You're not very keen on parties and you hate dancing, but a meal in a restaurant would be a good opportunity to talk to people from other departments. You certainly don't want a late night, because you like to get up early in the morning.

Tapescripts

My choice for *Pick of the Week* this week is the BBC2 documentary *How Michael Portillo Became a Single Mum*. I think this is probably the best programme I've seen all year. I don't usually choose to watch reality TV, but the title intrigued me and I wanted to find out more. And I wasn't disappointed; it was fascinating to see the private face of such a public man.

For those of you who didn't see it, Michael Portillo volunteered to step into single mum, Jenny Miner's shoes for a week, to look after her house and her kids and to take over at her two part-time jobs.

As a 'reasonably rich' MP, Michael Portillo is obviously used to a very different lifestyle in London. He never cooks or cleans or does the shopping – he pays someone else to do all that for him. And he doesn't have any children.

So life as a single mum is going to be a real eye-opener. Jenny Miner has four children, the oldest is eleven and the youngest is eight. Every day, Monday to Friday, she drives the kids to school and then she goes to work at her two part-time jobs, one as a classroom assistant and one as a supermarket cashier – and she doesn't pay anyone to do her housework for her!

1A Listening exercise 4 🔘 1.2

I always thought of Michael Portillo, the politician, as an arrogant and self-important man, but in this programme, Portillo comes across as being very different. Very modest, very friendly, very approachable. All in all, very likeable. He had a lot to learn in his week as a single mum, not least how to live on a tight budget of £80 to pay for all the family's day-to-day living expenses. He had problems, and he wasn't afraid to admit it, but he never lost his sense of humour – and he even seemed to be enjoying himself at times.

At one point, Tasha, the eldest of the children, is having a karaoke party for her friends and Portillo is obviously having a really good time. Tasha's friends are impressed by him and think he looks like George Clooney! It is one of the high points of his week.

In another clip, Portillo is working behind the cash till at the supermarket. He doesn't pretend to enjoy the work, but he says that the atmosphere and his colleagues are much nicer than in the Houses of Parliament.

His second job, in the primary school, is more difficult and, at the beginning, it looks as if he's bitten off more than he can chew. Will he be able to cope? We see him in the classroom where he is working as a classroom assistant. At one point, he's having problems with some eight-year-olds. He's trying, and failing, to explain a mathematics problem to them. But he listens carefully and patiently to the teacher and by the middle of the week he's doing much better.

His other great challenge – in fact, by far his biggest challenge – is little Ellie, the youngest child. She's eight years old and very stubborn, and she's going through a very rebellious phase. She flatly refuses to listen to him and at times you can see that all his people skills and lessons in political diplomacy will get him nowhere. In one typical situation, Portillo is trying to persuade Ellie that it's bedtime, but she's being particularly difficult. Although you can see she's really tired and really wants to go to sleep, she's refusing to go.

I think in the end Ellie is my favourite character in the programme – but Portillo came a close second. I don't know if Portillo is thinking about changing his politics, but I've certainly changed my opinion of him. Though I'm still not thinking of voting for him at the next election! So, if you missed it, and you too want to see the human side of Michael Portillo, watch out for a repeat, because this programme is sure to become a classic in the BBC archive.

1C Listening exercises 1 & 2 🔘 1.3–1.5

1   D = Dave   Dk = Derek   P = Peter   L = Linda

Dk: Thanks for coming, I won't keep you long. As you all know, Head Office has appointed a new director of this branch, and she will be starting with us today.

D: Ah, so that's why you're wearing that nice new suit! You look as if you're going to a wedding.

Dk: Yes, thank you, Dave. Can we just stick to business, please? Her name is Camilla Ridley and she'll be in my office. I've moved to the small blue office near the photocopying machine if you need me for anything. Avril's moving everything in there now. I'm sure that you will all want to welcome Mrs Ridley and make her feel at home here. We want to make a good impression, don't we?

P: What's she like – this new director woman?

Dk: I've only met her once or twice, and um, we didn't talk much. I know that she's very highly qualified. She's probably quite friendly when you get to know her. We'll find out soon enough. Oh, and Linda, she said that she wanted to start this morning by looking at the Accounts Department, so perhaps you could look after her.

L: Yes, all right, if I must.

Dk: And after that, if she's got time, she wants you, Dave, to explain the IT systems. She seems very interested in the technical side of things.

D: OK. Fine.

Dk: So, it's accounts first, then IT, personnel, sales and marketing, and then me, at the end of the day. This is going to be a long, important day for all of us, so let's do our best, eh?

2   A = Avril   Dk = Derek

A: Where do you want me to put this?

Dk: Mm? Oh, anywhere, Avril.

A: Don't say 'anywhere'. Your office will never be ready if you don't tell me where you want things.

Dk: You decide. You know best.

A: Is she here yet?

Dk: Who? Camilla?

A: Yes. Her.

Dk: No, she'll be here soon.

A: Well, she can wait.

Dk: Avril, we all have to get used to the idea that there's going to be a new boss around the office. I do. You do. We all do.

A: I still don't see why Head Office needed to send her here.

Dk: They think very highly of her at Head Office. To be honest, I was impressed myself.

A: Just because she's got an MBA, she probably thinks she's really special. I've met people like that before.

Dk: Oh, Avril. Wait until you meet her. Don't judge her until you know what she's like.

A: I'm not making any judgements. Just so long as she leaves me alone and doesn't expect me to work for her as well as for you. I haven't got time for extra work, as you very well know.

Dk: Oh, come on. Give her a chance. You'll like her. I think we'll all like her.

A: I doubt it. Anyway, what's she like, this Camilla of yours?

Dk: Well, she's, er, she's, er, she's nice. She, er, looks very calm and organized. She's very business-like, very intelligent, she's …

A: Anyone would think you had a soft spot for her.

Dk: Of course I don't. She's taking my job, but I have to respect her for her qualities.

A: If you say so.

3   P = Peter   L = Linda

P: Hi, Linda. Have you seen her yet?

L: Yes, she spent some time with me earlier this morning. We had a nice cup of tea together.

P: And?

L: She's all right. Actually, I quite liked her.

P: What does she look like?

L: That's typical of you, isn't it? Just because she's a woman, you want to know how good-looking she is.

P: That's not fair. I just want to know what she looks like, so I'll know who she is when I see her.

L: Mm, right.

P: So – what does she look like?

L: She's, er, she's wearing … she's got short dark hair, she's got a rather small pointed face. Scary black eyes, but she's got a nice smile, too. What else, er, blue jacket with shiny gold buttons, white skirt, expensive Italian shoes, red ones, and glasses – but she doesn't wear them most of the time. Come to think of it, she looks like a French flag!

P: Not my type, then?

L: No. Not your type.

P: How can you be so sure?

L: Well, for one thing, she's thinking of closing your department.

P: You're joking!

L: No, that's what she said. Look, I'm sorry. I've got a lot to do. Do you mind?

P: Er, yes, sorry.

2A Listening & reading exercises 1, 2 & 4 🔘
1.8–1.10

1: A Swedish pizza deliveryman has broken the record for the longest solo Vespa journey across Europe. Tommy Kallstrom, from Stockholm, arrived in Athens last week, after a four-month trip. Tommy visited fifteen countries on the way, including the principalities of Monaco and Liechtenstein. He kept a diary of his trip and, using his laptop computer, posted details and photos of his journey on his personal website. Tommy almost gave it all up when he had mechanical problems with his Vespa during a storm in the Swiss Alps. Fortunately, he was rescued by a farmer in a tractor who picked him up and took him to the nearest town, where he sorted the problem out. He eventually arrived in Athens on July 1st. Just in time to celebrate his 21st birthday! Tommy's website has won this year's Web Travel Site of the Year.

2: On TV later this week, you can see a documentary film of another incredible journey. Italian TV journalist Chiara Colucci and her husband, Luca, a wildlife cameraman, spent six months driving across Siberia in a Land Rover to make the film. They were looking for the rare Siberian tiger, of which only about two hundred still exist in the wild. However, the star of the film is a baby bear cub, called Tizio, that they came across near the River Amur. Tizio had been injured and the Coluccis took him with them so they could look after him. When Tizio got over his injury, he didn't want to leave the Coluccis, and the three became close friends. It's an extraordinarily beautiful film and you will not be able to stop crying when the Coluccis finally say goodbye to Tizio at the end of their journey in Vladivostok.

3

A: Hey, have you seen this?

B: What?

A: Here, look: 'University students hitchhike for charity'.

B: It's Alex and Isabelle! So what's the story?

A: Well, apparently they were part of a group of students who have hitchhiked from Land's End to John O'Groats to raise money for charity.

B: That's a long way to hitch … and what charity was it?

A: Let's see … yeah, a local children's hospital … yeah, and it seems although ten of them set out together, only four of them actually arrived.

B: What do you mean, only four of them arrived? Did the others get lost or something?

A: No, the thing was they had a time limit; they had to get to John O'Groats in less than two days. See there's a photo here of their friends and families seeing them off from Land's End last Friday, and it says here that they had to get to John O'Groats by midday on Sunday.

M: And they made it there in time?

F: Yeah, not only that, they broke the record too … it only took them ten hours and twenty minutes.

M: Ten hours? What did they do? Hire a helicopter or something?

A: Well, it says here that they were really lucky with their first lift. A van picked them up after only five minutes and took them almost all the way. It dropped them off just twenty minutes' walk from the finishing line.

B: And what happened to the others, then?

A: Looks like they gave up and turned for home.

2c Listening exercises 1 & 2 🌐 1.13–1.15

1   L = Linda   D = Driver   A = Avril   M = Man

L: Hi. Does this bus go to the town centre?

D: Sorry, what was that?

L: Are you going into the centre?

D: Yeah, we go there.

L: Er, a single to the town centre, please.

D: That'll be one twenty, please, love.

L: Er, yeah. Er, sorry, have you got change for a ten-pound note?

D: No, sorry love, exact change only.

L: OK, just a second … er … I don't think I've got it …

A: Linda! Don't worry, I've got it!

L: Oh, Avril I hadn't seen you there – thank you!

A: One single and one return, please.

D: Here you are.

A: There you go, Linda.

L: Thanks – you're a life saver. Erm, we're going to the pizzeria on Bridge Street. Could you tell us when we get to the bridge, please?

D: Yup. I'll let you know.

L: Thanks.

A: There's no need, I know where it is. I get this bus into town every day.

L: Excuse me, is this seat free? Excuse me, is this seat free?

M: Sorry, what? Oh, yes, yes, it is.

L: Avril, you take it.

A: Oh no, I couldn't, you take it.

L: No, no, no, you take it.

M: Don't worry, I'm getting off at the next stop, there'll be seats for the two of you.

A: So, how come you're on the bus then, Linda, problems with your car?

L: Mm, 'fraid so. Every week there's something else goes wrong with it. I'm surprised at you agreeing to come out. You don't normally go to work things, do you?

A: No, I didn't really want to come out. But Derek asked me if I was coming. I think he wanted a bit of moral support. I mean, what kind of nonsense is this? We could all be out of a job by the end of the month – and she suggests we spend an evening together for team building. All that nonsense they read on their management training courses. I don't know why the company brought that woman in. Derek was perfectly competent, but he'll be the first one to go. Poor Derek … I don't know why he's so nice to her … that's his problem, really, too nice by far …

L: Oh come on, give Camilla a chance … I mean, she's only doing her job …

A: Oh, look, here we are, this is our stop.

D: Next stop: Bridge Street. Next stop: Bridge Street.

2   Dk = Derek   D = Dave

Dk: How are you getting home? Have you got your car?

D: Er, no, I didn't bring it … I'm going to get a cab. Er, you live my way. Do you want to share one?

Dk: Well, er, OK, thanks, why not … I was going to get the bus, but, er, why not, if we're sharing.

D: Hello? Er, yes, I'd like a cab for the Pizzeria Roma on Bridge Street, please. Yes, on Bridge Street. Er, as soon as possible, please. Five minutes? Perfect. Yes, the name is Blackman. Yeah, thanks, bye. Well, it wasn't that bad, was it? The evening, I mean.

Dk: No, nice, very nice … good pizza. Good atmosphere.

D: Yeah, it was a bit mean though, don't you think … I mean, a pizza place … I thought she could have made more of an effort …

Dk: Yes, well, she is trying to make cuts, you know, save money …

D: Oh, standing up for Camilla, are you? I don't believe it. She's taken your job and you're standing up for her …

Dk: Well, she's not such a dragon off duty, is she? Though she hasn't got much of a sense of humour. She didn't seem to get any of your jokes.

D: No, she didn't, did she? Just as well, perhaps …

3   S = Station announcer   C = Camilla   I = Information clerk

S: Platform 14 for the 23.45 train to Brownsville. Platform 14 for the 23.45 train to Brownsville.

C: Excuse me, has the 11.40 for North Park left yet?

I: Not if you hurry, it's still at the platform, platform 10, it's running a bit late, you might catch it if you run … Oh, oh, no, that's pulling out now …

C: Rats! Could you tell me the time of the next train to North Park?

I: Er, the next one's tomorrow morning, madam. I'm afraid that's it for tonight.

C: Oh, I do not believe it! Er, can I get a taxi anywhere round here?

I: Yes, madam. There's a taxi rank at the front of the station. But you'll probably have a bit of a wait at this time of night.

C: Thanks, thanks. Hi. I've missed my train. Yeah, it was the last one, it was leaving just as I arrived. You can? Thanks! I was hoping you'd say that. OK, not too bad, I suppose, not the most exciting evening of my life, but it could have been much worse. Well, some of them are OK. They're being quite positive about the changes, but there are some who really hate me! Oh well, I'm used to that by now. Yeah, I'll tell you all about it when you come and pick me up. OK, see you in twenty minutes or so, then. Yeah, the café's still open, I'll be in there. Bye.

S: Platform 14 for the 23.45 train to Brownsville. Platform 14 for the 23.45 train to Brownsville.

3a Reading exercise 4 🌐 1.16–1.20

1: Disadvantages? I can't think of any, really. Maybe the monthly meetings that you have to go to. Some people never stop talking, and you have to sit there listening to people for hours. Er, I can't really think of anything else.

2: We're very happy here, but sometimes, yeah, I guess sometimes, it feels very small. I mean, everybody knows everything about everybody else. Sometimes it gets a bit too much.

3: We all have to help with repairs and things like that, but some folks do a lot more than others. The work isn't always divided very fairly. You know, it seems like some families don't have to do as much as other families.

4: Every now and then, someone cooks a really horrible meal. You can't say anything. Well, you can, but nobody ever does. We all sit there and eat it and smile.

5: I think that most of us agree that one or two of the children are a problem. You know, just difficult kids, but their parents never do anything about them. They're allowed to do anything. But it's no big deal.

3A Listening exercises 2 & 3 🌐 1.21–1.23

1
A: The best thing? The sense of freedom, I guess. The fact that we can decide to go where we want when we want. If we get bored, we go somewhere new. And if we don't like the neighbours, we can always move!
B: And the worst?
A: When the police or the local authorities make us move on. I mean, when we find somewhere where we want to stop, and we set up camp and make everything really nice and comfortable and then the police or the farmer or the local people don't let us stay. That happens quite often. They think we're dirty, or noisy or dangerous or something.
B: Do you have a favourite place to stop?
A: Yeah, we've got two or three places we go back to every year, where we've got friends, where the farmers are happy to let us stay on their land. We usually go at harvest time, to pick fruit or do other odd jobs …

2
A: The best thing? The views – no doubt about that. They're spectacular. And I love getting up to the sound of the sea. Not many people have the chance to live somewhere quite so beautiful. I particularly love the sea in winter, when the waves are enormous, and come crashing down on the rocks around the house. What other job lets you live somewhere so dramatic?
B: It certainly is dramatic, but doesn't it get a bit lonely out here sometimes?
A: Yes, it can get quite lonely. I usually spend three weeks here on the island and then I have three weeks off while my partner takes over. I usually go back to my home town and catch up with friends and family. I miss them a lot and you get a bit homesick at times. They don't allow us to have visitors, but the job keeps me pretty busy. And they let us keep pets. I've got three dogs, and they keep me company!

3
A: Do you live here all year round?
B: No! It's a holiday home really. We usually spend a month or so here in the summer.

A: Isn't it rather dangerous living halfway up a tree?
B: Obviously, the big drawback is the danger of people falling off. To start with, we were quite worried about it, especially when visitors came to stay … but nothing's happened yet. We don't let little kids come up on their own and we make dog owners leave their pets in the garden! And the other problem, of course, is fires … that really does worry us … we're very careful with candles and things like that so we don't allow smoking.
A: It looks pretty small, too. Why on earth did you choose this as a holiday home?
B: Well, we wanted something different, but what we really like about being here is the idea, the feeling of, you know, being part of nature. Hearing the birds, seeing all sorts of animals. Deer, for example. We often see deer – and rabbits. But it's probably the birds we like best.

3C Listening exercises 2 & 3 🌐 1.24–1.26

C = Camilla   Dk = Derek   N = Nigel

C: Hello, Derek. Come in, come in. You're early.
Dk: Oh, am I early? Sorry, sorry, I … I thought it was …
C: No, no, don't worry, Derek, absolutely no need to apologize. I was just doing some work, going over some accounts, actually. Come in, come in, it's cold out there.
Dk: Oh, nice house … er … very nice.
C: Thanks, yes. Nigel did all the decorating himself. Come and meet him. Nigel?
N: Here, in the kitchen.
C: Derek, follow me into the kitchen. Can I take your coat?
Dk: What? Oh yes, yes, thanks, and er, I brought, er, these …
C: Oh, flowers. Roses, how lovely. Thank you, Derek. It looks as if they need a bit of water. Ah, here we are. Derek, this is Nigel, my husband, Nigel. Nigel, this is Derek.
N: Pleased to meet you Derek, I've heard a lot about you.
Dk: Oh, er, pleased to meet you too. Mmm. Smells lovely … really lovely!
C: Nigel, can you put these in some water for me?
N: Yes, of course. One second. Derek, can I get you something to drink? Chablis maybe? White wine? Or I could open a bottle of red, if you like?
Dk: Er, … no, no, no, thank you. Better not. I'm driving. Do you think I could have a glass of water, please?
N: Sure, sure. What have we got? Er, still? Sparkling? Ice and slice?
Dk: Sorry?
C: H_2O, Derek. Do you want still or sparkling water?
Dk: Oh, I get you! No, no, could I have just straight tap water, please? Thanks.
N: OK, coming up.
C: Look, sorry to be a bore, but is it OK if I go and finish off those accounts? I'll only be five minutes.
Dk: No, no, no, no, fine …
N: Derek can help me out, can't you, Derek?
Dk: What? Oh, yes, yes … don't usually do much cooking … er, what can I do?

L: No, it's OK, thank you. Really. We'll do pizza another time. Promise.

C: Oh well, as you wish. Tell you what, though. If you're going to be a long time at the police station, do you want me to get a video for the kids to watch? While we're waiting for you to come back, I mean.

L: Oh, yes, that would be lovely.

C: All right, I'll do that, then. There's a video shop just by the pizza place.

L: OK, great. Thanks.

C: You sure about those pizzas?

L: No, really, thanks. We had one yesterday.

2

L: Linda here.

C: Linda? Hi, it's er, Clive here. Look, I've, er …

L: Clive?

C: I've, er, I've got a bit of a problem.

L: What is it? Are you all right?

C: Yes, I'm fine. It's just that I've, er, I've had a bit of an accident.

L: Oh no, not with the kids!

C: No, no, I was on my way to get them and, I was going a bit fast perhaps and this policewoman waved me down; she just appeared, I mean, and I had to stop, so I stopped, suddenly like, and this car went into the back of me.

L: Oh, what a relief!

C: So I can't, you know, I can't get the kids or anything. I mean, I know I promised, but I'm really sorry to let you down.

L: Oh, don't worry about that. The childminder will just have to wait a bit, won't she? But what about you? Are you all right?

C: Yeah, I'm all right, but the van's a write-off, I think. Oh, I've just thought; I hope I don't lose my job over this. What will that new boss say about it?

L: Oh, no. Don't worry about her. She's OK. Listen, can I do anything for you? I mean, do you want me to come and get you or anything?

C: No, I'll manage, thanks. Oh well, there is perhaps one thing …

L: Yes?

C: Well, I'll be here for a while sorting things out, so I'll probably be back quite late, and my mum'll be waiting, you know, for me to get her dinner and stuff, and …

L: Yes?

C: Well, she's all on her own …

L: Would you like me to ask her for dinner at my place?

C: Oh, that would be really nice.

L: Pizza?

C: She'd love that. I'll join you as soon as I'm finished here. In about an hour I expect.

L: OK. Well, good luck.

C: Yeah, cheers. See you later.

L: See you.

9A Pronunciation exercises 1 & 2 2.7

A = Ann B = Ben

A: Hi, where are you?

B: In the supermarket. I forgot the list – again! I can remember some of the stuff but not all of it.

A: Oh, so what have you got so far?

B: OK, I've got some bottles of beer …

A: Yeah …

B: And a can of carrot soup …

A: Aha …

B: A carton of cranberry juice and a jar of jam and some packets of crisps …

A: No, it wasn't crisps, it was peanuts. A couple of packets of peanuts.

B: Oh, right. And what else was there?

A: Er, let's see: some bottles of beer, a can of a carrot soup, a carton of cranberry juice, a jar of jam, some peanuts and a tin of tuna.

B: OK, peanuts and tuna – got it! Thanks! See you later.

A: See you!

9A Listening exercises 1 & 2 2.10

I = Interviewer K = Katy

I: So, Katy, you say you're a shopaholic, what exactly does that mean to you?

K: Well, it's not me that says it so much as most of … or maybe I should say, all the people who know me! All of them seem to agree that I'm a shopaholic. I enjoy shopping – any kind of shopping – I find it relaxing and satisfying and I don't think there's anything wrong with that … but I do know that my family and many of my good friends think I'm an addict!

I: And are you really an addict?

K: I don't know, but when I miss out on a shopping opportunity, I get pretty frustrated, and I suppose that most of the time I do go out of my way to make sure that I can visit the shops, wherever I am. And I hate seeing an interesting shop and not being able to go in …

I: Could you live without it?

K: Probably not!

I: When do you usually go shopping?

K: Whenever I can! At weekends, during my lunch breaks, when I'm on holiday …

I: And is there an ideal time to go shopping?

K: If the shops are open, any time is a good time to go shopping!

I: And where do you most like shopping?

K: Well, I love shopping malls. I know some people complain that they're boring, that all the shops look alike, that the shops are always the same, you know, once you've seen one mall you've seen them all, but I don't agree. I think they're a great invention! It doesn't matter what the weather's like, you don't have to cut your shopping trip short to go and find something to eat … they're perfect! But I also love exploring the little shops in old town centres – especially when I'm travelling.

I: Do you travel a lot?

K: Yes, I do, with my work, and I try to make sure I have time to do some shopping on most of my trips away from home!

I: What's your favourite country for shopping?

K: All of the countries I've ever visited! No, seriously, er, most countries are good for something. Let's see ... well, France is great for food, and no country I know is better than Italy for clothes, but I think Japan must be the best. I spent an absolute fortune in Tokyo on all sorts of electronic goods.

I: What do you most enjoy shopping for?

K: I love clothes shopping, of course, and I love buying presents for other people, but of all the things I buy, I think the one thing I most enjoy buying is – stationery.

I: Stationery?

K: Yes, you know, pens, pencils, notebooks ... I can spend hours in a stationery shop. I love handmade paper. That was another thing I spent loads of money on in Japan ...

I: When did you last go shopping?

K: This morning – on my way to the office!

I: And what did you buy?

K: A pair of shoes, a T-shirt and a set of coloured pens. Would you like to see them?

I: Katy, thank you very much for being with us this evening. So, let's see what you bought then ...

9c Listening exercises 1 & 2 🔊 2.12–2.14

1   Dk = Derek   C = Camilla

Dk: You said you wanted to see me?

C: Yes, Derek, come in. Have a seat. It's kind of you to spare the time.

Dk: Not at all, not at all. Did you want to see the sales figures?

C: Oh, yes. I'd forgotten about those. Have you got them?

Dk: Er, not just at the moment – I'll get them to you by the end of the day. They're nearly done.

C: Very well. Um, now, there's something I wanted to talk to you about.

Dk: Yes?

C: Well, I was looking at some of our office expenses earlier this morning. The files really are in a mess. I'm having problems finding anything.

Dk: Yes, they ... they need a bit of tidying up.

C: I'm glad you agree. Could you get someone to have a look at them? Your PA, perhaps. She doesn't seem terribly busy at the moment.

Dk: Certainly, certainly. I'll ask her to sort them out. Probably not until tomorrow, though. When she's finished working on the sales figures.

C: She needs all day to finish off the sales figures? I thought you said they were nearly done.

DK: Yes, well, nearly.

C: Anyway, I was going through the expenses and, by chance, I had a look at some of our telephone bills. I couldn't help noticing that they really are very high.

Dk: Really?

C: Extremely.

Dk: Hmm. I had no idea.

C: I'm afraid that's not good enough. It is your job, Derek, to keep an eye on this kind of thing.

Dk: Yes, of course. I'm sorry, but there has been a lot to do recently.

C: Well, I'm sure you'll find the time. Now, look at this bill, for example. A call to Japan. I didn't know we had any customers in Japan.

Dk: Strange. Maybe someone dialled the number by accident.

C: A twenty-minute phone call cannot be an accident. And, there have been nine calls to Japan in the last week.

Dk: Very strange.

C: Well, look into it, will you?

Dk: Will do. I'll get back to you at the end of next week. Is that all right?

C: No, Derek, this is top priority. This company is in trouble. If we don't do something soon, we are in real danger of closing. You, and I, could both find ourselves out of work.

Dk: OK. Right. Number one priority. In fact, I'll see to it this afternoon after lunch.

C: Good, I'm glad we agree. I'll speak to you again at the end of the day.

Dk: Fine. I'll catch you later.

2   D = Dave Dk = Derek

D: What's all this about then? 'Please refrain from making personal calls on the company phones.'

Dk: Cost-cutting.

D: What do you mean?

Dk: Well, Camilla reckons we're spending too much on phone bills.

D: What, and she thinks it's us, does she, I mean she reckons we're all sitting on the phone talking to friends and family all day? What a cheek! As if we had the time!

Dk: Yes, well, you know, every little counts ...

D: Yeah, well, it's just not on, I mean it's totally unacceptable, and I don't care who hears me say so. A quick conversation with my wife once in a while isn't going to break the bank! And what if there's an emergency? What do we do then? Go out on the street and use a phone box?

Dk: I know, I know, I'm really sorry, it wasn't my idea you know ... just following orders and anyway, you can always use your mobile ...

D: Oh, don't talk to me about mobiles!

Dk: Why, what's up? Is yours playing up again?

D: Yeah, I've had nothing but problems with it since I first got it. I was just going to make a call to get it sorted out ... but now of course, with this new development I can't even do that!

Dk: Oh, I think we can make an exception ...

D: Oh, yeah, like those calls to Japan, eh? Are those an exception too?

Dk: Yes, well, as I was saying, feel free to phone your mobile phone company ... just keep it short ...

D: Oh, I see, one rule for you and one ...

3   **W = Woman   D = Dave**

W: Customer service department. Can I help you?

D: Oh, hello. Er, I've got a problem with my phone. It's a KX 6700.

W: I'm sorry, sir. What seems to be the matter?

D: Well, I'm not too sure. I think there's something wrong with the power – the battery, maybe.

W: Oh, right. Your phone hasn't got wet, has it?

D: I'm sorry?

W: You haven't spilled water or coffee or something over it by mistake, have you?

D: No. Why?

W: No, it's just that the 6700 series power unit is very sensitive to water. Accidents do happen.

D: Oh, right.

W: You haven't dropped it, have you?

D: No, I haven't. Look, I'm sorry. I'm in a hurry because I'm calling from work. I just want to know where I can take it to get it repaired.

W: Yes, sir. I take your point. If you just go to the 'Services' menu on your phone, and then 'Help', the nearest repair shop to you will come up on your screen.

D: Yeah, but I can't do that because the phone doesn't work.

W: Oh yes, of course. I'm sorry, I'm not sure what to suggest. We don't have the addresses of the repair shops on file here.

D: Right. Um, listen, could I speak to the manager, please?

W: Yes, Sir. Can I tell him what it's about?

D: Yeah, it's about my phone that doesn't work. I'd like a refund – I want to have my money back.

W: Right-o. Can you just hold the line while I try to put you through?

10A   Listening exercises 2 & 3   ⊙ 2.18–2.19

M = Mary   D = David   G = Gary   A = Amanda
Me = Megan   Mi = Michael

Part 1

M: And welcome to the Mary Manners phone-in show. In today's programme, I'll be taking your calls about the latest scandal involving the royal family, your opinions on England's performance in the European Cup, but, first, what you think of the latest best-seller that everyone is talking about.

In case you haven't read it yet, *The Da Vinci Code* by Dan Brown is the story of Robert Langdon, a Harvard professor, who is in Paris on business. While he is there, the director of the Louvre museum, a man called Jacques Saunière, is murdered. The police suspect Langdon and plan to arrest him but he manages to escape from Paris. With the help of Sophie Neveu, who works for the French police, Langdon tries to find out more about the past of Jacques Saunière. He discovers that Saunière was the number one man in a secret organization, and that this organization is the guardian of an incredible secret, a secret that will change the future of the world. For those of you who haven't read the book yet, I won't tell you what the secret is,

because that would ruin the story, but let's just say that the book and its secret have upset a lot of people.

The Da Vinci Code is probably the best-selling adult book of all time. In addition, there are already at least ten books that have been published about it. There's *The Da Vinci Code: Fact or Fiction*; there's *The Truth behind the Da Vinci Code, A Guide to the Mysteries of the Da Vinci Code*, and loads more with similar titles. So, what's all the fuss about? Over to you. *The Da Vinci Code* – fact or fiction?

Part 2

M: And we've got our first caller on the line. David Sinclair from Edinburgh. David – *The Da Vinci Code* – fact or fiction?

D: Yeah, Mary, hi. I'd just like to say that the, I mean, the secret society in *The Da Vinci Code*, it's a fact. It even says so in the book on the first page. It's an organization that has been around for nearly a thousand years and I've read quite a few books about it.

M: And you think that this organization is keeping a secret that could change the world?

D: Yes, that's what most of the books say. I mean, we don't really know, but it's definitely a possibility. You know, that they may be waiting for the right moment before revealing the secret.

M: OK, David. Thank you. Let's see if our other callers agree with you. We've got Gary Hunt from Blackburn on the line. Gary – do you think that David has a point?

G: Hi. I don't know if David's right or not, but I definitely think the secret society in the book is based on fact. I mean, I saw a TV programme the other day about a thing called *Echelon*.

M: *Echelon*?

G: Yes. Apparently, the Americans have got this new technology with satellites and computers and they can read emails and listen to telephone conversations anywhere in the world. They said on the programme that they record three million communications every day. No, not three million. It was three billion, I think. Anyway, they're looking for terrorists and so on, but it's incredible to think how much they know about ordinary people like you and me.

M: I'm sorry, Gary. I don't see the connection between this Echelon thing and secret societies.

G: Oh, right. Yes, I see what you mean, but it's the same thing, isn't it? I mean, we're talking about secret societies, about powerful, secret societies, and what's the most powerful, secret society in the world?

M: You obviously have an idea.

G: It's the CIA, isn't it? And what is the CIA? It's an American government agency.

M: OK, Gary. Many thanks. Over to Amanda Hussey from Bristol. Amanda? Do you agree?

A: I'm sorry, Mary, but I think this is all complete nonsense, I mean, it's just a story, isn't it? I think Gary must be spending too much time in front of the TV watching things like *The X-Files*.

M: Er, could you say a little more?

A: Yes. The book says that there's some sort of secret society and they have this secret about Jesus having children.

M: Amanda, you've just given away the secret of the book!

A: Oh, sorry. But I don't think it matters, does it? This big secret – that Jesus had children – is just crazy. First of all, we know that Jesus was not married. And secondly, secondly, for a secret society, they can't be doing a very good job. I mean, it's not a secret any more. If you've read the book, it's not a secret, is it? And there's probably twenty million people around the world who've read the book.

M: You've got a point. Thank you. Our next caller is Megan Todd. Megan.

Me: I think we're talking about two different things. I saw that programme about Echelon, too, and after watching that, it's easy to believe that the CIA or someone might be listening to our telephone conversations. But that's got nothing to do with the secret society in *The Da Vinci Code*. They're completely different things.

M: Yes, but do you think it could be true?

Me: Yes, I do.

M: Right, I think we've got time for just one more call on this subject. It's Michael Sheng from Leeds.

Mi: Thank you, Mary. Yes, I read *The Da Vinci Code* and I thought it was very good, but I can't understand why everyone's talking about it. It's just a novel. Why does everyone want to believe it? It's mad!

M: And with that, let's turn to our big topic of the day. What is going wrong with Britain's royal family?

10B Grammar exercise 4 🔘 2.21–2.24

A Politician's clothes found on beach
It is not unusual for people to leave their clothes on the beach when they want other people to think they have died. But in 1967, Harold Holt, the prime minister of Australia, went swimming from the beach near Melbourne. Holt, who was 59, dived into the water and was never seen again. Many people believed that Holt did not die. Some thought he escaped because he wanted to live with his lover, and one journalist claimed that he was a secret agent who worked for the Chinese. But most people now accept that Harold Holt's death on the beach was an accident.

B Police find box of snakes on highway
In May 2004, the police in Little Rock, Arkansas, found a box that contained four dangerous African snakes on the side of the road. A few days before that, the police also found a dead man in a car at Little Rock airport. The cause of death was a snake bite. Before his death, the man had bought the snakes from a snake shop in Florida, but the police cannot explain why the snakes were in a box on the road.

C Alien attacks teacher
Kara Blanc, a teacher from Los Angeles, was the victim of an American TV show called *Scare Tactics*. Kara thought that aliens were attacking her, but in reality it was an actor who was wearing alien clothes. Kara did not find the joke funny and she took the makers of the programme to court.

D Six people see monster in Chinese mountains
In recent years, hundreds of people claim that they have seen a large animal, which is half-man and half-ape, in the mountains south-west of Beijing. In the 1980s and 1990s, scientists tried to find the animal, but they had no success. Many people believe that a similar animal, called *Bigfoot*, lives in the forests of North America.

10C Listening exercises 1 & 2 🔘 2.25

C = Camilla D = Dave P = Peter

C: Right, well, thanks for coming along bright and early like this. Let's get cracking, shall we? Dave, Peter, what have you got for us?

D: Er, yep, we've been looking at the software that can tell us what people are doing online. That's what you wanted, isn't it? Yes, well, it gives you a record of all the sites they go to, how long they spend there and that sort of thing. Er, it seems that quite a lot of companies are using this kind of thing these days.

C: And?

D: Well, I think it's a possibility. Definitely a possibility, but I think we should talk about it a bit more before we come to any decision. Er, to be honest, I'm having second thoughts about the whole idea.

C: Why? Is it expensive?

D: No, it's not that. It's just that, well, you know, I think we should think a little more about the pros and cons. I mean, the benefits of this are pretty obvious, but I think there may be one or two hidden drawbacks.

C: OK, tell me more.

P: Well, the good thing about this system …

D: Er, do you mind?

P: Oh, sorry. I thought you'd finished. Sorry, you go first.

D: No, after you.

P: No, no, after you.

C: Come on, stop wasting time. Peter, say what you want to say and get to the point this time, not like yesterday when you went on and on. Peter?

P: Yes, sorry. Er, yes, what I was saying was, er, yes, the good thing about this system is that it stops time-wasting. We don't really know how much time people are wasting when they should be working, but it's probably a lot. I've seen people doing their shopping, going to dating agencies … the other day, I even saw someone who had one of those online casinos on screen.

C: What? You saw someone gambling at work?

P: Er, yes, I think that's what he was doing.

D: I think we need to be a bit careful here. If someone wants to do that during their break, it's none of our business, really, is it?

C: I think it is, Dave. If people are gambling when they're at work, then it's got to stop. I don't want that kind of thing in my office.

D: Yeah, OK, I see what you mean, but …

P: Sorry, but there's a technical issue here, too, isn't there? The trouble is that every time they visit one of these sites – gambling sites, or whatever … the trouble is that our computer system is open to viruses. People can hack into our system any time they want.

D: Sorry, can I say something here? This is crazy. I mean, there's a risk. I mean, there's always a risk, but if someone goes to an online casino now and then, it's doesn't really change the security situation. You don't get more viruses there than anywhere else.

C: All right. We're talking about a number of different things here. Dave, I think you said that you were worried about some of the disadvantages of doing this.

P: Sorry, there's just one more thing that I wanted to mention.

C: Yes, go on. If you must.

P: It's just that, well, you were saying that you want people to understand how serious the situation is, you know …

C: Yes?

P: Well, I mean, if we use this programme and we tell everyone what we're doing, then they'll all know how serious it is. You know, they'll see that we're doing something to cut costs. I can't see any point in waiting. Let's get it now.

D: Oh, come on, I mean, people are not going to go around saying 'Oh, what a good idea.' I mean, hearing that your bosses are going to spy on you isn't exactly the high point of your day, is it? I've been reading an article about this in other companies. The experience there is that this kind of thing is very unpopular. I mean, the whole point of doing this is to make people work a bit harder. But if people think that the company is spying on them, well, they feel negative about it and they work less. You know, they start dragging their feet, extra five minutes break here, five minutes there.

C: Hmm, yes, I'd thought of that.

D: I think the other problem with this is, you know, the whole question of confidentiality. I mean, do we really have the right to spy on people like this? I don't think we do.

C: Hmm. Peter?

P: No, I don't really see it that way. We need to cut costs and improve productivity, don't we, and the good thing about this software is that it will help us to do just that.

C: But, Dave, you're saying that this may cost us money.

D: Yes, I think it's possible. The programme itself isn't too expensive, but it needs someone to look at the information afterwards, and then to speak to people, and so on. So, in the long term, I think it will cost us money.

C: So what do you suggest?

P: I think we should go for it. I don't think we should worry too much about, you know, is it moral, or is it not moral?

C: Dave? Should we get it?

D: No, I don't think so. Not yet. I thought that maybe we could tell the staff that we're thinking of using this software and explaining why, and asking them what they think. I think we should play it safe. Make people a bit more involved. I think there's a lot to be gained.

C: Good. I'll need to speak to some people in Head Office before I make any decision. Perhaps we could meet again tomorrow morning to decide where we go from there. Thanks for your thoughts and your time.

D: OK, see you later.

P: Would you like me to show you how the programme works?

C: Not now, Peter. Thank you.

11A Speaking & vocabulary exercise 3   2.26

A: It's very complicated to explain. Basically, you have to catch a ball and run with it to the other end of the field. You can pass it to the other players, but you can't throw it forwards. Oh, and you can kick it sometimes. I think you kick it if you have a penalty, but I don't really understand the rules of that.

11A Reading & listening exercises 3 & 4   2.27

I = Interviewer   J = Jan

I: In today's *Sport in Depth* feature we'll be talking to child psychologist Dr Jan Freeman about child sports stars. Jan, is it true that sports stars are getting younger?

J: Yes, it certainly is. In a lot of sports the average age of the competitors is getting lower and lower, and many of the new names and new champions are still young enough to be at school. Look at tennis stars these days. If they haven't won their first big competition before they turn sixteen, they might as well give up. And they start training from a very young age. I know one player whose parents bought him his first tennis racquet at the age of two!

I: And of course there are the others who are following in their parents' footsteps …

J: Yes, the father/coach figure is a fairly common figure.

I: The ex-Spanish tennis star Aranxa Sanchez, for example …

J: Yes, her dad taught her the basics of tennis at a very young age.

I: So when exactly did this child star phenomenon first appear? Was it with Olga Korbut in the 1972 Olympics?

J: Yes, that's right, and again four years later with little Nadia Comeneci in the 1976 Olympics. She won three gold medals for herself and her perfect scores helped win the gold for her team. She was only fourteen years old, and she was tiny. She looked even younger.

I: And everybody loved her.

J: That's right. And so did the judges. They gave her 10 for most of her performances – it made Olympic history. No gymnast had been given 10 before.

I: And wasn't she also the youngest gymnast ever to win a gold medal?

J: Yes, that's right. At the time she was an exception, but now it seems to be the rule. Younger girls are lighter and more agile. And they're easier to control and discipline.

I: But is it good for girls so young to be pushed so hard?

J: Basically, no. From a physical point of view, from a psychological point of view and from a very basic human point of view.

I: Could you be more specific?

J: Yes, of course. Gymnasts need to be small and slim in order to perform at their best. Many Olympic level gymnasts, as they get older suffer, from anorexia as they try to keep their weight down to compete with other younger competitors.

I: And psychologically?

J: The pressure to win is incredible. These young athletes are working eight hours a day, seven days a week in the gym. They eat, drink and sleep gymnastics. They are never given any time for themselves. Nothing else matters. Only winning.

I: That kind of pressure is difficult enough for an adult. I imagine it must be a 100 times more difficult for a child.

J: Mmm, exactly! Which brings us to the human side. These girls are not children, they are medal-winning machines. They don't have a childhood. Some have started training from the age of three or four, when they are far too young to have a choice. Their parents choose the sport and if the coach sees real talent, then he or she will push them to their limits in order to win that all important gold medal.

I: And maybe the coach is also the one who's taking all the glory as well?

J: Yes, quite often. And the parents promise the kids all sorts of rewards if they win, but it's really the parents who are getting all the money! Do you remember the case of Dominique Moceanu, the American gymnast who 'divorced' her parents because they were spending all her money? Well, that case is not so uncommon. And not only in gymnastics. It's just that gymnastics is such an extreme example.

I: Well, thank you Jan for being with us today ... Next, we'll be taking a look at ...

11c Listening exercises 1 & 2 🔘 2.30–2.34

1 D = Dave C = Camilla

D: Er, sorry, Miss Ridley? Have you got a second?

C: Dave. Come in. It's Mrs, actually. But I think we can use first names, can't we? Call me Camilla.

D: Oh, yeah, sorry, er, Mrs Ridley.

C: It's about the photocopying machine again, isn't it?

D: No, no, it's fixed. Sorted. Er, it's something completely different.

C: Well?

D: It's, um, I'm doing a cycle ride from London to Brighton at the weekend. On Saturday. And er, I wondered if you'd like to sponsor me?

C: Yes, I don't see why not.

D: We're doing it for Sport Relief. For children in Africa, you know.

C: Hmm, yes, fine. Shall we say £20?

D: Oh, great. That's very generous of you. Would you er, mind filling in the form here?

C: Sure.

D: Great. Thanks.

C: Just one thing, Dave. You're not taking any time off work for this, are you? You know how busy we are at the moment.

D: No, no.

C: Mm, just wanted to check, that was all. Well, best of luck, Dave.

D: Thanks, Miss Ridley.

C: Mrs. Camilla.

D: Sorry. Forgot. Thanks again, anyway.

2 D = Dave A = Avril

D: Hello, Avril. Er, have you got a second?

A: Not now, Dave. I've got to do these accounts. Her Majesty is waiting.

D: Well, it'll only take a second. I'm doing the London to Brighton cycle ride for Sport Relief. I wondered if you'd like to make a donation.

A: Oh! You said something about that last week, didn't you?

D: Yeah, it's this Saturday.

A: Well, you can put me down for £2.

D: Oh, can you fill in the form?

A: Do it for me, will you, Dave? There's too much I have to do at the moment.

D: Er, yeah, OK. It was er, just £2, wasn't it?

A: Yeah.

D: Thanks, Avril. Oh, by the way, is Derek in his office?

A: Yes, but he's making a call to the people in Japan. Give him five minutes, all right?

D: OK.

3 Dk = Derek D = Dave

Dk: Dave. Come in.

D: You look happy, Derek. Good news?

Dk: Excellent, I would say.

D: You've taken the job, haven't you?

Dk: Maybe. I'll tell you later.

D: Oh, well done, Derek, well done. We'll miss you, you know.

Dk: Er, keep this between you and me, Dave.

D: Of course.

Dk: Is that the sponsorship form?

D: Yeah, you er, want to make a little contribution?

Dk: Definitely. Pass it over. I see you've already asked Her Majesty. She hasn't given much, has she?

D: Hm, £20 – not too bad.

Dk: With her salary?

D: 50! Ah, you are a gentleman, sir. Thanks. Listen, I'll catch you later, all right. I want to ask a few more people before lunch.

Dk: Dave? Dave? Dave? Could you do me a favour? On your way out, ask Avril to make me a cup of tea. Time for a little celebration.

D: Will do. See you later.

4 D = Dave L = Linda

D: Hi there, Linda. All right?

L: Yeah, all right. I've got to do these accounts all over again. Avril's made a real mess of them. She's made mistakes on almost every page.

D: Nothing new there then.

L: No, but I get really fed up doing her work all the time.

D: Yeah, know what you mean. Anyway, you'll sponsor me for the cycle ride, won't you?

L: 'Course I will. How much are people giving?

D: It varies. Derek's down for £50, but, you know. Whatever you want to give.

L: £5? I have to do the shopping later and I'm a bit short of cash.

D: Oh, you don't have to pay me now. Next week's fine.

L: Oh, right. Well, better leave it at £5. We'll need all the money we can get if we lose our jobs.

D: Yes, fine, fine. It's kind of you. Here, do you want to fill this in?

L: Where do I put my name?

5 **P = Peter C = Clive**

P: Clive, did you give any money to Dave for his sponsored cycle ride?

C: Yeah, I put myself down for £30.

P: £30? You must be mad. I wish I had £30 to throw around like that.

C: No. I'll never give him the money, will I?

P: What do you mean, you'll never give him the money?

C: There's no way he's going to do 54 miles on a bicycle without having a heart attack. He's never done any sport in his life, has he?

P: 54 miles, is it? No, you're right. Five miles, maybe. Downhill, maybe.

C: Yeah, he'll do a few miles, then he'll get the train or something. My money's safe.

12A Listening exercises 1 & 2 🔘 2.35

M = Man E = Elaine

M: Right, moving on to the next point on the agenda. Elaine and Kate are going to talk us through the results of our recent market survey into young people's attitudes to money. Elaine …

E: Hi, as you know, we've got the results to the survey … you should all have a copy of the report on the table in front of you … Greg, there's a spare copy over there … got it? … Right, so there's a summary of the results on page 13. I think you'll find that they're quite interesting.

Now, as Bob pointed out, the whole point of the survey was to find out more about young people's attitudes to money. As we all know, we aren't attracting as many young customers as we'd like to, and we hope this survey will help us improve our advertising campaign.

So, on to the details. Right … We interviewed a total of 1,200 young people between the ages of 18 and 25. The interviews took place mainly in shopping centres, university student unions and multiplex cinemas. You can see a copy of the survey at the back of the report. The first two questions were very open and there were no surprises in the answers. When we asked if money was important to them, of course most people said that it was, but that it wasn't the only important thing.

So, as I said, no surprises there. I imagine we'd get the same answer from any group of people, no matter how young or old. And the second question was pretty predictable as well. When we asked them if they worried about money most of the people we questioned said yes. So far so good.

But there were some surprises in the next question. When we asked them what they did with their money, there was no surprise when they said they liked to spend it on enjoying themselves, but we were surprised to see that a large number, over 30%, said that they regularly donated money to charity, whilst only 2% said that they saved or invested it. This is something we really need to remember. At the moment our advertising campaign places far too much emphasis on investments and savings.

And the next question is quite an important one as well. When we asked what the main source of their income was, it was interesting to see that the majority said that it was their family, even though almost half of the people we talked to had a job. Which means that a lot of parents are still helping their children out financially when they first start to work. And, more importantly for our purposes, most of the people we questioned were still living at home. We really need to make sure we reflect this situation in any future advertising campaigns. We need to show more young people living at home with their parents. At the moment most of our ads show them sharing a flat with friends.

But even though they felt that they were still dependent on their families as far as money's concerned, they didn't seem to turn to their parents for advice on money matters. In the answer given to the question of who influenced them most in their money decisions, more than 60% said that the TV and papers influenced their decisions more than their own family and friends. This can only be good news for us!

Oh yes, and in case we're thinking of running another competition, the vast majority… that's almost 80% … wanted to win the limited edition Smart™ car!

Which brings us to the next part of our presentation. How do these results help us in planning our next advertising campaign? I'd like to hand over to my colleague, Kate, who's going to outline a possible plan of action …

12c Listening exercises 2 & 3 🔊 2.38–2.40

1 Dk = Derek D = Dave A = Avril W = Woman
C = Clive

Dk: Right. Is everyone here? … Thank you, thank you, Avril. Ah, everyone here? Good, let's begin by …

W: Aren't we going to wait for the boss?

Dk: Er, I had a call from Mrs Ridley and …

D: It's 'Miss', Derek.

Dk: Oh, Miss, Mrs, whatever, Dave. Anyway I had a call from Camilla, and she told me she was going to be a little late, so while we're waiting, there are a few announcements I need to make. Is Clive here?

A: He's over there.

Dk: Oh right. Clive, Clive. Most of us here have known Clive for a long time. In fact, when I joined the company as a young man, Clive was the first person I met. Always friendly, always ready to lend a helping hand, and it's because of people like Clive that it has been such a pleasure to work here for so many years. Now, what, er, what you may not know, actually, I don't think that even Clive knows it himself, in fact he told me the other day that he couldn't remember when he joined the company in, er, where was I, yes, what some of you may not know is that today, on this very day, 40 years ago, Clive joined the company. So, to mark the occasion, I'd like to take this opportunity to say congratulations to Clive and many thanks for all his years of hard work.

Dk: Clive, Clive I have here a little something for you.

Cl: Oh, goodness, it's a gold watch. I don't know what to say. Well, er, thanks. Many thanks. It's very kind of you, Derek.

Dk: Not at all, not at all. It's my pleasure. Now, I have one more bit of news …

2 C = Camilla Dk = Derek M = Man W = Woman

C: Hello, everyone. I'm sorry I couldn't be here earlier, but you've started the meeting already, I see. Very good. We don't want to waste any time, do we? Now, we all know that it has been a difficult time recently. I've just come back from a meeting at Head Office and I've got some very important news. As a matter of fact, I've got two bits of news. Would you like the good news first or the bad news?

Well, I think I'll start with the good news. Excellent news, as a matter of fact. I know that some of you have been worried about the possibility of this part of the company closing down, and I am now in a position to tell you that, thanks to all your hard work, we have reached our targets. And so, you will be pleased to hear that there will be no redundancies, we have no plans for any job cuts at all. We've made a healthy profit in the last twelve months and with the new computer system in place, things are going very well indeed. So, I'd just like to say congratulations to all of you and – keep it up!

Well done, again. Now, the bad news, I'm afraid. In the last few weeks, I've had a number of meetings with Derek here. After a lot of thought, Derek told me last week that he felt he needed a change. And, well, we have agreed that Derek will take early retirement. I'm sure you will all want to wish Derek good luck. The company would like to present Derek with this gold key as a leaving gift. Derek, all the best and good luck for your retirement.

Dk: Thank you. And the same to you. I mean, the same to all of you. Best of luck for the future.

M1: Good luck, Derek.

M2: It won't be the same without you.

W1: All the best, Derek.

M3: We'll miss you, Derek.

W2: Keep in touch.

C: Now, I won't keep you much longer, but I must tell you about one more change. We have decided, with immediate effect, that Mr Blackman – Dave – will be taking over Derek's duties as General Office Manager. I'm sure that Mr Blackman – Dave – will do a very good job. Dave, many congratulations, and I look forward to working with you as my assistant.

M4: Well done, Dave.

W3: Bad luck, Dave.

C: Right, I think that's all for now. Back to work, eh?

3 D = Dave Dk = Derek L = Linda C = Clive A = Avril

D: Well, cheers, Derek. We'll miss you.

Dk: Cheers, Dave.

L: So what's the big secret, Derek? You said you had something to tell us.

Dk: Oh, yes, that's right. Actually, I've got two things to tell you. Dave, here, he already knows part of it, but I asked Dave not to tell anyone.

L: Come on, Derek, don't keep us waiting. Tell us.

C: You've got some special plans for your retirement?

Dk: Yes, you could say that. The thing is, I'm not retiring.

Cl: But what's-her-name just told us all that you've decided to take early retirement.

Dk: Yes …

C: Oh, right, I get it. She's kicked you out. You're not retiring at all. She fired you. Oh, what a shame. That's really unfair.

Dk: No, no, no, no, no. I said to Camilla that I was more than happy to take early retirement and she offered me a very generous retirement payment.

L: I don't get it.

Dk: Well, what's happened is that I've been offered a job in Japan, and I've accepted.

C: So, it's not a holiday at all, then?

Dk: No.

L: That's fantastic news. Well done!

Dk: And there's something else that I need to tell you. I asked Avril if she wanted to come with me, didn't I, Avril?

A: Yes, that's right.

Dk: And, well, there's a bit more to it than that. Avril and I are getting married!

C: Oh, goodness!

D: Here's to Derek and Avril.

L: To Derek and Avril!

Irregular verb list

Infinitive	Past simple	Past participle	Infinitive	Past simple	Past participle
be	was / were	been	lend	lent	lent
beat	beat	beaten	let	let	let
become	became	become	light	lit	lit
begin	began	begun	lose	lost	lost
bend	bent	bent	make	made	made
bite	bit	bitten	mean	meant	meant
blow	blew	blown	meet	met	met
break	broke	broken	must	had to	had to
bring	brought	brought	pay	paid	paid
build	built	built	put	put	put
burn	burned / burnt	burned / burnt	read /riːd/	read /red/	read /red/
burst	burst	burst	ride	rode	ridden
buy	bought	bought	ring	rang	rung
can	could	been able	rise	rose	risen
catch	caught	caught	run	ran	run
choose	chose	chosen	say	said	said
come	came	come	see	saw	seen
cost	cost	cost	sell	sold	sold
cut	cut	cut	send	sent	sent
deal	dealt	dealt	set	set	set
do	did	done	shake	shook	shaken
draw	drew	drawn	shine	shone	shone
dream	dreamt	dreamt	shoot	shot	shot
drink	drank	drunk	show	showed	shown
drive	drove	driven	shrink	shrunk	shrunk
eat	ate	eaten	shut	shut	shut
fall	fell	fallen	sing	sang	sung
feed	fed	fed	sit	sat	sat
feel	felt	felt	slide	slid	slid
fight	fought	fought	sleep	slept	slept
find	found	found	smell	smelled / smelt	smelled / smelt
fly	flew	flown	speak	spoke	spoken
forget	forgot	forgotten	spell	spelt / spelled	spelt / spelled
forgive	forgave	forgiven	spend	spent	spent
freeze	froze	frozen	spill	spilled / spilt	spilled / spilt
get	got	got	spread	spread	spread
give	gave	given	stand	stood	stood
go	went	gone	steal	stole	stolen
grow	grew	grown	stick	stuck	stuck
hang	hanged / hung	hanged / hung	swear	swore	sworn
have	had	had	swim	swam	swum
hear	heard	heard	take	took	taken
hide	hid	hidden	teach	taught	taught
hit	hit	hit	tear	tore	torn
hold	held	held	tell	told	told
hurt	hurt	hurt	think	thought	thought
keep	kept	kept	throw	threw	thrown
kneel	knelt	knelt	understand	understood	understood
know	knew	known	wake	woke	woken
lead	led	led	wear	wore	worn
learn	learned / learnt	learned / learnt	win	won	won
leave	left	left	write	wrote	written

1 | Review

1 Correct the mistakes in the conversation.

A: Paul, hi, it's me. Listen, are you wanting to come out for a meal this evening?

B: Yes, sure, of course. But aren't you spending your birthday with Scott?

A: No, he's busy. He's doing something else.

B: What? On your birthday?

A: Yes, he's working late at the office today.

B: He's seeming to have a lot of work these days.

A: Yes, maybe. But I'm not believing him.

B: What? You're meaning that he's lying?

A: Well, I'm knowing that he's not telling me the whole truth.

B: Are you thinking that he's seeing someone else?

A: Maybe. He's behaving a bit strangely at the moment.

B: How terrible! Poor you.

2 Complete the postcard below. Put the verbs in brackets into the present simple or the present continuous.

3 Read the short text and complete the comprehension questions for these answers.

The Church of England decided that women could be priests in 1992. Two years later, 32 women became the first female priests in the country. At the time, some male priests complained. They thought that it was the end of the church.

1 Who _____? The Church of England.
2 When _____? In 1992.
3 When _____? Two years later.
4 How many women _____? 32.
5 Who _____? Some male priests.
6 What _____? That it was the end of the church.

4 Complete the questions with a word from the box.

as	of	to

1 Do most people see you _____ an approachable person?
2 Do you consider yourself _____ be very patriotic?
3 Do you think _____ yourself as right-wing or left-wing?
4 How many people would you describe _____ very good friends?
5 Do you think you are lucky _____ live in the 21st century?
6 Which is more important _____ you – friends or family?

5 Work in pairs. Ask and answer the questions in exercise 4.

6 Complete the missing letters in the words.

1 He has a very p _ _ _ _ _ _ t nose, like a big carrot.
2 He looks ill and has a very unhealthy c _ _ _ _ _ _ _ n.
3 He prefers to have grey hair than to be b _ _ d.
4 He's got a very m _ _ _ _ _ r build – he must spend hours in the gym.
5 Her eyes look very n _ _ _ _ w in her new glasses.
6 He looks as if he's just got out of bed – his hair's a mess and he hasn't s _ _ _ _ d.
7 She looks very t _ _ _ _ d, but I think it's fake – some sort of cream.
8 Sometimes her hair is straight and sometimes it's w _ _ y.

I arrived in London yesterday and I (1) _____ (have) a good time already. At the moment, I (2) _____ (watch) a cricket match. Tom (3) _____ (play) cricket every Sunday afternoon and today his team (4) _____ (play) in Kew – near the famous gardens. I (5) _____ (not / understand) the rules, but it (6) _____ (not / matter) – it's good fun anyway. It (7) _____ (look) as if it's going to rain later (typical England!), but for the moment, the sun (8) _____ (shine). We (9) _____ (drink) warm beer and I (10) _____ (eat) a cheese and cucumber sandwich. England is everything I imagined! You'd love it!

Love
Claire
XXX

Lauren Thompson
457 S. Monica Blvd.
Venice
CA
USA

2 | Review

1 Choose the correct time expression to complete the questions.

1 Did you do anything special *last weekend / over the last few weeks*?
2 Have you booked your next holiday *yesterday / yet*?
3 Have you made many friends *during your time at this school / when you were at primary school*?
4 Have you seen any good films *one month ago / recently*?
5 How many times did you take a taxi *during the last year / last year*?
6 How often have you been ill *in the last six months / last month*?

2 Work in pairs. Ask and answer the questions in exercise 1.

3 Complete the article. Put the verbs in brackets into the past simple or the present perfect.

SPECIAL PEOPLE

British TV viewers (1) _____ (*vote*) for Michael Palin as the UK's top TV star. Palin (2) _____ (*receive*) the award at a ceremony in London yesterday.

Michael Palin first (3) _____ (*become*) famous as a comedian in the 1970s with the Monty Python TV show. When the show ended, Palin (4) _____ (*make*) a number of successful films and in the 1980s he (5) _____ (*begin*) his new career as a maker of travel documentaries.

In the last 20 years, Palin (6) _____ (*be*) all over the world. His work (7) _____ (*take*) him to the Himalayas, the Sahara Desert and both the North and South Poles. He (8) _____ (*visit*) more than 80 countries and (9) _____ (*travel*) over 160,000 kilometres.

Following his trip to the Sahara, Palin, who is in his 60s, (10) _____ (*say*) that he was not a very good traveller, and recent news reports (11) _____ (*say*) that he intends to give up soon. However, at yesterday's ceremony, Palin (12) _____ (*insist*) this was not true.

4 Complete the sentences 1–8 with the phrases a–h.

1 A brown bear looks
2 He always drops
3 He often picks
4 I was surfing the net last night and came
5 It often takes a long time to get
6 She decided to give
7 She needs some help to sort
8 They've gone to see

a across a good site for hitchhikers.
b after her cubs for about two and a half years.
c off the kids at school on his way to work.
d off their friends at the airport.
e out a problem with a virus on her computer.
f over a serious illness like that.
g up hitchhikers in his truck.
h up the sport after her latest injury.

5 Rearrange the words to make sentences.

1 across before come him I never 've .
2 after her I if 'll like look you .
3 are picking them time up what you ?
4 came me nobody off see to .
5 could drop here me off please you ?
6 get it 'll over soon you .
7 give he it should up .
8 have it out soon sort to we .

6 Complete the conversation with verbs from the box. More than one answer is sometimes possible.

catch	get	get off	get on	miss	run
take	walk				

A: Excuse me, can you tell me how I can _____ to City Airport from here?
B: Yes, of course. The best way is to _____ a train to Stratford.
A: Thanks. How often do the trains _____?
B: Every ten minutes, so if you _____ one, you don't have to wait long. Platform 4.
A: Platform 4. OK. How long does it _____? Half an hour?
B: Oh no, only about fifteen minutes. You _____ the train at the last stop.
A: The end of the line. OK. And can I _____ to the airport from there?
B: No, you'll need to _____ the airport bus. It will be right outside the station.

7 Work in pairs. Practise the conversation in exercise 6.

3 | Review

1 Choose the best explanation for the signs.

1

Free car park
for residents only

a) Everybody has to pay to park here.
b) Nobody has to pay to park here.
c) Residents do not have to pay to park here.

2

Last check out 12.00

a) You don't have to check out before 12.00.
b) You must check out before 12.00.
c) You must not check out before 12.00.

3

No guests in rooms

a) Guests are not allowed in the rooms.
b) Guests must not leave their rooms.
c) You can take guests to your room.

4

Dogs welcome

a) You are allowed to bring a dog with you.
b) You don't need to bring a dog with you.
c) You have to bring a dog with you.

5

Restaurant
non-residents welcome

a) Non-residents can't eat here.
b) You don't need to be a resident to eat here.
c) You must be a resident to eat here.

6

Swimming pool
opening hours
08.00–20.00

a) Swimming is not allowed between 08.00 and 20.00.
b) You can swim between 08.00 and 20.00.
c) You mustn't swim between 08.00 and 20.00.

2 Complete the second sentence so that it has a similar meaning to the first.

1 In the Middle Ages, the church made most people give them one tenth of their money.
In the Middle Ages, most people _had to give_ one tenth of their money to the church.

2 Only important people could wear purple clothes in 16th-century England.
Only important people were _____ purple clothes in 16th-century England.

3 Between 1919 and 1932, Finnish people were not allowed to buy alcoholic drinks.
Between 1919 and 1932, the Finnish government _____ its people buy alcoholic drinks.

4 Before 1963, American law let employers pay a man more than a woman for the same job.
Before 1963, American employers _____ pay a man more than a woman for the same job.

5 The Soviet Union did not let some writers publish their work.
Some writers _____ publish their work in the Soviet Union.

3 Correct the mistakes in the sentences.

1 Could you possibly leaving your dog outside?
2 Do you mind if I opening the window?
3 Do you think could you pick us up at eight o'clock?
4 I wonder if could I invite a few friends for dinner.
5 Is it all right when I leave work early tomorrow?
6 Would you mind to pass the mayonnaise?

4 Choose an appropriate response for the requests in exercise 3.

1 *Yes, go ahead. / Yes, of course.*
2 *No, not at all. / Yes, sure.*
3 *No, that's OK. / Yes, no problem at all.*
4 *I'm sorry, but I'm busy tonight. / I'm afraid you can't.*
5 *No, that's fine. / Yes, that's fine.*
6 *Yes, here you are. / Certainly not.*

5 Complete the questions in column A with phrases in column B.

A		B	
1	Can you get to	a	alarm clock when you're on holiday?
2	Do you always make the	b	asleep at school?
3	Do you ever set your	c	bed every day?
4	Have you ever fallen	d	nap and then decided to stay in bed until the next morning?
5	Have you ever had a	e	sleep when there's a lot of noise?
6	How often do you wake	f	sleeper that you know?
7	What time do you begin to feel	g	sleepy in the evening?
8	Who is the heaviest	h	up in the middle of the night?

6 Work in pairs. Ask and answer the questions in exercise 5.

4 | Review

1 Choose the correct verb forms to complete the text.

```
┌─────────────────────────────────────────── chat time ──────────────┐
│ Coincidences                                                        │
│ Post reply reply/qoute email delete edit                            │
│                                                                     │
│ The other day I (1) thought / was thinking of a song, and when I    │
│ (2) turned / was turning on the radio, what (3) did I hear / was I  │
│ hearing? The same song, of course.                                  │
│                                                                     │
│ Earlier this morning, I (4) needed / was needing to call a friend.  │
│ I (5) looked / was looking for her number in the phone book         │
│ when the telephone (6) rang / was ringing. Guess who?               │
│                                                                     │
│ A few years ago, I (7) met / was meeting a woman when I             │
│ (8) flew / was flying to New York on business. Later that day,      │
│ I (9) saw / was seeing her again when I (10) had / was having       │
│ dinner in the hotel restaurant. She (11) stayed / was staying in    │
│ the same hotel!                                                     │
│                                                                     │
│ Post new topic                                                      │
└─────────────────────────────────────────────────────────────────────┘
```

2 Put the verbs in brackets into the correct tense (past simple, past continuous or past perfect).

```
┌─────────────────────────────────────────── chat time ──────────────┐
│ Post reply reply/qoute email delete edit                            │
│                                                                     │
│ Last night I (1) _____ (want) to watch a film on TV, but my       │
│ sister (2) _____ (watch) a quiz show. I (3) _____ (agree) to    │
│ wait until the end of her show. The contestant (4) _____ (sit)    │
│ in a big black chair. She (5) _____ (answer) nine questions       │
│ correctly and she (6) _____ (have) one more question to get       │
│ right for the jackpot. Her name (7) _____ (be) Emily – the        │
│ same as me – and she (8) _____ (wear) exactly the same            │
│ clothes as me! She (9) _____ (have) to give the name of the       │
│ river in Budapest. I (10) _____ (come) back from a trip to        │
│ Hungary only last week!                                             │
│                                                                     │
│ Submitted by Emily                                                  │
└─────────────────────────────────────────────────────────────────────┘
```

3 Decide if the pairs of sentences below have the same (S) or different (D) meanings.

1 The fire started while he was at the petrol station.
  When he was at the petrol station, the fire started.
2 She bought a new house when she won the lottery.
  She won the lottery after she'd bought a new house.
3 She screamed the moment she saw him.
  As soon as she saw him, she screamed.
4 By the time we arrived, they had already left.
  They left before we arrived.
5 They called for help as soon as their car broke down.
  Their car broke down as soon as they called for help.
6 He had an accident while he was playing on the balcony.
  When he was playing on the balcony, he had an accident.

4 In four of the sentences below, one word is missing. Insert the missing words.

1 Both them like a bit of a gamble.
2 Neither my friends my family think it's against the odds.
3 Neither us feel like giving it a go.
4 We both want to try our luck.
5 There's a lot at stake for both the company the workers.
6 They both think it's a lottery.

5 Match the sentences 1–6 to the short responses a–f.

1 I bought a _____ last week.
2 I can't _____.
3 I like _____.
4 I wasn't _____ yesterday.
5 I'm going to _____ tomorrow.
6 I've never been to _____.

a Neither can I.
b Neither have I.
c Neither was I.
d So am I.
e So did I.
f So do I.

6 Complete sentences 1–6 in exercise 5 so that they are true for you.

Work in pairs. Read your sentences to your partner. Your partner must respond to your sentences truthfully.

7 Complete the sentences with a word from the box.

ankle   black   bleeding   bruise
scratch   shock   sprained   unconscious

1 He _____ his wrist playing squash.
2 He wouldn't explain how he got a _____ eye.
3 Her finger is _____ after she cut it with a knife.
4 Many people were suffering from _____ after the explosion.
5 She's got a _____ on her arm where the ball hit her.
6 The cat was frightened and tried to _____ me.
7 The doctors think he may remain _____ for a few hours.
8 The parachutist twisted her _____ when she landed.

5 | Review

1 Look at the information in the table and say if the sentences 1–8 are true (T) or false (F).

A quick guide to local furniture stores

	range of goods	price	staff
Alum & Key			
Bettabeds			
Home Comforts			

1 Bettabeds is the least expensive of the three stores.
2 Home Comforts is slightly cheaper than Bettabeds.
3 Alum & Key is less friendly than the other shops.
4 The nicest staff are at Home Comforts.
5 Alum & Key has the biggest range of furniture.
6 It's easier to find what you want at Bettabeds than at Home Comforts.
7 On the whole, Bettabeds is better than Home Comforts.
8 Alum & Key is the worst place to go for good service.

2 Complete the sentences with a word from the box.

as	from	not	the	to

1 The prices in superstores are similar _____ the prices in local shops.
2 Local shops are _____ as convenient as superstores.
3 The staff in superstores are _____ friendly as in local shops.
4 Opening hours at local shops are different _____ superstores.
5 One superstore is _____ same as another.

Work with a partner. Decide if you agree with the sentences in exercise 2.

3 Choose the best word to complete the sentences.

1 He gets the *fewest / more* complaints.
2 He has the *least / less* experience of all of them.
3 I have a lot *fewer / less* energy than him.
4 I've taken *fewer / least* holidays this year.
5 She has *less / more* projects than the others.
6 She probably has the *fewest / most* work to do.

4 Complete the conversations with an appropriate phrase.

A: Hello. Could I (1) _____, please?
B: I'm afraid that Mrs Robinson isn't at home right now. Can I (2) _____?
A: Yes, please. This is Benjamin here.
B: I'm sorry. Could you (3) _____?
A: Yes. Benjamin. B-E-N-J-A-M-I-N. Could you (4) _____?
B: Yes, of course. I'll ask her to call you as soon as she gets back.

C: Sales and marketing. Can I (5) _____?
D: Yes, hello. Could I speak to Thomas, please?
C: I'm sorry, but Thomas isn't at his desk right now. I think he's at lunch.
D: Oh, right. Can I (6) _____? In about an hour?
C: Yes, I'm sure that he'll be back then. Could I (7) _____?
D: Yes, it's Mrs Laurence.
C: OK, Mrs Laurence. I'll tell him you called.

Work in pairs. Practise the conversations.

5 Complete the sentences with a positive or negative form of the adjectives in the box.

comfortable	correct	delicious
polite	popular	satisfied

1 It was a very _____ restaurant so they had to book in advance.
2 It was a very stylish place, but the chairs were very _____.
3 Last time they went, the food was _____, but this time it was not so good.
4 In addition, they didn't enjoy the meal because the waiter was extremely _____.
5 The bill was _____ so they asked for it to be changed.
6 They were _____ with the service so they decided to complain to the manager.

6 Four of the sentences below are strange or illogical. Put a cross (X) next to these sentences.

1 He made a few corrections with his pencil sharpener.
2 He ordered a couple of note pads from the stationery department.
3 Her secretary used a highlighter to show all the important information.
4 I need a new ink cartridge for my stapler.
5 She spent the day working in the filing cabinet.
6 She wrote an important biro to the new clients.
7 The photocopies were attached with a paper clip.
8 There are loads of reports in my in tray that I have to look at.

6 | Review

1 Choose the best verb forms to complete the conversation.

A: (1) *Are you going to do / Will you do* anything interesting this weekend?

B: Probably not. (2) *We're staying / We'll stay* at home, I guess. And you?

A: Yes, (3) *we're visiting / we'll visit* some friends at the coast. But according to the weather forecast, (4) *it's going to rain / it will rain*, unfortunately.

B: Well, I'm sure (5) *you're having / you'll have* a nice time anyway.

A: Yes, it doesn't matter too much. We're more worried about the traffic. It's a holiday weekend, so there (6) *are going to be / will be* a lot of cars on the road.

B: If you leave early, (7) *you're going to be / you'll be* OK.

A: Yes, but we can't leave until after nine because (8) *we're going to do / we'll do* a bit of shopping first.

2 Look at the conversation in exercise 1 again. Which examples of *going to* can you replace with the present continuous?

3 Put the verbs in brackets into the correct tense.

1 We're going to look for a hotel as soon as we _____ (*arrive*).
2 After we've checked in, we _____ (*find*) somewhere to eat.
3 We'll go for a walk around the city when we _____ (*eat*).
4 If the weather _____ (*be*) bad, we'll go on a bus tour.
5 Once we know the city a bit better, we _____ (*visit*) a museum or two.
6 We'll visit the National Gallery before we _____ (*leave*).

4 Correct the mistakes in the questions below.

1 Do you know what will your next film be?
2 Could you tell us which actor or actress would you really like to work with?
3 Can you tell us what do you like most about making films?
4 We'd all like to know how much did you earn for your last film.
5 Can you tell us if you ever do watch your own films?
6 Our viewers would like to know you're going out with anyone at the moment.

5 Work in pairs. Imagine that you are a journalist and a famous film star. Ask and answer the questions in exercise 4.

6 Complete the sentences with a word or phrase from the box.

arrive	book	check out	choose
do	find	pay	pick up

1 Don't forget the sunscreen when you _____ the packing.
2 Guests must _____ of the hotel before eleven.
3 Please _____ your excursions 24 hours in advance.
4 Signs in the town are written in English so it's easy to _____ your way around.
5 There will be a welcome party when you _____ at the hotel.
6 We have hundreds of exotic destinations to _____ from.
7 We kindly ask you to _____ a 5% deposit when you make your reservation.
8 You can _____ a brochure at our shop during normal shopping hours.

7 Complete the text with the best answers, a, b or c.

THE PHILIPPINES

Cebu Island, the Philippines' top tourist destination, has something for everybody. With both (1) _____ hotels and accommodation for travellers on a budget, you're sure to find the ideal place to stay. Cebu has many lively, (2) _____ resorts, where you can meet people from all over the world. These are perfect for (3) _____ holidays, with (4) _____ facilities for mountain biking, horse riding, trekking and water sports nearby.

Travellers looking for peace and quiet can choose one of the more (5) _____ holiday villages. And if you want to take things easy, you can relax on one of the hundreds of beautiful (6) _____ beaches, or go for a (7) _____ walk in the (8) _____ Cebu Mountains.

1 a) dreadful   b) painful   c) upmarket
2 a) awful   b) cosmopolitan   c) guided
3 a) shy   b) gorgeous   c) action-packed
4 a) dramatic   b) laid-back   c) superb
5 a) horrible   b) secluded   c) talkative
6 a) exhausted   b) sandy   c) unbeatable
7 a) memorable   b) discreet   c) ancient
8 a) exclusive   b) picturesque   c) respectable

7 | Review

1 Choose the correct verb forms to complete the conversation.

A: How long have you (1) *known / been knowing* him?

B: We've (2) *gone / been going* out for about three years.

A: Have you ever (3) *had / been having* any arguments?

B: Yes, a few, recently. I've (4) *worked / been working* late at the office and John doesn't like it.

A: He's jealous?

B: Yes, and I've (5) *thought / been thinking* that I'm not sure I want to get married to someone who gets jealous.

A: Have you (6) *spoken / been speaking* to him about it?

B: No, I've (7) *waited / been waiting* for the right moment.

2 Put the verbs in brackets into the present perfect simple or the present perfect continuous.

```
latest news                                    ▯▯▯
newsweb                    🌐

Royal wedding preparations nearly complete
(Filed: 09/04/05)

Staff at Windsor Castle (1) _____ (be) busy making the
final preparations for the wedding of Prince Charles and
Camilla Parker Bowles later today.

Castle workers (2) _____ (prepare) St George's Hall,
where the reception will take place. Four men (3) _____
(build) a small stage, from where the wedding speeches will
be made. When they (4) _____ (finish), the stage will be
covered in gold. Nearby, another group of servants
(5) _____ (polish) champagne glasses. 35,000 yellow
flowers (6) _____ (arrive) at the castle and eight flower
arrangers (7) _____ (work) around the clock to decorate
the hall. They expect to finish shortly before the arrival of the
royal couple.

Prince Charles (8) _____ (return) from Rome where he
was attending the funeral of the Pope.
```

3 Complete the gaps with *for* or *since*.

1 A few people have been waiting outside the castle _____ yesterday evening.
2 One man has been there _____ two weeks to be sure of getting a good view.
3 He has been a fan of the royal family _____ he met Prince Charles in 1992.
4 He has been to three royal weddings _____ then.
5 Journalists have been interviewing people in the streets _____ the last few hours.
6 Charles and Camilla have known each other _____ thirty years.

4 Complete the sentences with one word.

1 Have you _____ about looking for a job as a film extra?
2 Have you _____ looking for work on local TV?
3 I think you _____ forget the idea.
4 If I _____ you, I'd just go to Hollywood.
5 There's no _____ in taking a few acting lessons.
6 What you _____ to do is get on a reality TV show.
7 _____ don't you send your photo to an agency?

5 Work in pairs. Which is the best advice in exercise 4 for someone who wants to become a film star?

6 Complete the dictionary definitions with the missing words.

1 **live** _____ _____ phrasal vb [T] [**live** _____ _____ sth] to be as good as what was expected or promised: *The beautiful scenery certainly lived _____ _____ expectations.*
2 **live** _____ phrasal vb [T] [**live** _____ sth/sb] to think that someone or something is so important that they are your main reason for living: *She lives _____ her work.*
3 **live** _____ phrasal vb [T] [**live** _____ sth/sb] to depend on someone or something for the money or food that you need: *He's 25 and still living _____ his parents.*
4 **live** _____ phrasal vb [T] [**live** _____ sth] to experience a dangerous or unpleasant situation and still be alive after it: *There are people who have lived _____ two world wars.*
5 **live** _____ phrasal vb [T] [**live** _____ sth] to have a particular amount of money to buy the things that you need to live: *They have to live _____ a pension of £350 a month.*

Extracts from Macmillan Essential Dictionary

7 Complete the sentences 1–6 with the phrases a–f.

1 Even when you're heartbroken, you have to move
2 It's when we're adolescents that we embark
3 It's quite common for couples to go
4 It's usually a good thing when our lives take
5 Most people's lives don't really take
6 When your life is at a

a an unexpected turn and we take a new direction.
b crossroads, it's best to ask an elderly relative for advice.
c off until they're middle-aged.
d on and find someone else.
e on the most important stage of our lives.
f their separate ways when they're in their early twenties.

8 Work in pairs. Do you agree with the statements in exercise 7?

8 | Review

1 Choose the best response.

1 Do you think it will rain?
I wouldn't say so. / Yes, I would.
2 Do you want to come for dinner this evening?
I'd love to. / I'd never do that.
3 How about spending the weekend in Paris?
I wouldn't know. / That would be great.
4 I don't think you should tell him.
No, he wouldn't understand. / Yes, I would think so.
5 Shall we stop for a break?
I wouldn't care. / I wouldn't mind.
6 Will we get a pay rise this year?
I'd never forgive myself. / I'd be very surprised.

2 Work in pairs. Think of at least two ways to complete the sentences below.

1 If I was the look-alike of someone famous, I …
2 If someone offered me a role in a movie, I …
3 If I had a private jet, I …
4 If I was the owner of a daily newspaper, I …
5 If I found a bomb in the street, I …

3 Rewrite the sentences beginning with the words given.

1 The nurses weren't happy with their salaries so they went on strike.
If the nurses _____.
2 The newspapers reported the demonstration because the protesters dressed as Elvis Presley.
If the protesters _____.
3 The police stopped him because he drove through a red light.
If he _____.
4 Stiglitz lost his job because he asked the wrong questions.
If Stiglitz _____.
5 He didn't do more TV work because he didn't have enough time.
If he _____.

4 Put the verbs in brackets in the correct tense.

1 I _____ (*not / need*) to go to the launderette if I had a washing machine.
2 If it _____ (*be*) less left-wing, the paper would have better circulation figures.
3 If you _____ (*study*) engineering, you'd have found a better paid job.
4 They _____ (*not / vote*) for the government if they'd known about their plans for the war.
5 They wouldn't have gone in the fountain if they _____ (*not / be*) hot.
6 Would you walk naked down the street if I _____ (*give*) you £100?

5 Rearrange the words to make offers.

1 anything   can   do   for   I   you ?
2 a   give   hand   let   me   with   that   you .
3 if   I'll   do   like   the   washing-up   you .
4 a   bottle   champagne   I   of   open   shall ?
5 drive   like   me   there   to   would   you   you ?
6 a   coffee   cup   do   make   me   of   to   want   you ?

6 Cross out one noun in each group which cannot form a compound with the noun in bold.

1 credit / ID / rest   **card**
2 face / safety / seat   **belt**
3 mobile / pay / pie   **phone**
4 police / strip / train   **station**
5 speed / time / toy   **limit**
6 money / street / traffic **lights**
7 driving / gun / war   **licence**
8 bag / danger / no-parking **zone**

7 Match the headlines 1–5 to the beginnings of the news stories A–E.

1 **Journalist killer arrested**

2 **New bomb clue**

3 Thieves get long sentence

4 **Protesters not guilty**

5 **Witness disappears**

A   A judge has sent two men to prison for fifteen years after a jury found them guilty of taking part in the Bettabeds Superstore robbery. The men had

B   Dutch police have caught a man who fired a gun into the offices of a left wing newspaper, resulting in the death of one member of staff. It is believed

C   Three women who were arrested for violent behaviour at an anti-globalization demonstration have been found innocent. The judge said that the

D   A woman who worked for Richie Preston failed to appear in court today to give evidence in the Cardiff gangster's trial. Police think that she may

E   A Metropolitan Police spokesman announced earlier today that they have found new evidence in their investigation into last week's explosion at the

8 Work in pairs. Use your imagination to complete the unfinished sentences in exercise 7.

9 | Review

1 Complete the sentences with with *a/an*, *the* or Ø (zero article).

Have you ever had (1) _____ problem finding (2) _____ right birthday present for (3) _____ friends? Have you ever spent (4) _____ hours at (5) _____ shops only to return with (6) _____ empty bag and (7) _____ growing sense of (8) _____ frustration? If so, (9) _____ internet is (10) _____ only place to go.

2 Complete the sentences with *some* or *any*.

Type 'weird gifts' into (1) _____ search engine on the internet, and you'll find (2) _____ really original ideas. At (3) _____ sites, like stupid.com, you won't find (4) _____ normal ideas at all. But you will certainly find (5) _____ of the strangest gifts on the net. Even if your friend doesn't actually need (6) _____ of these things, they may find (7) _____ of them quite amusing.

3 Choose the best way to complete the text.

How about buying a piece of land on the moon? There are (1) *lots of / too much* online shops that have moon property on offer. It doesn't cost (2) *many / much* (about $15), and there are (3) *much / plenty of* people who are happy to pay. Unfortunately, (4) *few / little* of them will ever get the chance to visit their property.

If you think that $15 is (5) *a few / too much* for something that you'll never see, there are (6) *many / much* other interesting ideas. If you only have (7) *a little / not enough* time, go to the 'weird stuff' section of Ebay. If you've got (8) *a lot of / many money* and (9) *not enough / a few* sense, you can buy a mystery brown box for $200. And if you really have (10) *few / too much* money, you can join (11) *a few / enough* other people and buy a bag of Iowa air for $1. What a bargain!

4 Put the conversation in the correct order.

☐ A whole week? I'm afraid that's not good enough. I can't spend a week without one.

☐ Good morning. I think there's a problem with the watch I bought yesterday.

☐ Good morning, sir. How can I help you?

☐ And I'm sorry, but that's totally unacceptable. I'd like to speak to the manager.

☐ I see. Well, if you'd like to leave it with us, we'll look into it. Could you come back next Monday?

☐ I'm sorry, sir, but there's nothing else we can do.

☐ Oh yes? What seems to be the problem?

☐ There's something wrong with the alarm.

5 Work in pairs. Practise the conversation in exercise 4.

6 Find four items on the shopping list that are in the wrong container.

1 bottle of red wine
1 large box of washing powder
2 cartons of organic marmalade
4 cans of diet cola
1 tin of pineapple slices
4 cartons of orange juice
1 jar of skin cream
2 small jars of beefburgers
1 packet of spaghetti
1 box of olive oil
3 tins of Italian tomatoes
1 small tin of fresh salad leaves
2.5 litre tub of vanilla ice cream

7 Complete the definitions 1–7 with the phrases a–g.

1 A discount is
2 A high street is
3 A shop assistant is
4 A shopaholic is
5 A shoplifter is
6 A shopping mall is
7 Window-shopping is

a a large building with a lot of shops, restaurants, and sometimes a cinema.
b a reduction in the price of something.
c someone who enjoys going to shops or buying things.
d someone who steals something from a shop.
e someone whose job is to serve people in a shop.
f the activity of looking at things in shop windows but not buying anything.
g the main street in a town or city, with a lot of businesses along it.

8 Complete the missing letters in the words.

1 I found the house in a real m _ _ _ when I got home.
2 I found the right answer totally by c _ _ _ _ _.
3 I have all your details on f _ _ _.
4 I met her ex-husband completely by a _ _ _ _ _ _ _.
5 I think we're in d _ _ _ _ _ of missing the last train.
6 I'd like the bill now, please. We're in a h _ _ _ _.
7 I'll be in t _ _ _ _ _ _ if Tom finds out about this.
8 I'm sorry, I took your keys by m _ _ _ _ _ _ last night.

10 | Review

1 Complete the conversation with *must, might, could* or *can't*. Sometimes more than one answer is possible.

A: What's that noise? I think there (1) _____ be someone in the flat.
B: No, it (2) _____ be coming from our flat. The noise is too far away.
A: What do you think it (3) _____ be?
B: It (4) _____ be someone next door.
A: It (5) _____ be the neighbours. They've gone away.
B: If it's not the neighbours, it (6) _____ be a thief. Go and have a look.
A: I'm not going. They (7) _____ have a gun or something.

2 Rewrite the sentences beginning with the words given.

1 There's a chance you will meet someone through a dating agency.
  You might _____.
2 That definitely wasn't an alien.
  That can't _____.
3 I'm sure she's completely crazy.
  She must _____.
4 Perhaps they buried the treasure.
  They might _____.
5 I think she's spying on us.
  She may _____.
6 He probably buried the murder weapon.
  He may _____.
7 It's possible that he's working as a secret agent.
  He could _____.
8 There's a possibility that it won't rain.
  It might _____.

3 Work in pairs. Read the story. How many possible explanations can you think of?

It may have been a treasure map.

IN ABOUT 1890, the priest of Rennes-le-Château in the south of France discovered some very old, secret documents in his church. He could not understand the documents, so he took them to an expert in Paris. When the priest returned to his village, he was extremely rich. He never explained where the money came from and he took his secret with him to the grave.

4 Complete the sentences with a word from the box.

about   from   in   of   with

1 One of the good things _____ his job is he travels a lot.
2 The main problem _____ his work is that he can't tell anyone what he does.
3 Another drawback _____ his work is that he can't visit certain countries.
4 It also has the disadvantage _____ being very dangerous at times.
5 He works for the benefit _____ his country.
6 The trouble _____ working for the government is that the pay isn't very good.
7 There is a lot to be gained _____ carrying a gun in his job.
8 There is no point _____ asking him his name – he won't tell the truth.

5 Complete the text with words from the box.

audiences   magician   perform   pretended
revealed   stage   tricks   vanish

The world's greatest (1) _____ was probably Harry Houdini. When he first went on (2) _____, he did (3) _____ with playing cards and made women (4) _____ from magic boxes. He later became popular with (5) _____ around the world when he started to (6) _____ incredible escapes as part of his show. Houdini also (7) _____ the secrets of many people who (8) _____ to be able to communicate with the dead.

6 Replace the words in italics with a word from the box.

accused   admitted   claimed
pretended   refused   seemed   tried

1 He *acted as if* he was deaf.
2 He *said that it was true* that he had met an alien.
3 There was some vandalism in the school and the police *said it was* my brother.
4 One of the boys has *said that he was* bullying younger children.
5 She *made an effort* to calm down.
6 The casino *said they didn't intend* to pay.
7 They *appeared* to be using new tactics.

11 | Review

1 Rewrite the sentences beginning with the words given.

1 His tea is made by his secretary.
His secretary _____ .
2 You must do all the work before tomorrow.
All the work _____ .
3 When are your accounts going to be finished?
When are you _____ ?
4 Someone's made a few mistakes with this.
A few mistakes _____ .
5 My car's being repaired at the moment.
The garage _____ .
6 They cancelled the marathon at the last moment.
The marathon _____ .
7 You haven't filled in your form.
Your form _____ .
8 They estimate the cost of the games to be more than $3 billion.
The cost of the games _____ .

2 Four of the sentences contain one unnecessary word. Cross out the unnecessary words.

1 I promised to my boyfriend a ticket for the cup final for his birthday.
2 A friend got the ticket for me on the black market.
3 I paid for her a fortune for it.
4 Then, my boyfriend was offered a well-paid job in Los Angeles on the day of the final.
5 So, I bought to him a pair of socks.
6 I found him a very nice pair with the English flag on them.
7 I gave them to him when he returned home.
8 As usual, he didn't bring for me anything from America.

3 Rearrange the words to make sentences.

1 am   cut   going   hair   have   I   my next   to   week .
2 bed   breakfast   had   have   I   in   never served .
3 delivered   have   house   I   my   often pizzas   to .
4 dyed   hair   have   I   my   never   would .
5 a   car   have   I   my   once   serviced   year .
6 tested   eyes   have   I   must   my   soon .
7 all   by   clothes   have   I   ironed   mother my   my .
8 decorated   flat   have   I   love   my   to would .

4 Work in pairs. Are the sentences in exercise 3 true (T) or false (F) for you?

5 Complete the question tags with an auxiliary verb.

1 You've been to Wimbledon, _____ you?
2 The weather's never good, _____ it?
3 The tickets are very expensive, _____ they?
4 British players never win, _____ they?
5 Wimbledon started over one hundred years ago, _____ it?
6 They play on grass, _____ they?
7 You can't park near Wimbledon, _____ you?
8 You haven't got an extra ticket, _____ you?

6 Complete the text with words from the box.

catch	championship	pass	penalty
players	run	team	throw

Netball is similar to basketball, and (1) _____ have to (2) _____ a ball in a net to score goals. However, they cannot (3) _____ with the ball. When they (4) _____ it, they must (5) _____ it to another member of their (6) _____ .

If a player breaks a rule, the other team is given a (7) _____ . The world netball (8) _____ is often won by Australia.

7 Choose the correct word to complete the sentences.

1 If you are *determination / determined* enough, you can usually get what you want.
2 It's better to have good looks than *intelligence / intelligent*.
3 Men don't usually like *ambition / ambitious* women.
4 Most people lose their *enthusiasm / enthusiastic* when they become adults.
5 People with natural *talent / talented* will always be successful.
6 Women have more mental *agility / agile* than men.
7 Women will always be less *power / powerful* than men.
8 You need to be absolutely *ruthlessness / ruthless* to succeed in the business world.

8 Work in pairs. Decide if you agree or disagree with the sentences in exercise 7.

12 | Review

1 Rewrite the quotations in reported speech.

1 I don't want money. It is only people who pay their bills who want that, and I never pay mine.
Oscar Wilde

2 A bank is a place that will lend you money if you can prove that you don't need it.
Bob Hope

3 The only reason I made a commercial for American Express was to pay for my American Express bill.
Peter Ustinov

2 Put the bank manager's questions in direct speech.

(1) The bank manager asked me what I would do with the money. (2) He wanted to know when I was going to pay the money back. (3) He asked how much I earned. (4) Then, he asked if I had any investments. (5) He wanted to know how much money I had saved last year. (6) He asked if I had ever had any credit card debts. (7) Finally, he asked me if I could give him the names of two referees.

1 *'What will you do with the money?'*
2 '_____?'
3 '_____?'
4 '_____?'
5 '_____?'
6 '_____?'
7 '_____?

3 Work in pairs. Imagine that one of you wants to borrow £1,000 from the bank. Roleplay the interview between the bank manager and the customer.

Now work with a different partner. Tell him/her about the customer's answers to the bank manager's questions.

4 Complete the news story on the right at the top using a maximum of three words for each gap. Use sentences 1–6 to help you.

1 'You must appear in court.'
2 'We want the demonstrations to be stopped.'
3 'Could you limit the number of protesters to a maximum of ten?'
4 'Can you allow us to continue?'
5 'You can't go within 50 metres of the factory.'
6 'Stop making weapons!'

A group of protesters who demonstrated outside a weapons factory were in court in Brighton today. The anti-war protesters were told (1) _to appear_ in court after the factory asked the judge (2) _____ the demonstrations. The company's lawyer asked the judge (3) _____ the protesters to ten people on Thursday afternoons.

In reply, the protesters claimed they had a legal right to demonstrate and asked the judge (4) _____ them to continue. In his ruling, the judge told the protesters (5) _____ within 50 metres of the factory, but he did not agree to limitations on the number of people or the day of the week. It is believed that protests will continue. The protesters have told the factory (6) _____ making weapons if they want the demonstrations to stop.

5 Choose the best response for each exchange.

A: It's been nice meeting you. See you again soon, I hope.
B: (1) *Yes, another day, maybe. / Yes, keep in touch.*

A: I'm really sorry, but I've lost the pen you lent me.
B: (2) *Oh, never mind. / Oh well, all the best.*

A: It was really nice of you to show us around. Thanks.
B: (3) *Not at all. / The same to you.*

A: Katy's not feeling well, so she's decided to stay at home tonight.
B: (4) *Guess what? / What a shame!*

A: You've been so kind to me. I'll never forget it.
B: (5) *Congratulations! / My pleasure.*

A: I've got the interview for the new job tomorrow.
B: (6) *Have a safe journey. / I'll keep my fingers crossed.*

6 Complete sentences 1–8 with the phrases a–h.

1 He denied that he had made
2 I couldn't withdraw
3 I don't think I can pay
4 It's very easy to get into
5 She became very rich by investing in
6 We'll need to save
7 When I was little, my parents opened
8 You'll need to take out

a a mortgage to buy the house.
b a savings account for me.
c all my bills this month.
d any cash because the machine was out of order.
e debt when you lose your job.
f his money by selling heroin.
g some money before we can afford it.
h stocks and shares.

Macmillan Education
Between Towns Road, Oxford OX4 3PP
A division of Macmillan Publishers Limited
Companies and representatives throughout the world

ISBN 1-4050-1065-7

Text © Philip Kerr and Ceri Jones 2006
Design and illustration © Macmillan Publishers Limited 2006

First published 2006

Designed by Oliver Design

Illustrated by Arlene Adams pp 70; Ross Cuthbert pp 126, 130, 133, 134; Paul Davies pp 42, 56-57; Mark Duffin pp10, 36, 48, 69, 81, 90, 92, 122; Gary Kaye pp 59; Roger Penwill pp 40, 46, 120; Colin Thompson pp12-13, 22, 32, 38, 52, 62, 72, 80, 92, 102, 112, 123 and Gary Wing pp 43, 71.

Cover design by Macmillan Publishers Limited

Cover photographs reproduced with kind permission of Action Plus, Alamy, Corbis, Getty, Lonely Planet, Photolibrary.com, Rex and Dean Ryan.

Author's acknowledgements
The authors would like to thank Katy Wright, Kenna Bourke, Shona Rodger, Nicola Gardner, Barbara Mercer, Laila Meachin, Andrew Oliver, James Richardson and everyone involved in the sound recording.

The author and publishers would like to thank the following people for their help and contribution:
Carolina Mussons, Mari-Carmen Lafuente, Eliseo Picó Mas, Carmen Roig-Papiol and Lourdes Montoro, EOI Sta Coloma de Gramanet, Barcelona. Maggie Hawes, Tony Isaac, Tom Radman and Anita Roberts, British Council, Barcelona. Rosie Dickson and Sarah Hartley, Merit School, Barcelona. Christina Anastasiadis, Andrew Graydon, Steven McGuire, Alan Hammans, Heather Shortland and Roger Edwards, International House Zurbano, Madrid. Guy Heath, British Council, Madrid. Ramón Silles, EOI Majadahonda. Javier Martinez Maestro, EOI Parla. Rosa Melgar, EOI Valdezarza. Susana Galan, The English Centre, Madrid. Yolanda Scott-Tennent Basallote, EOI Tarragona. Ceri Jones.
Marzenna Raczkowska. Yaffite Mor, Alicja Fialek and Ricky Krzyzewski, UEC-Bell School of English, Warsaw. Steve Allen, Joanna Zymelka, Marek Kazmierski, Przemek Skrzyniarz, Colin Hinde, Mireille Szepaniak, Gabriela Pawlikowska and Simon Over, English First, Warsaw. Fiona Harrison-Rees, British Council, Warsaw. Karina Davies and Katarzyna Wywial, Szkola Jezykow Obcych 'Bakalarz', Warsaw. Peter Moran and Joanna Trojanowska, International House, Krakow. Walter Nowlan, British Council, Krakow. Agnieszka Bieniek, Anna Galus, Malgorzata Paprota and Joanna Berej, U Metodystow, Lublin. Mr Paudyna, Alicja Grajek, Eliza Trojanowska and Monika Bochyn'ska, Studium Jezykow Obcych, Minsk Mazowiecki. Paola Randali. Paola Povesi. Roberta Giugni. Mirella Fantin. Rossella Salmoiraghi. Marco Nervegna and Rebecca Kirby, Linguaviva, Milan. Peter Sheekey, Oxford Group, Milan. Irina Kuznetsova, Elena Ivanova, Olga Kekshoeva and Yulia Mukoseeva, Tom's House, Moscow. Asya Zakirova, Tatyana Tsukanova, Natalia Brynzynyuk, Anna Karazhas, Anastasia Karazhas and Nadya Shishkina, Mr English Club, Moscow. Inna Turchin, English First Zhulebino, Moscow. Tatiana Shepelenko, Ljuba Sicheva and Tatiana Brjushkova, Higher School of Economics, Moscow.
David Willis. Susan Hutchison. Kirsten Holt. Kater Pickering. Cathy Poole. Jenny Roden. Michael West. Howard Smith, Clare Dunlop, Clare Waring and Andrew Mitchell, Oxford House, London. Garth Cadden, Lefteris Panteli and Vicky McWilliam, St Giles College, London. Sarah James, Sarah Lurie, Karen Mathewman, Chris Wroth, Olivia Smith, Sue Clark, Alan Greenslade-Hibbert, King's School of English, Oxford.
Sara Fiorini, CEFETI Centro de Linguas, São Paulo. Neide Silva and Maria Helena Iema, Cultura Inglesa Pinheiros, São Paulo. José Olavo de Amorim and Amini Rassoul, Colégio Bandeirantes, São Paulo. Maria Antonieta and Sabrina Teixeira, Centro Britânico, Perdizes, São Paulo. Loreliz Kessler, Unilínguas, São Leopoldo. Marli Zim, Acele, Porto Alegre. Luciane Duarte Calcara, Britannia, Porto Alegre. Magali Mente, Lingua Lindóia, Porto Alegre. Maria Higina, Cultura Inglesa Savassi, Belo Horizonte. Eliane Peixoto, Green System, Belo Horizonte. Adriana Bozzolla Vieira, Britain English School, Belo Horizonte. Roberto Amorin, ICBEU Centro, Belo Horizonte.
Patrícia Brasileiro, Cultura Inglesa Casa Forte, Recife. Eleonor Benício, British Council, Recife. Roseli Serra, Cultura Inglesa Madalena, Recife. Alberto Costa, Cultura Inglesa Olinda, Recife. Glória Luchsinger, English Learning Centro, Recife. Angela Pougy Azevedo and Márcia Porenstein Toy Centro, Rio de Janeiro. Julian Wing, British Council, Rio de Janeiro. Karla Koppe, Colegio Tereziano, Rio de Janeiro. Márcia Martins. Ricardo Sili and Janine Barbosa, Cultura Inglesa, Rio de Janeiro.

Ágnes Tisza, Ring Nyelvstúdió, Budapest. Katalin Nemeth and Edina Varga, Novoschool, Budapest. Szilvia Hegyi, Mack Alasdair, Eva Lukacsi and Katalin Jonas-Horvath, Babilon Language Studio, Budapest. Nikolett Pozsgai, Európai Nyelvek Stúdiója, Budapest. Krisztina Csiba and Anett Godó, Oxford Hungária Nyelviskola, Budapest. Zsuzsanna Tóth and Szilvia Fülöp, H-Net, Budapest. Judit Csepela, TIT Globe, Budapest. Judit Volner and Rita Erdos, Dover Nyelvi Centrum, Budapest. Ildikó Tóth and Piroska Sugár, Katedra, Budapest. Katalin Terescsik Szieglné and Magdolna Zivnovszki, London Stúdió, Budapest. Agota Kiss and Gabriella Varga, KOTK, Budapest. Rita Lendvai and Judit Szarka, Atalanta, Budapest. Péter Gelléri, Tudomány Nyelviskola, Budapest.

The author and publishers would like to thank the following for permission to reproduce their material:
Extract from 'Who do we think we are?' copyright © The Guardian 1999 first published in The Guardian 20.01.99, reprinted by permission of the publisher.
Extract from Bedrooms Through The Ages by Richard Wood (Wayland Publishers Ltd, 1999), reprinted by permission of Hodder and Stoughton Limited.
Extract taken from www.nationallottery.co.uk, reprinted by permission of The National Lottery Commission.
Extract from The Guinness Book of Oddities by Geoff Tibballs (Guinness Publishing, 1995), reprinted by permission of the publisher.
Extracts from 'World's luckiest man wins the lottery' taken from Ananova.com 17.06.03; 'Toddler locked mum out on balcony' taken from Ananova.com 15.10.03; 'Man fired after being stranded on mountain top' from Ananova and 'Fried egg cost teenagers' mum £675.00' both from Ananova.com 04.11.03 all copyright © Ananova 2003, reprinted by permission of the publisher.
Extract from The Lord of the Rings by J.R.R. Tolkien copyright © J.R.R. Tolkien 1954 (George Allen and Unwin, 1954), reprinted by permission of HarperCollins Publishers Ltd.
Extract from 'Maria prepares to celebrate her 110th birthday' by Jonathan Lessware copyright © The Scotsman 2003, first published in The Scotsman 27.10.03, reprinted by permission of Newsflash Scotland.
Extracts from 'Coin through elbow' and 'The self-tying handkerchief' both taken from www.conjuror.com.

Extracts from Macmillan Essential Dictionary (Macmillan Publishers Limited, 2003), text © Bloomsbury Publishing Plc 2003, reprinted by permission of the publishers.

The author and publishers would like to thank the following for permission to reproduce their photographs:
Action Plus/N.Tingle p110(r); Alamy/Photolibrary Wales p11(l), H.Sykes p11(ml), B & C Alexander p18(E), S. Caplan p18(a), T.Kraft p18(d), S.May p23(t), Mira p26-27, N.Joseph p28(B), IML Image Group p28(C), G&M Schwartz p28(E), J. Wiedel pp28(F), 116(l), R.Cooke p28(D), Travel-Shots p28(A), C.Hill p61(tr), Pictures Colour Library p88, B.Croxford p99(t), D.Noton p118 (beach), K-Photos p122(l), D.Barba p122(r); Bridgeman Art Library/C.E.Butler/Private Collection Christopher Wood Gallery London p99(b); Corbis/W.P-Conway p18(c), V.Streano p26(t), Hulton Deutsch pp31(t),(b), B.Kraft p38(l), F.Trapper p38(r), Photomorgana p46(tr), D.Cumming p58, R.Bruderer p68(r), R.Ressmeyer p77, Firefly Productions p107, C.Collins p122(m), Corbis RF p20(mr); DigitalSTOCK p20 (ml) & (r); Empics/ PA p11(r), D.Cheskin p68(l), T.Boyd/AP p98; Europix p40;
Getty Images/V.Besnault p18(f), M.Funk p23(main), Hulton Archive p30, M.Tcherevkoff p46(tl), P.Hince p46(br), Hulton Archive p48, B.Thomas p67, Getty p78(t), J.McDonald p110(l).
Lonely Planet/R.Cummins p61(b); Mark Duffin pp81 collage, 122(ml), (mr), (b); Mary Evans p11(mr); Photodisc pp 127,128 &132; Rex Features/L. Oy p46(bl), R.Gardner p103(b), Sipa Press p108; Ronald Grant Archive pp6, 100; The Scotsman /S. Bell p70; Topham p82(inset), PA pp33, 78(b), 93, Polfoto p106, T. Hindley p110(m), National Pictures p113; Zefa/M.Buckhart p10.

Photograph of Tony Hawkes reproduced with kind permission of Ebury Press p17.
Photographs of Alvaro Neil reproduced with kind permission of Alvaro Neil, p16.
Cover of 'Why Men Don't Listen and Women Can't Read Maps' by Allan & Barbara Pease. ISBN: 0-75284-619-1, reproduced with kind permission of Orion Books. P62.

Commissioned photography by Dean Ryan pp18(B), 51, 52, 87, 116 (r), 118, 134.

Whilst every effort has been made to locate the owners of copyright material in this book, there may have been some cases when the publishers have been unable to contact the owners. We should be grateful to hear from anyone who recognises copyright material and who is unacknowledged. We shall be pleased to make the necessary amendments in future editions of the book.

Printed and bound in Spain by Edelvives

2010 2009 2008 2007 2006
10 9 8 7 6 5 4 3 2 1